# WHO SANK THE
# TITANIC?

Dedicated to the best of all friends

Annette Clarke

'Friendship is being there when someone's feeling low and
not being afraid to kick them.'

Randy K. Mulholland, Something Positive

# WHO SANK THE
# TITANIC?

*The Final Verdict*

## ROBERT J. STRANGE

Pen & Sword
**MARITIME**

First published in Great Britain in 2012 by
PEN & SWORD MARITIME
an imprint of
Pen & Sword Books Ltd
47 Church Street
Barnsley
South Yorkshire
S70 2AS

Copyright © Robert J. Strange, 2012

ISBN 978 1 84884 470 4

Typeset in Ehrhardt
by Chic Media Ltd

Printed and bound in England
by CPI Group (UK) Ltd, Croydon, CR0 4YY

*Pen & Sword Books Ltd incorporates the imprints of*
Pen & Sword Aviation, Pen & Sword Family History, Pen & Sword Maritime,
Pen & Sword Military, Pen & Sword Discovery, Wharncliffe Local History,
Wharncliffe True Crime, Wharncliffe Transport, Pen & Sword Select,
Pen & Sword Military Classics, Leo Cooper, Remember When,
The Praetorian Press, Seaforth Publishing and Frontline Publishing

*For a complete list of Pen & Sword titles please contact*
PEN & SWORD BOOKS LIMITED
47 Church Street, Barnsley, South Yorkshire, S70 2AS England
E-mail: enquiries@pen-and-sword.co.uk
Website: www.pen-and-sword.co.uk

# Contents

# Foreword

The basic facts of the *Titanic* disaster have long been accepted throughout the 100 years since the then biggest ship in the world sank beneath the waves of the Atlantic Ocean. On her maiden voyage from Southampton to New York, the Royal Mail Ship *Titanic* struck an iceberg late on the evening of 14 April 1912. She sank in the early hours of the following morning after an estimated 3,845,000 gallons of water had poured in below her waterline. The crew had launched all of her too few lifeboats to try and save as many women and children as possible. But her officers were so badly trained that lifeboats were lowered away with far fewer people than they were designed to hold.

The precise number of passengers and crew who sailed on *Titanic* has been much debated over the years, but the authoritative British Wreck Commissioner's report recorded at the time that 2,201 souls were on board that night. Only 711 people were saved in the boats, leaving 1,490 others to drown or freeze to death in the bitterly cold, but abnormally calm, water.

Were you to have been caught up in the tragedy, your gender, financial position and social class would all have influenced your chance of survival. More than three-quarters of all the women were rescued, but less than one fifth of the men. Every child in First Class was saved, but two out of three of Third Class children were not. At greatest risk of all were the 454 men booked in Third Class; only around one in ten of them managed to get into a lifeboat.

In the aftermath of the tragedy, two lengthy and expensive inquiries – one on each side of the Atlantic – produced new safety recommendations. Neither hearing attached any significant blame to any company, government department or individual involved in the management, construction or safety regulations of the ship. No shipping company boss lost his job. Nobody involved in building the ship was dismissed. No politician responsible for safety at sea resigned or was thrown out of office. There were no criminal prosecutions.

During the century since those inquiries were concluded, a wealth of additional information about *Titanic*'s sinking has entered the public domain. Previously secret government files have been released into the national archive collections of both Britain and the USA. Personal and political memoirs have been written. Scientists have uncovered the secrets of *Titanic*'s construction by studying metal fragments retrieved from 2½ miles under the Atlantic

Ocean. The recollections, stories, excuses and self-justifications of everybody caught up in the disaster are now being examined in the light of this mass of new evidence.

Many famous men are now being found to be wanting.

# Acknowledgements

T his book owes much of its existence to the expertise of the staff of a number of national archives houses and a wide range of specialist local history and university libraries throughout the UK. Without the excellence and efficiency of such institutions it would be impossible to uncover the first person accounts and true history of events such as the construction of *Titanic*. I have received unstinting help from a long list of institutions including, but not limited to: the UK National Archives (PRO) at Kew in West London, the Public Records Office of Northern Ireland (PRONI), the US National Archives and the Library of Congress in Washington D.C., various American universities who have safeguarded the archives of many obscure and defunct newspapers from cities throughout North America, the British Library (especially the ever-helpful staff of the library's newspaper archive at Colindale), the National Maritime Museum at Greenwich, the Morgan Library and Museum in New York City, the Merseyside Maritime Museum in Liverpool, the Kelham Island Industrial Museum in Sheffield, the Modern Records Centre of the University of Warwick, the Southampton Maritime Museum, the Corus Record Centre in Deeside, the Staffordshire and Stoke-on-Trent Archive Service, and the Clydebuilt Maritime Heritage Centre in Glasgow. My special thanks must go to Miss Gemma McCallion of PRONI in Belfast for her help at a time when the museum was suffering severe disruption from a then imminent closure and move to new headquarters at the city's refurbished 'Titanic Quarter'.

Outside of such archive repositories, I received invaluable help and advice from a range of pubic and commercial organizations including, but again not limited to, the International Ice Patrol of the United States Coast Guard service, the Royal National Lifeboat Institution, the National Union of Seamen, the Federal Emergency Management Agency of the US Department of Homeland Security, the Mission to Seafarers, Harland and Wolff Heavy Industries Ltd., Tyssenkrupp Marine Systems, General Dynamics Electric Boat of Groton, Connecticut, Fairview Lawn Cemetery of the Halifax Regional Municipality in Nova Scotia and the city councils of Southampton, Belfast, Liverpool and Cobh. Special thanks are again due to the archivists of the Royal Belfast Academical Institution, and to Susan Crossland, of Harrow School, in London.

This book began life after an attempt to develop a television programme to coincide with the centenary of the sinking of *Titanic* and, although that project never came to fruition, my gratitude is due to all I worked with at Pioneer Film and Television Productions Ltd. The book would never have been possible without the invaluable assistance of my literary agent, Doreen Montgomery of Rupert Crew. Above all, it depended on the specialist, in-depth research and assistance of my son, David Strange, who spent countless hours unearthing dusty files, which had rarely before seen the light of day, from within the bowels of the PRO at Kew and at PRONI in Belfast. His support was mirrored by the assistance and constant encouragement of my younger son, William Strange, and, most importantly of all, of my wife, Pam.

# Chapter One

# 'I reported it as soon as I seen it . . .'

**11.35 pm**
**Sunday, 14 April 1912**
**Crow's-nest of RMS** *Titanic*
**Dead reckoning position: 41° 46' N, 50° 41' W**
**North Atlantic Ocean**

A twinkling canopy of stars provided the only light on the freezing, crystal-clear, moonless night. At the rear of *Titanic's* crow's-nest, which was gently swaying from side to side 100 feet above the dark waters of the Atlantic Ocean, two loosely-tied sheets of rough canvas flapped gently in the icy wind. They offered little protection against the bite of the bone-chilling Arctic cold for the two sailors, whose breath continually frosted the air around their precarious lookout perch. Unsurprisingly, the two men were hunched down deep into the folds of their heavy greatcoats. Even so, staring into the darkness ahead of the speeding ship, both were alert and determined to do their duty. They were each well used to the hardship of a lookout's life. This job in the crow's-nest earned each of them an extra five shillings per voyage, a welcome bonus on top of their £5 a month wages. More importantly, it meant they needed to work for just two hours on duty and four hours off; a far easier routine than the longer shifts and harder physical labour endured by many of their fellow seamen on board the Royal Mail Ship *Titanic*.

The senior of the two men, 41-year-old Able Seaman Reginald Robinson Lee, had a quarter of a century's experience of sailing across most of the oceans of the world. An intelligent man, the son of an Oxfordshire schoolmaster, he was one of just eight sailors trusted to serve as specialist lookouts on this, the newly-built *Titanic's*, maiden voyage. Just ten minutes earlier, Lee had heard 'Seven Bells', 11.30 pm ship's time, ringing out across the deck below. The bells were normally a welcome sound for any sailor nearing the end of his shift; even more so when he worked in this highest and chilliest post, on board the biggest ship in the world. On a normal night they signalled that just thirty minutes of the lookouts' shift remained, but with a muttered sailor's curse, Lee remembered that tonight was not a normal night. The ship's clocks were being set back that evening as *Titanic* powered westwards across the Atlantic.[1] Lee's lookout's shift was to be twenty-three minutes longer than normal. He later recalled the deep chill of that night's duty:

> It was a clear, starry night overhead. There was no moon; quite a calm sea, and no wind whatever, barring what the ship made herself. Very freezing ... the coldest we had had that voyage.

His watch had begun at 10.00 pm when he had squeezed through a small hatch hidden below decks and climbed up to the crow's-nest. For the passengers, this ship was the most luxurious vessel afloat; for the crew it was a world of plain-painted metal walls and cold metal ladders. Reaching the crow's-nest was not a task for the claustrophobic; the near-vertical ladder ran up *inside* the windowless, 3-foot diameter steel tube that formed the lower section of *Titanic's* foremast. An upper hatchway in the front face of the mast exited directly onto the 6-foot wide, semi-circular lookout platform. Stepping out of the hatch, Lee always had to be careful not to bump his head on the signal bell hanging immediately in front of him.

Lee's younger companion in the nest was Frederick Fleet. Then aged twenty-four, Fleet had overcome the most deprived of childhoods to earn his place in *Titanic's* crew: a father he never knew and abandonment by his mother, who ran away with a boyfriend and left her young son in the care of a children's home. He had followed the route of many 'Barnardo's boys' before him by joining a training ship at the age of twelve and being sent to sea four years later. Fleet had served with *Titanic's* operators, the White Star Line, for almost seven years and, despite his age, was already then an experienced lookout. During his previous four-year-long posting he had performed the same duty on what had been, until recently, the company's flagship, the SS *Oceanic*.

The two men knew each other well and, over many shifts closeted together high on the foremast, had developed an easy working relationship. Content to speak no more than was necessary, each gravitated naturally to his own favoured side of the thin-plated, steel crow's-nest basket. Although neither man could tell you why, Able Seaman Lee always preferred the port side of the nest and Fleet naturally stood to starboard. Despite those different viewpoints, they each spent most of their time looking dead ahead to where the greatest danger usually lies. Both were resolute in their duty.

They had a particular reason tonight to pay close attention to the ocean directly ahead. The lookouts they had relieved ninety minutes earlier had passed on instructions from the junior officer on the ship's bridge below: 'Watch out for small ice and growlers,' – 'growlers' being the sailors' name for the hard to spot, low-lying small icebergs often seen in these northern Atlantic waters.

Lee was one of the oldest ordinary seamen on board but he still rated his eyesight as excellent. On that night, however, he was finding it hard to see as clearly as he would have wished.

'There was a haze right ahead,' he later explained. 'In fact, it was extending more or less round the horizon. My mate happened to pass the remark to me. He said, "Well; if we can see through that we will be lucky." We had all our work cut out to pierce through it.'[2]

Even with the reduced visibility, Lee's experienced seaman's instincts told him that ice was somewhere near. 'You could smell it,' he said. 'There was a sudden change in the temperature.'

Late on that Sunday evening, RMS *Titanic*, the newest pride of the White Star Line's transatlantic fleet, was four days into her maiden voyage from Southampton to New York. She was expecting to dock at New York City's Pier 59, comfortably on schedule, in three days' time. In the warmth below deck, far beneath the two lookouts' icy perch, most of *Titanic's* 1,305 passengers and the majority of her 896 crew were in their cabins. Many were already asleep. On the bridge, Quartermaster Robert Hitchens and Sixth Officer James Moody were ensuring that the ship never deviated from its assigned course and speed. After a good dinner in the First Class restaurant, and confident that all was well with his ship and the world, Captain Edward Smith had retired to his own cabin. He was already sleeping peacefully with the pride of a man with a job well done. On her first Atlantic crossing, RMS *Titanic* was so far proving to be an unqualified success.

Even further below the two feet-stampingly cold sailors in the crow's-nest, *Titanic's* three propellers were powering the ship through the Atlantic waters at a little over 20 knots, around 23 miles per hour. The 45,000-ton ship was seemingly an irresistible force. But disastrously, around half a mile ahead and directly in the ship's planned path, lay an almost immoveable object: a million-ton iceberg.

The enormous iceberg would have been easy for lookouts Fleet and Lee to spot were it not for one remarkable scientific phenomenon: water undergoes a peculiar change when it freezes. Cubic metre for cubic metre, the solid ice weighs around ten per cent less than it does when it is liquid water. That makes ice float, whether as ice cubes in a cocktail in one of *Titanic's* luxurious restaurants, or as an Atlantic Ocean iceberg. But because the density differential between liquid and solid is so small, most of the ice lies underwater. Like all of its kind, the mountain of ice facing *Titanic* was hiding nine-tenths of its gargantuan bulk beneath the waterline. Lying in wait for the unsuspecting ship, the iceberg had already travelled on its own decade-long voyage to reach that spot.

## Notes

1. USA Senate Inquiry, Mr Hitchens: 'I do not know whether they put the clock back or not. The clock was to go back that night 47 minutes, 23 minutes in one watch and 24 in the other.'
2. Fleet's account was different. He denied the quote attributed to him by Lee and claimed: 'I told him there was a slight haze coming. It did not affect us, the haze … we could see just as well.'

# Chapter Two

# '. . . competent to produce disastrous results'

**Summer of 1902**
**Sea terminus of Jakobshavn Glacier**
**Disko Bay**
**West coast of Greenland**

The ice began life, tens of thousands of years ago, as billions of individual, freshwater snowflakes falling across the island of Greenland. Over millennia, the weight of more and more layers of snow crushed those flakes into ice that flowed outwards from the mountainous interior towards the sea. What had once been snow had now become part of the Jakobshavn Glacier, one of the fastest flowing rivers of ice on Earth.

A decade before *Titanic's* launch, the freshwater ice had reached the shores of Disko Bay, on Greenland's west coast. To this day, the shoreline there is the birthplace of most Atlantic icebergs. With what would have been an ear-splitting crash had there been human ears to hear it, a wall of ice calved from the face of the glacier and splashed spectacularly into the already ice-packed waters of the Ilulissat Icefjord: the leading edge of the Jakobshavn had just given birth to the most infamous iceberg in history.

The breadth and depth of the iceberg meant that its keel scraped along the sea bottom and its sides jostled for space against bergs big and small in the fjord's shallow channel. Progress was slow for the next six or seven years. Finally, inexorable pressure from the still-moving glacier at its rear squeezed the iceberg out of the fjord and into open water. Wind and waves pushed from all directions on the portion of ice that peeped above the waterline. But, with most of the iceberg's massive bulk under the surface of the water, its course was determined predominantly by the complex ocean currents. Finally freed into open water at the end of the fjord, it set off on a year-long journey towards Melville Bay on the northwest coast of Greenland. A further year saw it traverse Baffin Bay and float midway down the coast of Baffin Island.[1]

Growing fractionally smaller year by year as it melted freshwater into the surrounding ocean, the iceberg drifted relentlessly to the south-east.

All of the major shipping lines carrying passengers on the busy North Atlantic run between Europe and the USA knew about the dangers of ice. They had agreed among themselves to always travel on what they believed to be safe routes across the ocean. The mutually agreed, one-way routes to and from America had several advantages: they helped avoid collisions, they increased the chance of shipwreck survivors being found by another vessel, and, in theory, they kept all ships to the south of any drifting fields of Arctic ice.

But the ice season in 1912 was to prove an extraordinary one. The Hydrography Office of the United States Navy had recorded more reports than usual of icebergs drifting further south. The abnormally cold weather of early January of that year may have helped the bigger icebergs survive for longer in unusually cold Atlantic waters.

In addition, there was another unusual set of circumstances that was to affect the fate of *Titanic* on that April night in 1912. A high-pressure weather system had been sitting over the Northern Atlantic, bringing clear skies, low night-time temperatures and barely a breath of wind. On a dark night, most icebergs are more easily seen when waves are breaking into spray and pure white foam around their base. But the dead-calm seas through which *Titanic* was sailing were producing no waves at all.

Silent and unseen, on seas as still as a millpond, the iceberg drifted slowly onwards into the shipping lanes of the North Atlantic Ocean.

### Notes

1. This version of the iceberg's origins and course relies on 2011 interviews with experts of the US-based International Ice Patrol. One scientist commented: 'The question about the iceberg's fate is easier. It probably didn't survive very long, perhaps a few weeks. Most frequently, the cold waters of the Labrador Current move north-eastward. At this point, very warm water is not very far away.'

*Chapter Three*

# 'A most extraordinary circumstance'

**11.40 pm**
**Sunday, 14 April 1912**
**Crow's-nest of RMS** *Titanic*
**Dead reckoning position: 41° 46' N, 50° 41' W**
**North Atlantic Ocean**

Despite the younger lookout's lesser experience, but perhaps because of his younger eyes, it was Able-Seaman Fleet who first spotted danger. Initially, he made out just a vague shape, perhaps half a mile away.

> It kept getting larger as we were getting nearer it. I reported it as soon as ever I seen it.

Fleet struck hard on the crow's-nest bell hanging just above the two lookouts' heads: once, twice and then a third time, the alarm signal denoting a sighting dead ahead. He pushed past Lee to snatch up the telephone on the starboard side of the nest and punched the button that instantly connected him to the ship's bridge down below. His call was answered by *Titanic's* Sixth Officer, James Moody, although Fleet at the time had no idea to which officer he was speaking.[1]

> I got an answer straight away – 'What did you see?' I told him an iceberg right ahead. He said: 'Thank you.' It was so close to us. That is why I rang them up. It was not very large when I first saw it, as large as two tables put together; it kept getting larger as we were getting nearer it. When we were alongside, it was a little bit higher than the forecastle head; 50 or 60 feet above the water.

His fellow lookout, Lee, later described the moments leading up to the impact to the British Wreck Commissioner's Court Inquiry:

> As soon as the reply came back, the helm must have been put either hard-a-starboard or very close to it, because she veered to port, and it

seemed almost as if she might clear it ... but I suppose there was ice underwater.

It was a dark mass that came through that haze and there was no white appearing until it was just close alongside the ship, and that was just a fringe at the top. The ship seemed to heel to port as she struck the berg ... you could hear a rending of metal right away. It seemed to be running right along the starboard side.

The actual impact with the iceberg was a glancing blow. At first it appeared to have done little more than send a judder throughout the massive steel ship. Many passengers actually slept through the collision in blissful ignorance of what had happened. *Titanic* was supposed to be 'practically unsinkable', and able to survive with any two of its watertight compartments open to the sea. Yet, below the waterline, steel plates had buckled and riveted joints had sprung apart. Although the ship's officers did not yet know it, seawater was already being forced at high pressure into six different watertight compartments. The ship was already mortally wounded; nothing could now prevent her from sinking.

*Titanic* was at that time the biggest man-made object ever to have moved on the face of the planet. She was destined to sink beneath the waves within 2 hours and 40 minutes. There were far too few lifeboats on board ... and the clock was ticking.

The two lookout men, Fleet and Lee, were both fated to survive the sinking, but would soon realise that they were prime candidates to be blamed for the disaster. Like many of their surviving *Titanic* shipmates, they gave evidence at official inquiries in both America and Britain. Each was understandably nervous, and somewhat defensive. Frederick Fleet spent several gruelling hours in the witness box at the London inquiry. He was particularly stressed by the repeated questions from batteries of lawyers. Fearing that he was being set-up as the scapegoat, Fleet finally lost his patience: 'Is there any more likes to have a go at me?' he demanded.[2]

But, in fact, neither Fleet nor Lee had done anything wrong. In the freezing cold, high above the ocean, ill-equipped, with no binoculars on hand, and as the sole guardians of *Titanic's* safety, Fleet and Lee were blameless that night; ordinary sailors who did their duty as well as anyone could have expected. The abnormal weather and ocean conditions that made it harder for them to spot the iceberg were later described by *Titanic's* most senior surviving officer, Charles Lightoller:

In the first place, there was no moon. Then there was no wind, not the slightest breath of air. And most particular of all in my estimation is the fact, a most extraordinary circumstance, that there was not any swell. Had there been the slightest degree of swell I have no doubt that berg would have been seen in plenty of time to clear it. The moon we knew of, the wind we knew of, but the absence of swell we did not know of. You naturally conclude that you do not meet with a sea like it was, like a table top or a floor, a most extraordinary circumstance.

There were indeed guilty men on the night that *Titanic* struck the iceberg: men who shared responsibility for the deaths of 1,490 people; but none of them were in *Titanic's* crow's-nest that evening. With one exception, the guiltiest men of all were not even on board the great ship that night. None were ever convicted – or even charged – for their negligence, greed and overwhelming hubris that culminated in their nemesis of the *Titanic* disaster. They were all to survive, each carrying his own burden of guilt, into a comfortable old age, unlike so many of their victims, left struggling for survival as *Titanic* slowly filled with water.

### Notes

1. James Moody was the most junior office on board and was also the only one of *Titanic's* junior officers to die in the disaster. His body was never recovered.
2. Frederick Fleet's death was to be as unfortunate as his childhood. Having survived the sinking, he hanged himself at the age of seventy-seven in the garden of his home in Southampton.

## Chapter Four

# 'Gross breach of a relevant duty of care . . .'

**11.55 pm**
**Sunday, 14 April 1912**
**Mail Room of RMS** *Titanic*
**Dead reckoning position: 41° 46' N, 50° 41' W**
**North Atlantic Ocean**

The sights and the sounds were sufficient to chill the blood of any sailor. The water level inside the post room, deep in the bowels of *Titanic*, was visibly rising before his eyes, and the thunderous roar of rushing seawater was filling his ears. For a few seconds, 4th Officer Joseph Boxhall was rooted to the spot. He had been so sure that *Titanic* had escaped any serious damage; his earlier cursory check of the lowest accommodation decks had shown that all was normal, and he had reported that fact to the captain on the bridge. Only afterwards, having been sent deeper below decks to check once again, had Boxhall realised the full extent of that mistake:

> I met the carpenter and he wanted to know where the captain was. He said the ship was making water fast. I continued with the intention of finding out where the water was coming in, and I met one of the mail clerks. He also asked for the captain, and said the mail hold was filling. I went down to the mail room and found the water was within a couple of feet of G deck, the deck I was standing on ... It was rising rapidly up the ladder and I could hear it rushing in. I saw mail bags floating around on deck.

A few minutes earlier First Class Stewardess Mrs Annie Robinson had also seen the water rising up the mail room steps and had met the carpenter, John Hutchinson, whose duties included 'sounding the ship' to test the depth of any water in the bilges:

> He was the first man I saw. He came along when I was looking down at the water, and he had the lead line in his hand. The man looked absolutely bewildered, distracted. He said nothing.[1]

As the stewardess began gathering warm clothing and lifebelts from nearby cabins she saw Captain Edward Smith and the ship's designer, Thomas Andrews, come down to inspect the damage. Neither man was to survive the sinking:

> We had already got the blankets and the lifebelts out of the rooms which were unoccupied at the foot of the staircase. Mr Andrews said to me, 'Put your lifebelt on and walk about and let the passengers see you.' I said to him, 'It looks rather mean,' and he said, 'No, put it on,' and then after that he said to me, 'Well, if you value your life put your belt on.

Robinson did put her lifebelt on and immediately started to wake up and warn the eight First Class passengers under her care. All of her charges were early on deck and found spaces in a lifeboat. Not all on board were to be so lucky.[2]

Imagine, if you will, a similarly tragic, but hopefully imaginary, disaster striking one of today's packed holiday cruise ships on a voyage from Southampton to New York City. As the crisis unfolds – perhaps an uncontrollable fire, or a collision with another vessel far out to sea – the ship proves far weaker than she should have been. Water floods in below the waterline … and she slowly starts to sink. Her desperate captain reluctantly gives the one order that he hoped he would never need to issue: 'Man the lifeboats.'

But therein lies a problem. There are far too few boats to save everyone on board. This vast, floating palace has lifeboat seats for fewer than half of her unsuspecting passengers and crew. In the desperate scramble for survival, many passengers honourably remember – and obey – the most venerable law of the sea: 'Women and children first'. But, as the last lifeboats pull away to safety, almost 1,500 terrified victims are left behind to drown or slowly freeze to death in the cold Atlantic waters.

In our fictitious scenario, the world of today would be understandably outraged; a public outcry would demand justice for the innocent victims. Under our modern laws any, or all, of the cruise line owners, the designers, the builders, and even the politicians who failed to effectively regulate the number of her lifeboats, would be at risk of criminal prosecution.

The comparison with the fate of those who boarded *Titanic* a century ago is clear. With her swimming pool, gymnasium, electric elevators, wood-panelled interiors and elegant furnishings, the ship attracted some of the richest men and women in the world to join her maiden voyage. When she sailed out of Southampton on 10 April 1912, the ship possessed a passenger certificate from the British Board of Trade to carry up to 3,547 passengers and crew. Luckily, her owners had been unable to sell all of the tickets for her first sailing to New York; one-third of her accommodation was empty. The most luxurious ship the world had ever seen complied with all of the laws of the land. Yet, even had *Titanic's* lifeboats been packed to capacity, they had spaces for just 1,167 people.

In all human tragedies, great or small, there is rarely a single cause that leads to disaster: innumerable small decisions, myriad random-chance moments, countless lucky or unlucky throws of the dice, can mean the difference between life and death. Around the world, road, rail, air and sea disasters cost thousands of lives every year. Each tragedy may have had an obvious and immediate cause: the railway signal mistakenly left at green; the aircraft take-off checklist forgotten; or the bow doors of the ferry improperly secured. But there is always a lengthy chain of events leading up to the instant when disaster strikes: a multitude of times when small deviations in the vagaries of fate, or in people's attitudes and decisions, might have made it all so different.

And so it was for *Titanic* a century ago. Few could doubt the obvious and immediate cause of the accident: the ship hit an iceberg. But that collision, a glancing blow as the crew desperately attempted to alter course, need never have killed anybody. Nobody died as *Titanic* struck the iceberg; nobody died for two hours afterwards. She sank slowly, with ample time for all her lifeboats to be loaded and launched in fortuitously calm seas. The terrible deaths came later, in the frigid waters of the Atlantic Ocean, even as rescue boats steamed towards the scene. Because most of the victims were wearing their life-jackets, very few of them even drowned; mostly, they froze to death. *Titanic* was supposedly a triumph of the shipbuilding arts of one of Britain's greatest shipyards; the most modern and luxurious ship on the seven seas. She was reputedly the safest ship afloat. Nobody needed to die on *Titanic*.

Behind that simple truth lies a complex web of negligence, greed and bad human decisions that tragically altered the course of maritime history. This book attempts to look beyond the sensational, inaccurate headlines, and the inadequate public inquiries that followed the sinking of *Titanic*. From recently released files in national archive libraries and private collections on both sides of the Atlantic, it examines what motivated the myriad decisions that were to seal the fate of so many innocent men, women and children.

It studies, in particular, the roles of five powerful and influential figures. Some were household names at the time, such as the up-and-coming British Cabinet minister, Winston Spencer Churchill. Others, such as Board of Trade mandarin, Sir Alfred Chalmers, were little known outside of the corridors of Whitehall, where they wielded absolute power. British ship-owner, Bruce Ismay, had already created commercial empires in partnership with Lord Pirrie, the Chairman of *Titanic's* shipbuilders, Harland & Wolff. Now, they were busy social climbers, seeking respectability and recognition in the class-obsessed Britain of the day. The fifth man was already wealthy beyond measure: John Pierpoint Morgan, the American banker who effectively owned and controlled *Titanic*.

This investigation deals with events of a century ago, but also has messages for today. All those involved had their faults; some were merely lazy, others lusted after money, career enhancement, political influence or social position and respect. All shared some degree of the guilt for *Titanic's* demise. Laws governing corporate responsibility for people's health and safety have been changed substantially over the 100 years since *Titanic* sank. Companies whose actions kill people have long been liable to prosecution for 'gross negligence manslaughter'. Such prosecutions have, however, been rare, and often unsuccessful. For that reason, The Corporate Manslaughter and Corporate Homicide Act 2007 was introduced into British law. The legislation widens the scope of possible corporate prosecutions. British Crown Prosecution guidance explains:

> The new offence was created to provide a means of accountability for very serious management failings across the organisation. The offence is now considerably wider in scope ... and it now includes liability for organisations which could never previously be prosecuted for manslaughter.

The Act offers a clear definition of the offence:

> An organisation to which this section applies is guilty of an offence if the way in which its activities are managed or organised: causes a person's death; and amounts to a gross breach of a relevant duty of care owed by the organisation to the deceased.

Nobody faced criminal prosecution of any kind after the *Titanic* tragedy. This book looks at how different that position might have been had *Titanic* sunk today, when those responsible could have faced a criminal trial for violating health and safety regulations, gross negligence manslaughter, or corporate manslaughter laws.

Outlining the prosecution case against any of the men involved is not an easy task. Many decisions made over months, years and even decades before *Titanic* was launched all contributed to the final, tragic outcome. Events that may appear to have been unconnected – spread out over the years and over the wide oceans of the world, all played their part. The first of those events to affect the *Titanic* story was a tragedy in itself. It involved a desperate crime of murder – and cannibalism; a crime that was to shape the way in which the world looked upon human survival in lifeboats at sea.

### Notes

1. Receiving the tip of a gold coin, Hutchinson reputedly exclaimed: 'It's such good luck to receive gold on a first voyage.' He did not survive the voyage.
2. Annie Robinson may have suffered from post-traumatic stress disorder. Two years after surviving *Titanic* she panicked when a ferry sounded its foghorn. She jumped overboard and drowned.

## Chapter Five

# 'Drinking his blood will save our lives . . .'

25 July 1894
A becalmed lifeboat
Estimated position: 27° 10  S, 9° 50  W
1,600 miles off the Cape of Good Hope
Southern Atlantic Ocean

Cabin boy Richard Parker had not stirred for many hours. He sprawled, bent, cramped and apparently unconscious, across the narrow wooden plank that normally would serve as the seat for an oarsman in the bows of the open boat. This lifeboat, however, had no oars and no oarsman; merely a makeshift sail, fashioned from scraps of its near-dead crew's clothing. The four men in the boat were dying from thirst and starvation. For three weeks they had suffered together, adrift in this tiny 13-foot long wooden rowing boat. They had no food or fresh water. They were at least 1,000 miles in any direction from the nearest land.

Unbeknown to anyone at the time, the desperate plight of those unfortunate sailors was to reverberate down through the years to come and directly impact upon the fate of *Titanic*; a disaster that was still then almost twenty years in the future. The imminent death of the young cabin boy was to be one of the many factors determining the number of lifeboats to be carried on board *Titanic* – and therefore how many of that ship's company were to die.

The tragic story of Richard Parker, and the explanation of how his murder affected the *Titanic* disaster, began in May 1894. Captain Thomas Dudley, a respected, deeply religious and teetotal Master Mariner, was recruited to sail the 33-foot British yacht *Mignonette* to Australia. Dudley, temporarily retired from the sea and working as a greengrocer in Surrey, was at first uncertain about taking the job. It meant many months away from his family, and a perilous voyage. He was to have just two other trained crewmen, and young Parker, to assist him. But, married to a Hampshire schoolmistress and as the proud father of three young children, the captain badly needed the £200 he was offered for the voyage. The yacht's new owner, a wealthy Australian politician and businessman, had purchased the *Mignonette* on a recent visit to London. He was paying handsomely for its safe delivery to the other side of the world. Putting his fears aside and heading out from Southampton, Captain Dudley set course for the Cape of Good Hope ... and sailed into a nightmare.

All had gone well with the voyage until the day when, sailing southwards across the Atlantic, a sudden squall hit the *Mignonette*. It had been a sight to terrify any sailor; a rogue great-wave towering above the surrounding waters and bearing down on the tiny craft that was already struggling to stay abreast of heavy seas. Captain Dudley was certain he was about to die. He screamed a warning to his crew and wrapped himself around the mainmast, literally clinging on for his life. The boat lurched sickeningly to the side as the vast wave crashed over the captain's head. He heard timbers cracking around him and his aching arms all but lost a wrenching tug-of-war with the seething waters. Then, the seas receded. For a moment, Dudley dared to hope that all would be well; gasping for breath, he lifted his head – and saw that his vessel was lost.

Five weeks into its epic, 15,000-mile voyage from Southampton, England, to Sydney, Australia, the lee bulwarks of the yacht *Mignonette* had been smashed into matchwood and washed overboard by the storm. Without their protection, waves crashed freely over the open deck. Captain Dudley hauled himself to the rail and looked down over the ship's side. The damage was even worse than he had feared; the great wave had laid open the butt-ends, and water was pouring into the cabin below. The *Mignonette* was dying and was about to take her crew down with her.

Dudley had just one hope. The yacht's 13-foot long open lifeboat was still lashed to the afterdeck. First Mate Edwin Stephens and Seaman Edward Brooks were struggling to cut the boat free of the now fast-sinking yacht. Dudley wrenched the binnacle, the wooden case holding the ship's compass and navigational equipment, free of its housing on deck. He knew that the navigational aids might save their lives in the days to come.

He called to cabin boy, Richard Parker, to haul a 'beaker' container of fresh water up from the water-filled cabin. In his panic to get to the lifeboat, the 19-year-old boy threw the beaker into the ocean. He had hoped that they might salvage it from the waves after the yacht had sunk. In his own, last desperate act, Dudley scooped up an armful of food tins and threw them at the lifeboat; most fell into the water and sank – just two of the containers bounced into the bottom of the boat.

Achingly tired, soaked to the skin, shocked, and fearing for their lives, the former crew of the *Mignonette* took stock of their plight. As the remains of their yacht vanished below the waves they realised that, for the moment, they were safe. They had their lives and a small but seaworthy boat. They had the clothes they were wearing and the compass bravely pulled to safety by Captain Dudley. Most importantly, they had two 1lb tins of what they hoped was preserved meat. Disappointingly, those meagre provisions later proved to be cans of stewed turnips. They had not a drop of fresh water.

A frantic search of the ocean around them failed to find the water container that Parker had thrown over the side. Just knowing they had no water made all four men instantly thirsty. Yet, astonishingly, they were to survive for the next three weeks adrift on this lonely southern ocean. In the days that followed, the crew caught a little rainwater in the salt-soaked scraps of clothing they still wore and rationed out the last of their turnips. They pulled one small turtle into the boat and devoured it, down to the tiniest morsels of shell and bone. They even tried to save the turtle's blood but it was contaminated with seawater and undrinkable. After days without water, with mouths parched dry and tongues swelling, they began drinking their own urine. The cabin boy, Parker, fell ill and semi-conscious. His companions suspected he had succumbed to unbearable thirst and had repeatedly drunk seawater.

It was only on the twentieth day, when all on board were suffering the extreme pains of true starvation – and Parker seemed to be on the verge of death – that the captain unsheathed his knife. The sea had been calmer that morning, and even the irregular pitching movement of the broad, Atlantic swell had been unable to rouse the lad as it had done in earlier days. Richard Parker's long, sun-bleached fair hair lay, as if spread on a pillow, across the captain's rough-tanned and blackened sea boots. Captain Dudley gently wriggled his foot to see if the silent boy reacted to the movement. The unconscious 17-year-old boy, a would-be adventurer who wanted to see the world, was now dying thousands of miles from his Southampton home. He was beyond the point of registering his own pain or the captain's movements. Still scanning the unchanging horizon in his endless search for a sail, Captain Dudley whispered quietly to his other two shipmates.

'He's going, lads. He's been drinking seawater, he's burned, he's starving and he's dead to the world. There's the look of death about him. We've got to do him quick. Drinking his blood could save our lives.'

'Who's going to do it,' asked First Mate Edward Brooks. 'I've the fear of God about me when it comes to it, but I'll do my duty, if that's what it needs.'

'No, it's my job. I'll not ask your help, it wouldn't be right. But you need to hold him fast when I use the knife; get hold of the can, and make sure you catch every drop of that blood.'

In the stern of the small craft, crouching down below the gunwale, holding his head in his hands, Able Seaman Edwin Stephens tried, unsuccessfully, to block out the murderous conversation continuing in the bow of the boat. He was the only one of the survivors who had refused to contemplate the awful twin crimes of murder ... and cannibalism. A truly God-fearing man, Stephens was concerned for his immortal soul for even thinking of breaking the most Holy of Commandments: 'Thou Shalt Not Kill.'

Six feet away, Dudley and Brooks prepared to do just that. The captain held his razor-sharp, fish-gutting knife to the boy's throat, and murmured a prayer for both his victim and himself. 'Our Father, who art in heaven ...' All of the sailors were shocked when their intended victim suddenly spoke out: 'Is it time?' he murmured.

Overcome with emotion, Captain Dudley bent lower and used the hard-dried sleeve of his rough cotton shirtsleeve to wipe the sweat and seawater droplets from the dying boy's brow.

'Aye lad ... Richard, my boy, your time has come.'

Even as he comforted the boy, Captain Dudley drew his knife in one long, sweeping motion fast across the lad's neck. Warm, thick blood spurted in a rising arc from his victim's severed carotid artery and splashed noisily into the empty can that the Mate held in place to catch the precious liquid. All tenderness abandoned in his desperation to slake his own thirst, Dudley let the dead boy's head drop heavily to the floor. He snatched at the now warm can, lifted it to his lips ... and drank greedily.

Crouching by Dudley's side, Brooks was resisting an overwhelming urge to snatch the can from the ship master's hands and take his own drink. He grasped at their victim's throat, squeezing hard to try and stem the flow, until the blood could be caught once again in the only receptacle they had. When his turn came to drink, the blood had cooled slightly, but Brooks gulped half a can of the partly-congealed, faintly salty liquid down his throat. Then he turned and offered the life-saving fluid to Stephens.

Overcoming waves of revulsion and his fear of Holy retribution, the 26-year-old sailor also drank in a frenzy of thirst, until the can was snatched from his hands, to be refilled from the flow that then gurgled, rather than spurted from the gaping wound in Parker's neck. No further words were exchanged as the corpse was lifted and tilted sideways to drain every drop of consumable blood from the body. These men had survived in the lifeboat for almost three weeks, with virtually no food and precious little water. In the days to come, Richard Parker's body was to be systematically butchered and cannibalised by his fellow shipmates. Evidence at their eventual murder trial would reveal that the three men first ate the body parts most likely to spoil in the heat: the heart, the liver and the kidneys. Next went the major muscle areas of the thighs and upper arms; to be followed by thinner meat strips, dried for days in the sun. In court, Dudley admitted that he killed the boy, before a natural death from thirst and starvation intervened, for fear that Parker's blood would congeal rapidly once his heart had stopped pumping. The sailors had needed that blood to survive; their crime was a crime of absolute need.

It was also a crime that induced such revulsion among the British public that, for years afterwards, it influenced people's view about survival in lifeboats at sea. Within the next two decades, the cannibal consumption of young Richard Parker in a lifeboat impacted directly upon a far greater tragedy, the death of 1,490 souls on board *Titanic*. Public sensibilities about this and similar 'cannibalism at sea' cases helped influence government thinking about the necessity of having lifeboats for all of the passengers and crew on board any ship.

Just four days after the murder, Captain Dudley, Brooks and Stephens, all sustained by the bounty of Parker's blood and flesh, were finally rescued by the crew of a passing German cargo ship. They made no secret of how they survived. Requesting that the cabin boy's 'torn and mangled body' be buried at sea, Dudley freely confessed to the killing, and repeated every detail of the case to Customs officials when they landed, still weak from their ordeal, at Falmouth Docks in Cornwall. In those latter days of the nineteenth century, cases of 'survival cannibalism' were far from unknown at sea. In one infamous case, a starving seaman had suggested drawing lots to see who should die; then drew the shortest straw himself. He had willingly accepted his fate for the greater good. The difference in Captain Dudley's case was that his victim had clearly been too weak to have volunteered his own death.

At their family home in Myrtle Road, Sutton, Surrey, Captain Dudley's worried wife, Phillipa, was relieved to receive a telegram with news that her husband was safe and well in Cornwall. It was not until the following day that the local schoolmistress read newspaper accounts of his dreadful ordeal and learned of the murder at sea. The Falmouth police were at first reluctant to arrest the surviving sailors but finally did so on orders from the Home Office in London. Dudley and Brooks were charged with Parker's murder and remanded in custody. The third crewman, Stephens, who had eaten and drunk from the victim's body but who took no part in the killing, became an unwilling witness for the prosecution.

The sensational court case, and the appeal court hearings that followed, polarised opinion throughout the country. Although the court hearing was taking place 250 miles away, the London *Evening Standard* was moved to comment:

> Although the loss of the *Mignonette* involved the sacrifice of one life only, it possesses all the elements of the most fatal tragedies of the sea.

Many agreed with the prosecution claim that killing an innocent man or woman to save one's own life could never be acceptable; others referred to ancient 'laws of the sea', believing that the sailors had been driven to murder from necessity only after unimaginable suffering. A public appeal had no difficulty in raising substantial sums from well-wishers anxious to pay for the sailors' defence.

A *Daily Telegraph* editorial about the case summed up the depth of feeling:

Repulsive as the last resort of this boat's crew appears, it is but just to
remember that it was arrived at only through and after an anguish of
suffering which would dethrone reason and reduce manhood to a raving
crave for food and drink utterly beyond the limits of restraint and
wholly unimaginable to any save the victims. These are they that came
out of great tribulation.

Guided by the Judge, the Cornish jury returned a 'special verdict', a rare legal
procedure that had not then been used for more than 100 years. That verdict
detailed the accepted facts of the killing, but requested the court to rule on the
men's guilt or innocence. Many were shocked when both of the accused were
pronounced guilty of murder. The Judge donned the traditional black cap and
sentenced both men 'to be taken to the place of execution and hanged by the
neck until dead.'

Home Office files, stored for more than a century in the British National
Archives, reveal the depth of concern that the sentence caused within the
corridors of establishment power. The captain's wife, Mrs Phillipa Dudley,
wrote to Queen Victoria, eloquently begging that his life should be spared:

He is a good husband and a good father to his children. He did all he
could to save the lives of his crew ... the elements mocked them with
rain clouds that dispersed with no rain. This case has no known parallel
and God grant that it never may have again. The publicity and misery
of the tragedy have been too painful almost for human endurance.

On the margins of a file that went to the Queen, the then Home Secretary, Sir
William Harcourt, the official who had initiated the prosecution in order to
clarify the law regarding 'murder by necessity', added his own, poignant,
handwritten note:

This is a sad–sad case, one of the saddest I should think that has ever
come under the notice of a Minister of the Crown.

In Holloway Prison, awaiting transfer to a condemned cell as prisoner No. 31-
5331, Captain Dudley was allowed to write or receive just one letter every
three months. But his lawyer brought him news of an upwelling of public
support that saw donations flood in to fund his family and support any
possible appeal. The money was never needed for a legal battle. Days later,
Queen Victoria acted on the advice of her Home Secretary and respited the
men's death sentences. They were replaced with six months of imprisonment.

Dudley and his first mate were duly released on 20 May 1895,[1] a year to the
day since their disastrous voyage began. His campaigning wife, Phillipa,
pleaded with the British Board of Trade to legally enforce the provisioning of

lifeboats to prevent such a tragedy in future. The files show they thought her suggestion 'self-evident and requiring no action'.

More significantly, the case of the *Mignonette* and other 'survival cannibalism' cases at sea reinforced a belief, common among law-makers in the nineteenth century, that the provision of lifeboats simply prolonged human misery, and could even promote the fearful sin of eating human flesh. It was a fear that was voiced frequently in the House of Commons, even by the most senior government officials responsible for safety at sea. As early as 1876, the then President of the Board of Trade, Sir Charles Addersley MP, argued vehemently against the idea of providing enough lifeboats to save everybody on board a sinking ship. The example he cited proved to have chilling parallels with the future fate of *Titanic*.

> Suppose a ship [be] wrecked in the middle of the Atlantic, with all the lifeboats proposed on board, and that all the passengers were lowered safely into them, what would become of them? They would simply be starved, and die by inches, instead of being drowned in the ship.
>
> The decks would be crowded with boats, two-thirds of which would probably become rotten and unstable, and certainly all of them could not be lowered or manned in case of emergency. A great number of boats would be the worst kind of deck-loading, and would impede the working and navigation of the ship. Even if the passengers were got in, the only difference would be that they would be drowned in the boats, instead of being drowned in the ship.[2]

By today's standards, the willingness to let seafarers drown with no hope of salvation may appear to be a cruel and abnormal concept. Yet fuelled by the greed of ship owners who never wanted to pay for boats or for the men who could launch them, it was to be the norm for almost fifty more years. It was only to end on the night, in April 1912, when almost 1,500 of *Titanic's* doomed men, women and children found the ship was sinking under them – and too few boats were left to save them.

### Notes

1. On his release, Dudley refused substantial financial offers to exhibit himself 'in places of public entertainment'. He always believed himself wrongly convicted, and initially refused to speak of his ordeal. He and the ever-loyal Phillipa are believed to have emigrated to Australia.

2. Addersley was ridiculed for his own lack of seafaring experience but refused to amend his 1876 Merchant Shipping Act, and won a decisive majority in the subsequent division.

## Chapter Six

# 'Many more could have been saved . . .'

12.20 am
15 April 1912
The confectioner's cabin
RMS *Titanic's* E deck, amidships on the port side
Dead reckoning position: 41° 46' N, 50° 41' W
North Atlantic Ocean

The natural home of Charles Joughin, the chief baker on *Titanic*, was far below decks in the comparative peace and quiet of his bakery. He had never enjoyed the clatter and confusion of the ship's main galleys, where food orders were shouted out from dawn till midnight among the chefs and their myriad assistants. Instead, since joining the ship as part of the original delivery crew in Belfast, Joughin had been spending his days, and much of his nights, working quietly alongside his staff of thirteen bakers. Together they turned out of his ovens the thousands of loaves, rolls, biscuits and pastries needed to feed the 2,201 people on board.

Just 32-years-old, Joughin was a married man, originally from Birkenhead, on Merseyside. He was proud to hold his responsible post with the new flagship liner of the famed White Star Line. Joughin was well qualified for the job; he had worked in kitchens at sea since the age of eleven. He knew that producing fine bread required skill, and patience. His years of seagoing experience had taught Joughin never to panic. He had already heard that *Titanic* had struck an iceberg, but a simple thing like his ship sinking from under him was not going to start him panicking now. The baker had just heard the general order: 'All hands out; all hands out of your bunks,' instructing the crew to go on deck. There was, however, just one thing that Joughin needed to do first ... he was badly in need of a drink.

Joughin, one of *Titanic's* least recognised heroes, had already been far from idle in the three-quarters of an hour since the collision roused him from his bunk in his cabin on E deck. His first task was to 'provision the boats'. Joughin had rushed to his bakery on D deck, one floor above, and despatched every one of his team with armfuls of soft bread for the lifeboats. He later explained:

> The boats are provided with hard bread, what we call biscuits. I sent thirteen men up with four loaves apiece; 40 pounds of bread each, as near as I could guess.

Despite his years of seafaring experience and his outwardly calm demeanour, not all of the baker's actions were to prove to be entirely sensible for a man who feared he may be swimming for his life if the ship were to sink.

'Some curious things are done at a time like this,' he said. 'Why did I lock the heavy, iron door of the bakery ... and stuff the heavy keys in my pocket?'

Having properly fulfilled his lifeboat catering duty, Joughin headed for his cabin. He had moved from the accommodation originally allocated to him, and had taken over the nearby 'confectioner's cabin'. It had a little more space and enjoyed the benefit of light from a porthole. On his way downstairs, the baker had passed men, women and children struggling upwards from cabins on the lower decks. They were Third Class passengers trying to find a way through what, for them, was alien territory; areas of the ship that were normally reserved for the crew and those with upper class tickets. The lost refugees were hoping to reach the First Class upper deck, from where lifeboats were already being launched.

'There was an emergency door from the Third Class, into the Second Class, leading up the broad staircase that was open very early,' said Joughin. 'Coming along the alleyway were some women, with two bags in their hands. They would not let go of them.

'Just outside of this emergency door there are two wide staircases, which, under ordinary conditions, is private for the crew, but I suppose they walked through it. One man had two bags slung over his shoulder and one in his hand – an Italian, or some nationality like that.'

Joughin later told the London inquiry that even though there were no locked gates to obstruct the Third Class passengers, their route to the boat deck was far from straightforward. He had seen an interpreter and stewards from Third Class trying to make passengers understand that, in this moment of crisis, they were allowed to pass through an emergency door.

> At normal times it is kept private. They could walk past it, but it is never open. They would not know unless they were given instructions. I saw the interpreter passing the people along that way, but there was a difficulty in getting them along because some of the foreign Third Class passengers were bringing their baggage and their children. It hampered the interpreter and the men who were helping him because they could not prevail on the people to leave their luggage.

I saw Third Class passengers coming straggling through the kitchen,
and they even had their baggage then.

These first signs of panic among refugees from the lower decks were totally
understandable. Nobody had told them that *Titanic* was sinking, but the decks
already had a slight, but noticeable, tilt downwards towards the bow. Inch-by-
inch, the front of the ship was being dragged down by the weight of seawater
flooding in below the waterline. Seams between the overlapping steel plates of
her hull had buckled. The rivets in this forward part of the ship were made of
iron and the impact had sheared off many of their heads. The weakened joints
were letting in water.

Ignoring the growing unease among the crowds, Joughin escaped to the
peace and quiet of his cabin. He sat down on the small settee, up against what
the crew termed the 'skin' of the ship, and poured himself a large glass of
strong spirits. Suitably fortified, he headed back upstairs to fulfil his next
important duty of the night. On the day that *Titanic* departed from
Southampton, a lifeboat list for the catering crew had been affixed to the D
deck galley wall. It assigned the Chief Baker to be in charge of the crew of
lifeboat No. 10, the foremost of four lifeboats towards the rear of the ship, on
the port side. Like the great majority of *Titanic's* crew, Joughin was a sailor,
not a boatman. He was not trained to handle an oar. He was, however,
determined to do whatever duty was asked of him. By around half-past
midnight he arrived at the side of boat No. 10 on the upper deck of *Titanic*:

> They were getting the boat ready for getting the passengers in. Mr
> Wilde (the Chief Officer) shouted out for the stewards to keep the
> people back, to keep the men back, but there was no necessity for it. The
> men kept back themselves, and we made a line and passed the ladies and
> children through; stewards and seamen; they were all together. The
> discipline was splendid.

Joughin helped load boat No. 10 until no more women and children could be
found.

> We got it about half full, and then we had difficulty in finding ladies for
> it. They ran away from the boat and said they were safer where they
> were. I heard ladies saying that. Myself and three or four other chaps
> went on the next deck and forcibly brought up women and children;
> they were all sitting, squatting down on the deck. Many more could
> have been saved, had the women obeyed orders. In those circumstances
> the crew are helpless.

Determined to save as many people as possible, Joughin ignored the women's
reluctance to leave the supposed safety of the ship and face the dangers of a

60-foot descent in a lifeboat. He and his colleagues manhandled women and children upstairs towards the boats.

> There are only about ten stairs to go up. I brought up two children and the mother – and a mother and a child, and other stewards were bringing up other women.

Back up on the boat deck with his reluctant charges, Joughin found that *Titanic* was listing more heavily. Lifeboat No. 10, which had been alongside the deck, now hung 4 feet or more away from the ship's side. Undaunted, Joughin threw two children across the gap and into the boat ... but their mother held back.

> We wanted to throw her in, and I think she preferred to try and step in. She missed her footing ... this steward named Burke got hold of her foot and she swung head downwards for a few minutes, but somebody caught her into B deck ... no ... on A deck.

A month after the sinking, Joughin's testimony was to have a startling impact at the British Wreck Commissioner's Inquiry. The packed hall fell silent as *Titanic's* cool-headed baker was asked what had become of the mother who was dragged, upside-down, onto the deck below.

'Did you ever see her again?'
'No.'
'The children were saved?'
'The children were saved.'[1]

With his lifeboat now 'pretty well filled' with women and children, Joughin expected that he would be ordered to take his place in charge of the boat crew. He knew that each lifeboat had been assigned seven or eight men to row it clear of the sinking ship. And Joughin had checked that all of his bakery staff were ready, able and willing to tackle that task:

> I sung [sic] out the names of all the victualing department connected with the boat, and they were – every man – there. I was supposed to be captain of the boat by the crew list. I was standing waiting for orders, by the officer, to jump in, and he then ordered two sailors in and a steward. I would have set a bad example if I had jumped into the boat. None of the men felt inclined to get in. We stood back till the officers should give us the word, and we never got it ... so that we never jumped for the boat.

As lifeboat No. 10 began its precipitous, 60-foot descent down the side of *Titanic*, the men who should have been manning its oars were left behind on the deck with no new orders to follow. Joughin, however, knew precisely what to do. He needed another drink.

I went down to my room and had a drop of liquor that I had down there.

But in the forty minutes that Joughin had been helping out on deck, *Titanic's* plight had grown distinctly more perilous. Compartments near the bow were so deeply flooded that water was flowing over the top of the ship's bulkheads and spreading rapidly through the front sections of the Third Class decks. Even Joughin's E deck cabin was no longer the safe haven it had been. He found that the floor was running wet with water:

> I saw it in my room; just enough to cover my feet, that was all. My idea was she had shipped some water forward, and had run down; but I did not give it a second thought, because it was not serious.

Sitting on his sofa, up to his ankles in seawater, Joughin poured out another half-tumbler of neat spirits ... and carried on drinking.

### Notes

1. Although Joughin did not see the woman again, other crewmen saw her pulled onto the ship and climb back in the boat to be reunited with her children.

# Chapter Seven

# 'Who, if anyone, told you to enter that lifeboat?'

**1.00 am**
**Monday, 15 April 1912**
**Upper deck of RMS *Titanic***
**Dead reckoning position: 41° 46' N, 50° 41' W**
**North Atlantic Ocean**

While Joughin, the baker, was savouring his drink in his E deck cabin, hundreds of women and children were still being loaded into the last few of the sixteen wooden lifeboats on the uppermost deck of the ship. Around an hour and twenty minutes after striking the iceberg, *Titanic* was dipping lower and lower in the water. Her pumps were at full capacity, discharging more than 30 tons of water per minute from the stricken ship's lower decks. They were, however, fighting a losing battle with the overwhelming power of the ocean. Seawater was flooding in at a rate of 360 tons per minute and all of the pumps on board could only briefly delay the inevitable.

Even so, many of the passengers remained ignorant of the imminent danger; convinced that they were safer on board the vast, 45,000-ton vessel than they would be in an open lifeboat at sea. With many of the boats by then launched and rowing away from the ship, around 1,800 people were still trapped on *Titanic*, many of them nowhere near the lifeboats on the upper deck. The crew, trying to persuade women and children into the boats, had been joined by an unexpected volunteer: Bruce Ismay, the 49-year-old president of the American corporation that owned *Titanic*, had been working alongside them on the open deck.

Ismay, a British ship-owner who had inherited one of the world's greatest shipping empires from his father and grandfather before him, was the man most directly responsible for the design, construction and operation of *Titanic*. Now he was struggling to comprehend the magnitude of the disaster that had befallen him, his company, and *Titanic's* remaining passengers and crew. Ismay already knew that he was living through a disaster of almost unimaginable proportions. What he could not then have appreciated was that the repercussions of the tragedy would echo through the years to come and blight the remainder of his life. The events then unfolding on the boat deck were to ruin Ismay's reputation forever and brand him as, arguably, *Titanic's* most despicable coward.

Ismay's sole reason for sailing on *Titanic* had been to judge how well the ship would operate on her maiden voyage. He had been on deck for more than an hour. Moving from lifeboat to lifeboat, he had urged women to save themselves and encouraged the sailors to 'lower away' the boats. Most of the crew had not even recognised the president of their shipping line, and some had not welcomed his assistance. At one point, *Titanic's* 5th officer, Harold Lowe, told Ismay, his own employer, to 'Go to Hell ... '[1] because his unwanted instructions were confusing everybody.

'The occasion for using the language I did was because Mr Ismay was over-anxious and he was getting a trifle excited.' Lowe explained later:

> He said, 'Lower away! Lower away! Lower away! Lower away!' I told him, 'If you will get to Hell out of that, I shall be able to do something.' He was, in a way, interfering with my duties, and also, of course, he only did this because he was anxious to get the people away and also to help me.
>
> I said, 'Do you want me to lower away quickly? You will have me drown the whole lot of them.' He did not make any reply. He walked away and went to No. 3 boat.

Combining Bruce Ismay's testimony to both the American and British inquiries builds up a detailed picture of his actions that night. The millionaire ship-owner consistently claimed that all he wanted to do was save as many lives as possible:

> I assisted, as best I could, getting the boats out and putting the women and children into the boats. I do not think I ever left that deck again. We simply picked the women out and put them in the boat as fast as we could. The natural order would be women and children first; as far as practicable.
>
> I put a great many in. We took the first ones that were there and put them in the lifeboats. I rendered all the assistance I could. All the women that I saw on deck got away in boats. They were swung out, people were put into the boats from the deck, and then they were simply lowered away down to the water.

Ismay's critics, however, took a different view of his actions. He was one of the few people on board who knew the terrifying truth: that *Titanic* was inevitably going to sink that night. How convenient then was Ismay's self-appointed role as an unofficial, junior lifeboat assistant? It gave the ship-owner the perfect reason to stay close by the boats; and the perfect means of saving himself should the opportunity arise.

By Ismay's own account of events, he clearly understood the danger far better than any other passenger on board. Finding himself all alone the previous evening, Ismay had invited an old friend, *Titanic's* surgeon, Dr William O'Loughlin, to dine with him in the First Class restaurant. The two men, colleagues for almost forty years, had eaten early and finished their meal before 9.00 pm. Ismay then returned to his cabin, put on his pyjamas and fell asleep.

> I presume the impact awakened me. I lay in bed for a moment or two afterwards, not realising, probably, what had happened. I really thought we had lost a blade off the propeller.[2] I went along the passageway out of my room and I met a steward. I asked him what had happened; he told me he did not know.
>
> I went back to my room, put a coat on and went up on to the Bridge, where I found Capt. Smith. I asked him what had happened, and he said, 'We have struck ice.' I said, 'Do you think the ship is seriously damaged?' He said, 'I am afraid she is.'

Ismay, who had known and respected Smith for decades, was to see the captain twice that night; first soon after the impact, and then during a second visit to the bridge around thirty-five minutes later. By then, *Titanic* was already dipping lower into the water. In the interim, Ismay had returned to his cabin and donned a suit and an overcoat over the top of his pyjamas. Yet, in the confusion, he forgot to put on his shoes and spent the rest of the night wearing only his slippers.

> I heard Captain Smith give an order to lower the boats. I think that is all he said. He simply turned around and gave the order. As soon as I heard, I left the bridge. I walked along to the starboard side of the ship, where I met one of the officers. I told him to get the boats out – I saw the first lifeboat lowered on the starboard side. What was going on on the port side, I have no knowledge of.

Armed with his insider's knowledge about *Titanic's* inevitable fate, Bruce Ismay stood directly opposite one of the last boats waiting to be launched on the starboard side of the ship. It was one of four collapsible, canvas-sided boats that *Titanic* carried in addition to the sixteen wooden lifeboats that hung from her davits. 'Collapsible-C' had already been manhandled onto an empty davit in preparation for its descent. As it began inching lower Ismay looked around, moved forward ... and stepped into the boat. The lifeboat rocked slightly as he took a seat among the few dozen women and children already on board.

Ismay subsequently attempted to justify his actions throughout repeated question-and-answer sessions with Senator William Alden Smith, the Chairman of the US Senate Hearings. He defiantly explained how and why he escaped with the women and children, just before *Titanic* finally slipped beneath the waves:

'Mr Chairman, I understand that my behaviour on board the *Titanic* has been very severely criticised. I want to court the fullest inquiry, and I place myself unreservedly in the hands of yourself and any of your colleagues, to ask me any questions in regard to my conduct; so please do not hesitate to do so, and I will answer them to the best of my ability.'

'Who, if anyone, told you to enter that lifeboat?'

'No one, Sir.'

'Why did you enter it?'

'Because there was room in the boat: she was being lowered away. I felt the ship was going down, and I got into the boat. I was immediately opposite the lifeboat when she left. The boat was there. There was [sic] a certain number of men in the boat, and the officer called out asking if there were any more women, and there was no response, and there were no passengers left on the deck. And as the boat was in the act of being lowered away, I got into it.'

'At that time the *Titanic* was sinking?'

'She was sinking.'

'Was there any attempt, as this boat was being lowered past the other decks, to have you take on more passengers?'

'None, Sir; there were no passengers there to take on.'

'And that at the time there were no other persons around; no women, particularly?'

'Absolutely none that I saw, Sir.'

'Was that the last lifeboat, or the last collapsible boat, to leave?'

'It was the last collapsible boat that left the starboard side of the ship. It was not filled to its capacity. I should think there were about forty women in it, and some children. There was a child in arms. I think they were all Third Class passengers, so far as I could see.'

'Were all of the women and children saved?'

'I am afraid not, Sir.'

'What proportion were saved?'

'I have no idea. I have not asked. Since the accident I have made very few inquiries of any sort.'

As the most senior executive of the company that owned *Titanic*, Ismay's apparent indifference to the fate of her passengers and crew was used against him by his critics in the months after the disaster. His evidence in America revealed that, for some days after the sinking, he had spoken to just one of the surviving officers, and to none of the traumatised passengers. With the sole exception of the Second Officer, Charles Lightoller, Ismay admitted that he did not even know the names, ranks or the positions of the other *Titanic* officers who had lived through the ordeal.

Ismay was unable to give even a rough estimate of the proportion of women and children who had been saved. The British inquiry into the sinking did, however, calculate the figures.[3] Out of 439 female passengers and crew, 336, or 77 per cent, did survive. Out of 105 children on the ship just 52, or 49 per cent of them, were saved. Both statistics were in stark contrast to the proportion of men who died; out of the 1,662 men on board, a mere 319, just 19 per cent, survived the accident. One of the survivors was Bruce Ismay.

Ismay's decision to save himself by taking one of the precious lifeboat seats when so many others, including hundreds of women and children, were left behind to die was to haunt him for the rest of his life. One American newspaper headline at the time condemned him as 'Brute' Ismay.

The questionable morality of Ismay's decision to save his own life was perhaps best highlighted at the British inquiry by Clement Edwards, an MP and barrister representing many of the 686 crewmen and women who had died. His cross-examination, in the face of sometimes monosyllabic answers from the wealthy ship-owner, expressed the views of many 'ordinary men in the street' about Ismay's conduct that night:

'When you got into the boat you thought that the *Titanic* was sinking?'

'I did.'

'Did you know that there were some hundreds of people on that ship?'

'Yes.'

'Who must go down with her?'

'Yes, I did.'

'Has it occurred to you that, except perhaps apart from the captain, you, as the responsible managing director, deciding the number of boats, owed your life to every other person on that ship?'

'It has not.'

'If you had taken this active part in the direction up to a certain point, why did you not continue and send to other decks to see if there were passengers available for this last boat?'

'I was standing by the boat; I helped everybody into the boat that was there, and, as the boat was being lowered away, I got in.'

'Is it not the fact that you were calling out, 'Women and children first', and helping them in?'

'Yes, it is.'

'What I am putting to you is this, that if you could take an active part at that stage, why did you not continue the active part and give instruction, or go yourself to other decks, or round the other side of that deck, to see if there were other people who might find a place in your boat?'

'I presumed that there were people down below who were sending the people up.'

'But you knew there were hundreds who had not come up; that is your answer; that you presumed that there were people down below sending them up?'

'Yes.'

'And does it follow from that that you presumed that everybody was coming up who wanted to come up?'

'I knew that everybody could not be up.'

'Then I do not quite see the point of the answer?'

'Everybody that was on the deck got into that boat.'

Ismay had earlier revealed that only one other male passenger had escaped in his boat, but that a few of the crew had stowed away on board.

> We found four Chinamen stowed away under the thwarts after we got away. I think they were Filipinos, perhaps. I believe one was a cook, another was the butcher, and another was the quartermaster.

The Inquiry Commissioner, Lord Mersey, who had earlier tried to deter any public discussion of Ismay's escape from the ship, finally brought the continuing cross-examination to a halt. He briefly, and bad-temperedly, summarised the Union barrister's case against Ismay:

'Your point, Mr Edwards, as I understand, is this: that, having regard to his position, it was his duty to remain upon that ship until she went to the bottom. That is your point?'

'Frankly, that is so; I do not flinch from it a little bit.'

The official hearings on both sides of the Atlantic later exonerated Ismay[4] from the suggestions of cowardice and dishonour that were widespread among the public and press. Despite that, the circumstances of his survival and his deep personal involvement in the construction and management of *Titanic* were such that neither Ismay's reputation, nor the man himself, ever fully recovered. Reputedly at the insistence of his American-born wife, Florence, he never again publicly discussed the tragedy. Even before *Titanic* sailed, Ismay had been planning to retire from his taxing role as the public figurehead of one of the world's most diverse shipping empires.[5] The following year he duly resigned and brought to an end his family dynasty's long history of control over the famed White Star Line.

Unbeknown perhaps even to Ismay himself, there was a terrible irony, never made public before, in the fact that he was saved by one of *Titanic's* last lifeboats. Over decades leading up to the sinking, the British Board of Trade had consistently refused to update regulations governing the number of boats to be carried on the vast new ocean liners of the day. The irony is that files now released within the British National Archives have revealed for the first time the name of the one man who bears much of the responsibility for the grossly inadequate number of boats on *Titanic*. He was a man who rejected suggestions that ships should carry 'lifeboats for all'. He bullied and cajoled Board of Trade committees to keep lifeboat numbers below the numbers that safety required. That man was Thomas Ismay – Bruce Ismay's father.

Among the most prominent ship-owners of his day, Thomas Henry Ismay was personally responsible for Board of Trade rules that allowed British ships to sail with insufficient lifeboats. The regulations he created were to remain in force for decades. They allowed *Titanic* to sail from Southampton with lifeboat places for less than half of her passengers and crew.

The story of how Thomas Ismay helped to cause the death of almost 1,500 people – and in the process almost killed his own son – began fifty years earlier, on the far side of the world.

### Notes

1. Lowe was reluctant to reveal what 'swear-word' he had used. He wrote it on a piece of paper and handed it to the Chairman. The word 'Hell' was then ruled to be admissible for the official record.
2. Ismay knew that *Titanic's* sister ship, *Olympic*, had lost a propeller blade on a similar transatlantic crossing.
3. Confusion in official passenger and crew lists meant that statistics about the number of people on *Titanic* were recalculated by officials towards the end of the inquiry. It produced slight statistical variations in all of their figures of death or survival. The confusion has never been fully resolved.
4. In his final report, Lord Mersey dismissed criticism of Bruce Ismay: 'There was room for him and he jumped in. Had he not jumped in he would merely have added one more life, namely, his own, to the number of those lost.'
5. In yet another strangely prophetic moment, Ismay wrote, before the disaster, about his plans to retire the following summer. He concluded by saying: "... of course the 30 June 1913 is a far cry, and much may happen between now and then.'

## Chapter Eight

# 'The stench was like that from a pen of pigs . . .'

8.00 am
5 August 1851
White Star Line's cutter SS *Phoenician*
Estimated position: 52° S, 34° W
South of the Falkland Islands
Southern Atlantic Ocean

A murmur of excited voices could be heard from below as the last of the wooden clips were hammered away from the battened-down hatch. As the canvas cover was finally lifted, the smell of human excrement and sweat from scores of unwashed bodies rose like a warm, damp fog from the heart of the ship. After days of stormy weather, this was a rare opportunity for the passengers of the Aberdeen White Star ship, SS *Phoenician*, to see the sky and feel the sun upon their faces. The steerage passengers wearily climbed out onto the deck, at last free to savour the luxury of fresh air, untainted by the stink of themselves and the enforced nearness of their neighbours.

On the raised poop deck of the *Phoenician*, then sixty-one days out of London on its voyage to Sydney, Australia, Captain Hugh Sproat was keeping a wary eye on the strength of the wind. The ship's sails were billowing wildly and the White Star flag was flapping against the mainmast. The five-pointed symbol, set against a blood-red background, flew over every ship of the White Star Line. An identical flag was destined, some sixty years in the future, to grace the rigging of a vastly larger White Star ship; a link through the years between the company's 485-ton cutter, *Phoenician*, and her luxurious, 45,000-ton, far-distant cousin, *Titanic*.

Captain Sproat's nose wrinkled in disgust as the smell of his passengers blew to him on the wind. At the age of forty-one, and with years of experience working 'the Australia run', Sproat had seen before the levels of degradation to which these lowest class of emigrant passengers could sink. He knew what happened on these long voyages halfway across the globe. Men and women unused to the demeaning hardship of ocean life sometimes found even the basic decencies of washing and human hygiene beyond their capabilities. One of his fellow seafarers had given evidence to an earlier British Parliamentary inquiry about just how bad conditions could be on the run to Australia:

> It was scarcely possible to induce the passengers to sweep the decks after the meals or to be decent in respect of ordinary personal cleanliness; in many cases, in bad weather, they would not go on deck, as their health suffered so much that their strength was gone and they had not the power to help themselves.
>
> Hence the 'tween decks were like a loathsome dungeon. When the hatchways were opened, under which the people were stowed, the steam rose and the stench was like that from a pen of pigs. The few beds they had were in a dreadful state, for the straw, once wet with seawater, soon rotted. At that time the passengers were expected to cook for themselves, and from their being unable to do this, owing to either ignorance or seasickness, the greatest suffering arose. Thus, though provisions might be abundant, the emigrants would be half-starved.

In the years that followed the discovery of gold in Australia, the emigrant ships, and living conditions on board, had improved steadily. Yet, even on the faster cutters such as the *Phoenician*, passengers still faced a substantial risk of death or disease. Powerful commercial pressures pushed ships' crews to reach Australia quickly. To satisfy their owners' demands they needed to unload the would-be prospectors, load up with precious gold dust and sail back to Britain in the shortest possible time.[1] Under her Scottish master, Captain Sproat, the SS *Phoenician* had been setting records. She had previously completed the entire round trip from London to Sydney in a little over eight months.

The 1851 Australian gold rush had brought hardships to the *Phoenician's* passengers, but prosperity to her owners, the Aberdeen White Star Line. Over the next few years they had invested extravagantly in new ships to fight off increasing competition from other British shipping lines.[2] It was a fatal error of judgement. The gold trade was fading fast. Many emigrants, realising that there was no easy path to golden riches in the Australian outback, had switched to raising sheep instead. The subsequent decline and the then fast-approaching bankruptcy of the Scottish-based White Star Line had been closely observed by young Liverpool businessman, Thomas Henry Ismay.

In 1867, after years of working in his wealthy father's shipping business, 30-year-old Thomas Ismay had been looking to buy some ships of his own. He was a family man and wanted to build a shipping empire that he might, one day, pass on to his 5-year-old son, Bruce. Thomas Ismay had made White Star's struggling owners an offer they could not refuse. For the sum of £1,000 he took over the

White Star trading name, its flag and the dwindling goodwill of its clients. Many years in the future, Thomas Ismay's purchase of White Star was to have momentous consequences for the doomed passengers on board the *Titanic*: it would make Ismay the most powerful ship-owner in Britain – and directly influence how many lives were to be lost on the night when *Titanic* sank.

Thomas Ismay and the White Star Line soon prospered. His fledgling business was helped by financial backing from Gustav Christian Schwabe, a long-time family friend. Schwabe, a multi-millionaire Liverpool financier, much preferred doing business with family and friends and had shareholdings in many of his relatives' businesses in Britain and abroad. He loaned the young and ambitious Ismay enough money to buy a fleet of new ships, calculating that the shipping line would fit in well with another of his recent family investments. Schwabe had given his nephew, Gustav Wilhelm Woolf, the money to buy a junior partnership in a newly established shipbuilding company. Now, the canny financier saw an easy way of benefitting both of the firms in which he had an interest. As a condition for his loan Schwabe demanded that all White Star's new ships were to be constructed by his nephew's company – the Belfast shipbuilders, Harland and Wolff. It proved to be a long-term partnership that was good for both the shipping line and the shipbuilders. Planning his fleet of new ships, Thomas Ismay and his new shipbuilding partners made bold design decisions. A contemporary study of ship design revealed how radical their changes were:

> Mr Ismay was not a man to be bound by any precedent. It was his business to attract passengers by attending to their creature comforts and he realised that in steamers of ever-increasing dimensions the most comfortable place for passengers must be right amidships, just forward of the engine space. Hence the new White Star steamers, in addition to their novel dimensions, had their quarters for passengers placed where motion and vibration would be least observable.

The 'novel dimensions' of White Star's Belfast-built ships made them longer, slimmer and faster than the more traditional ships of their day. They attracted new customers to the previously ailing line, despite their rivals' suggestions that Thomas Ismay was courting commercial popularity at the cost of safety at sea. In the years immediately after Ismay took over the White Star Line, marine safety had become a major political issue as the shipping trade boomed, and more and more lives were lost at sea.

In a House of Commons debate, the Government had revealed worrying statistics: In 1872, more than 3,500 British sailors and passengers had died in the sinking or disappearance of ships of the British merchant marine; two years later, those annual losses had soared to 4,171 seafarers' deaths. Hoping to improve that safety record, the recently formed Board of Trade wrote to major ship-owners seeking their views on the necessity of 'life-saving appliances' on their vessels. It was perhaps indicative of Thomas Ismay's level of regard for safety that his White Star Line was the only one of nineteen British companies that failed to answer the question.

The Board of Trade's concerns about lifeboats was understandable. For decades the legal regulations about lifeboats had been linked, not to the number of people on board a ship, but to its registered tonnage. The arrangement was a convenient one for the undermanned and hard-pressed force of Board of Trade's surveyors who were charged with enforcing the rules. They had a printed scale of tonnage to show both the surveyor and the shipbuilder precisely how many lifeboats needed to be provided. But, by the time Ismay took over the White Star Line, the 'lifeboat scale' was already hopelessly out of date. It had been drawn up in the 1850s, at a time when the biggest ships being built were just a few hundred tons and carried a few hundred passengers. Its architects had failed to imagine how much larger ships might become in the future.

WHICH? FATE? — OR ECONOMY IN LIFE-BOATS?

Contemporary cartoon reflecting on the one-in-three chance that *Titanic*'s passengers had of finding a place in a lifeboat.

Some safety improvements had, however, been made. Against fierce opposition in the House of Commons, Derby MP Samuel Plimsoll had roused public opinion against the terrible toll of lives lost at sea. He finally pressurised the Government into passing the Merchant Shipping Act of 1876. Plimsoll wanted load lines to be painted on ships to stop greedy owners packing dangerously heavy cargoes onto their vessels.[3] As the debate continued, another MP suggested an even more novel idea. Colonel Francis Beresford asked the Board of Trade for a dramatic increase in the number of lifeboats carried on British ships. His amendment proposed:

> Certificates should not be granted to passenger ships unless they are provided with lifeboats and deck rafts sufficient to save *all on board* [author's italics] in case of disaster or shipwreck.

It was a radical suggestion. Had Colonel Beresford's amendment been accepted, the old 'lifeboat scale' would have been replaced with the simple requirement that ships carried lifeboats for everybody on board. It would have saved countless lives – including those of all the men, women and children fated to die on *Titanic*. But ship-owners knew that more boats meant more expense, and needed more crewmen to man them. So Beresford fell afoul of the powerful and wealthy shipping lobby among MPs and the Civil Service. The Board of Trade's president, Sir Charles Addersley, the minister who had earlier warned of the dangers of starvation in lifeboats at sea, vehemently opposed any change. He claimed:

> Existing rules, based on the tonnage of ships rather than the number of souls on board, are ample, if not excessive.

Fellow MPs with financial interests in the shipping business lined up to support his view. MP George McIver claimed:

> Steamers are already compelled to carry more boats than could be properly stowed, and heavy boats getting adrift and damaging hatchways are a real source of danger. I have no great faith in life-saving apparatus of any kind. There are exceptions to all rules; but, upon the whole, I think ships' boats have lost more lives than ships' boats will ever save.

Summing up the debate, Sir Charles was adamant that no ships could ever carry enough lifeboats to save everyone on board:

> If the proposal were carried into execution it would be impracticable to have on board a crew sufficiently large to man the boats, or even to lower them. Even if the passengers were got in, the only difference would be that they would be drowned in the boats, instead of being drowned in the ship.

A two-to-one majority voted down the lifeboat amendment and the carnage at sea continued unabated. In 1882, more than a thousand shipwrecks killed nearly 3,500 passengers and crew.

It was not only Westminster legislators, however, who were concerned about the increasing numbers of people dying at sea. British Imperial laws governed ships throughout the far-flung British Empire, and colonial authorities were pushing for change. Those in Australia, the colony whose citizens faced the longest sea passages of all, were especially vociferous. The states of Victoria, South Australia, Queensland and Tasmania all demanded new laws to make ship-owners offer lifeboats for all.[4]

Eventually the Government agreed to take action. It was, however, perhaps the slowest form of action known to mankind: a 'Royal Commission on Safety at Sea'. It was appointed in 1884 – and finally reported three years later. As the businesses of Thomas Ismay and Britain's other ship-owners continued to flourish under ineffective safety legislation, the Royal Commission plodded its way through growing piles of evidence. Its voluminous files, preserved for posterity in the archive repository at Kew, reveal how slowly it proceeded. One folder stores the letters from British embassies all over the world who were asked about local laws on the provision of lifeboats. Endless responses, from countries as diverse as Mexico, Brazil and Turkey, all proved to be irrelevant, even though conscientious embassy staff produced lengthy, handwritten reports about their discussions with local merchant marine and naval officials.

'Are we to send any more of these to the Committee? I think they have arrived at their report,' one, clearly frustrated, civil servant wrote on the cover of the bulging Board of Trade file. His irritation is understandable; the British Embassy in Rome had sent him a 100-page booklet of Italian lifeboat law written in Italian, without a translation.

Playing its own part in the Royal Commission circus, the Board of Trade's Marine Division asked three of its own 'nautical men' to investigate the safety of emigrant boats sailing between the UK and America. In the light of what later befell the *Titanic*, their report was highly prophetic:

> Supposing a vessel leaves with 1,000 passengers and 200 crew. Under the present statutory requirements, she needs only carry sufficient boat accommodation for 216 of these people. Thus, it will be seen that the boats carried by this class of vessel are quite inadequate as an effectual means of saving life should a disaster happen to a ship with her full complement of passengers on board.

The three officers spoke to sailors in ports all over Britain, deliberately shunning advice from shipbuilders and ship-owners with a vested interest in resisting further regulation. Their 'nautical men's' report called for more boats:

… so that each ship shall have sufficient life-saving gear for all on board at any one time. We believe that in nearly all the ships of this class, room for the extra boats could be found with very little trouble and expense beyond the cost of the boats and their fittings.

The report omitted to mention the danger of icebergs, but did warn of the perils of heavy seas, storms and fog in the North Atlantic. It suggested that only good fortune had so far prevented major loss of life among the millions of emigrants then being shipped to America. The officers were so convinced of the need for 'lifeboats for all' that they 'respectfully declined' to suggest lesser measures. It was an unusually brave statement for any nineteenth century civil servants to make to their employer, and their honest, though undiplomatic, opinion was not welcomed by the Board of Trade. A handwritten note on the file suggests:

We should send a copy to the Royal Commission on Life-Saving At Sea, and this is perhaps all we should do, except acknowledge receipt and thank the committee for their efforts, which we might call 'clear and valuable'.[5]

The department subsequently did all that it could to downplay their own officers' report:

The Board of Trade are not prepared to accept it as expressing the opinion of the department. They send it rather as embodying the opinions of three gentlemen of undoubted nautical experience and ability.

The Board of Trade have no doubt that the Royal Commission will agree with them that before anything approaching a definite conclusion is arrived at, steps should be taken for ascertaining and considering the views of ship-owners, shipbuilders, and others interested in the matter.

One final detail in the 'men of undoubted nautical experience's' report was also ignored by the Board of Trade. It was to prove highly significant in the light of the coming *Titanic* disaster. The officers revealed that different shipping companies had widely differing policies about lifeboats:

We are glad to be able to say that there are many liberal and careful ship-owners who do all in their power to provide for the safety of their passengers by equipping their vessels with boats [that] are in excess of the number required by statute. But at the same time there are others, carrying large numbers of emigrants, who do no more than they are required to do by law.

An accompanying table detailed the proportion of passengers and crew that could be saved by the lifeboats of various transatlantic ships. At the bottom of the list were one distinctive set of ships' names: the steamships *Baltic*, *Germanic* and *Britannic*. Each carried so few boats that less than one in five of their passengers and crew could have been saved in the event of a disaster. All were owned by one company, the White Star Line – the future owners of *Titanic*.

In due course the long-awaited Royal Commission failed to make any significant changes to the lifeboat laws. Instead, they recommended further consideration of the need for more boats ... by yet another committee. The Board of Trade had just the man in mind to guide that committee's decisions. He was a leading light in the shipping industry; a man whose company's ships carried the fewest lifeboats of any major line in Britain ... a man who had not even bothered to respond to surveys on lifeboat safety ... the Liverpool-based managing director of the White Star Line, Thomas Henry Ismay.

Asking Thomas Ismay to frame the lifeboat laws was perhaps the ultimate example of asking poacher to turn gamekeeper. From the start, Ismay steered his committee away from the idea of any drastic changes. Lifeboats cost money, needed more crew and blocked the view from profitable First Class cabins on his ships. His leadership of the grandly-named 'Advisory Committee On Life-Saving Appliances' would have appalling consequences for *Titanic's* victims in years to come.

### Notes

1. In February 1852 the Aberdeen White Star Line's *Phoenician* sailed into Plymouth harbour with the first Australian gold shipment to reach British shores. The ship carried seventy-four bags of gold dust worth more than £80,000.
2. White Star's greatest competition came from the Black Ball Line and 'Bully' Baines, a captain infamous for driving crews onwards through storms with two loaded pistols and the threat: 'It's to Melbourne ... or to Hell.'
3. The new law at first failed to specify where the so-called 'Plimsoll lines' were to be painted on a ship. Some owners put them on the funnel.
4. Board of Trade file M12260 reveals how little notice was taken of the colonial pleas. Some governors were told their letters would 'receive consideration', others received no reply at all.
5. National Archive file M12883 of 1886 reveals that the three 'nautical men' were never told that their advice was 'clear and valuable'. Each received a bland letter of acknowledgement from a junior departmental official.

## Chapter Nine

# '. . . irritating, meddling and muddling to the benefit of nobody'

**10.30 am**
**Thursday 7 February 1889**
**Committee Room Three**
**Board of Trade**
**Whitehall Gardens**
**London**

Sitting at the head of the Board of Trade's polished mahogany boardroom table, Thomas Henry Ismay knew he had a problem. As newly-elected Chairman of the Marine Safety Act's Life-Saving Appliances Committee, the Liverpool ship-owner needed to be fair to all sides. His role was to facilitate an open discussion, allowing equal weight to the opinions of all, listening to arguments that he disagreed with every bit as eagerly as those with which he shared a like mind. His problem was that some opinions now being expressed were manifestly costly and dangerous nonsense. Ismay had expected such behaviour from the handful of seamen's unions' representatives invited onto the Committee, but other more moderate voices were unexpectedly supporting them.

The distinguished shipping industry figures seated amid the grand surroundings of the London headquarters of the Board of Trade were a representative gathering of the great and the good, with a few ordinary seamen thrown in for good measure. Over a series of meetings that had started the previous November, they had been debating the vital safety issue of how many lifeboats British ships should carry at sea. Although they could not possibly know it then, their deliberations in this room would one day decide the varying fates, be they good or bad, of everybody on board the maiden voyage of RMS *Titanic*.

As the morning progressed, one of the sailors on the Committee renewed a request that had already divided the Committee at earlier sessions. He demanded that 'lifeboats for all' should be the rule for all British ships, whatever their size and however many passengers they might carry. Ismay, the managing director of one of the country's greatest merchant shipping fleets, knew only too well how costly it would be for him and his shipping industry colleagues to provide that many boats. Lifeboats were expensive, they occupied valuable deck space, and each extra one increased the number of seamen needed to man any ship. Fortunately, years of experience in controlling business meetings and Whitehall committees had fully equipped Ismay for such a moment. He quickly selected the next speaker, his friend and fellow ship-owner, Sir Francis Dunlop.

'It's an interesting idea, but totally impracticable and harmful to safety at sea,' explained Sir Francis. 'Boats are heavy and there isn't a ship being built that can comfortably carry more than twelve lifeboats cluttering up her decks. We've been asked to recommend a scale of "minimum numbers" of boats to be carried. Nothing prevents any owner from putting on more boats if they so wish.'

Before anyone else could argue the point, Ismay rapidly picked his second pet speaker; Henry Anderson was a dependable colleague from the Council of Shipping Owners. His views could not have been more predictable:

> Preposterous idea that you can have boats for all. Some ships can carry a thousand passengers, or more; give them all lifeboats and you won't get the crew that could man them.

With the mood of the meeting successfully steered back onto an acceptable path, Ismay's next course of action was clear:

> Well, Gentlemen … a good time for lunch, I feel? The meeting stands adjourned.

The Board of Trade had carefully packed the 1888 Life-Saving Appliances Committee with men who could be relied upon to protect the British merchant shipping industry; British ships that at that time transported more than fifty per cent of the entire world's trade and that were vital to the country's home and colonial interests in those latter days of the nineteenth century. For those reasons, a substantial majority of its fifteen members were ship-owners and shipbuilders, or represented associations of masters and owners across the country. Only three of the delegates were working able seamen with experience of the dangers of deep ocean voyages. Even the *Official Minutes Book* differentiated between the different social classes represented within the group. Individual ship-owners and shipbuilders speaking on behalf of the rich men who controlled the British shipping industry were respectfully referred to by name; seamen's representatives were frequently simply called 'the nautical men'. In the grand surroundings of the Board of Trade's London headquarters, in the company of such wealthy and distinguished fellow members, a humble sailor's opinion carried little weight.

From the establishment's point of view, Thomas Ismay was the ideal choice to be a co-operative chairman. From the earliest days of his reign as the managing director of the White Star Line, Ismay had gone out of his way to please the rich, the famous and the influential. Important customers of the White Star Line were courted with sycophantic, personal letters from the managing director. He was regularly invited to serve on numerous government committees and inquiries after favouring the Admiralty with an offer to place White Star steamers at their disposal in case of war.[1]

Under Ismay's leadership, investors in his company had prospered so much that a group of shareholders had commissioned a portrait of him from the renowned artist Millais. It hung in pride of place in Ismay's luxurious Liverpool home. Ismay had become a wealthy man with a fortune in excess of £1 million, a vast sum approaching the end of the nineteenth century. He had an impeccable background to serve the purposes of the Board of Trade.

The tactic of appointing 'advisory committees', whose composition could be suitably arranged to produce any advice that might be desired, had been popular for decades among civil servants within the Board of Trade. Controversial decisions and unpopular policies could be referred to advisory boards, on the grounds that only experts could possibly understand the technical issues involved. The concept allowed government ministers to defend unpopular decisions by claiming that they had acted on the expert advice received from a committee. Some commentators, however, had grown wise to the Board's methods. The creation of yet another committee led the *Northern Daily Mail* to pour sarcasm on the qualities of some of those appointed:

> ... not the best representative men in the estimation of the seamen and the other classes but the men that may find favour in the sight of the President of the Board of Trade, who may be a tool of bungling officials.
>
> Official mediocrity or stupidity will have the advantage of doing precisely what it thinks fit, whilst seeming to be acting under the influence of a representative committee. We have here a prospect of irritating, meddling and muddling to the benefit of nobody.

Even into the early years of the twentieth century, the frequently biased make-up of advisory committees was being attacked by government critics. During a 1906 Parliamentary debate, shortly before the keels of *Olympic* and *Titanic* were laid in Belfast, seamen's union MP, Joseph Havelock-Wilson, was scathing about their use:

> If the Government would give the seamen and officers the same representation as ship-owners, then I am sure [they] would be able to hold their own. But I have had 26 years' experience of advisory committees, and they are composed of ship-owners, and people interested in ships, and then, as a kind of makeweight, they throw on a seaman, who is practically helpless, and whose voice exerts no influence.

The responsible minister, David Lloyd-George, responded with a practiced air of wounded innocence:

> I do not understand. The Hon. Gentleman must not assume that the Board of Trade would not set up such a Committee without the seamen being adequately represented. I certainly had it in my mind that there should be representatives of a class whose lives depend on these regulations.

And again, in 1907, questions were asked about the undue influence of ship-owners in the advice given to by ministers about safety issues. John Jenkins, then the MP for the thriving dockyard port of Chatham, in Kent, asked the President of the Board of Trade about the composition of his latest advisory committee:

> ... how many of the members are ship-owners or persons interested in shipping; how many are shipbuilders, and whether they are also owners or share-owners in shipping property ... and whether he will take into consideration the appointment of additional representatives on the Committee who have no interest in shipping property.

Lloyd-George admitted that the majority of the advisory committee did have shipping interests but was clearly determined not to upset the status quo:

> I regard the Committee as fairly representative of the interests concerned; and I am not prepared at present to add to the number of its members.

The 1888 Committee, chaired by Thomas Ismay, had been charged with deciding how many lifeboats the law should insist were carried on passenger ships. The Committee's surviving records show how skilfully Ismay manipulated the decisions of an already biased body.

But Ismay went far further than simply steering discussions in the direction that he desired. He went on to falsify their records. Board of Trade file MT 9/320B, kept confidential for fifty years after the *Titanic* had sunk, reveals that the Committee Minutes were altered when civil servants submitted them to the Chairman. The original documents still clearly reveal that passages were crossed-out of the record when they failed to agree with Ismay's views:

(7th February 1889)
Each individual gave an opinion on whether it should be lifeboats
for all. ~~The general opinion of the nautical members was that~~
~~appliances of some kind sufficient for all on board should be~~
~~provided.~~

The committee decide that the number of boats under davits
should not be reduced ~~as they are all sufficiently few now.~~

(15th March 1889)
Ismay decided, and it was unanimously agreed that short hand
notes should not be recorded ~~Mr Callaghan (able bodied seaman)~~
~~thought that appliances should be provided for all on board and~~
~~Capt. Ward (Shipmasters Society) made it clear that he thought it~~
~~should be boats for all, with appliances as extras.~~
[Strike-throughs in original document.]

Ismay's apparent disregard for safety, in the cause of increasing his shipping
company profits, was shared by many of his wealthy colleagues. Any laws that
threatened to interfere with a ship-owner's right to run his business in any way
he saw fit attracted immediate criticism from the industry's tame MPs, and
from a powerful lobby of associated business interests. Even the threat of new
laws emerging from Ismay's committee sparked off a flurry of complaints.

The influential 'General Ship-owners' Society' of London were quick to
complain. Their 1888 letter of objection to the President of the Board of
Trade ridiculed the need for additional lifeboats on the 'practically
unsinkable' steel steamships of the day. The Society's Secretary, Mr W.H.
Coke, reported:

I am directed by the Committee to point out to your Lordship that ship-
owners are at present, of their own accord, doing a great deal in the way
of making their vessels *practically unsinkable* [author's italics] by sub-
dividing them into watertight compartments scientifically planned.

Provisions such as these are more valuable to an almost
immeasurable degree as a means of saving life at sea than any
multiplication of lifeboats and suchlike appliances.

The clearly optimistic Mr Coke went on to claim that modern steamers were
also 'practically safe' from the risk of fire. 'Regulators,' he concluded, 'should
rather be directing attention to improvements in construction than to placing
reliance on subsidiary appliances, the value of which is too likely in practice to
prove inadequate.'

Other ship-owners soon joined the attack. Among the letters that poured
into the Board of Trade's Marine Division, were several from the long-

established Hull shipping line of Thomas Wilson & Sons. They insisted they had carried passengers 'without accident' for years. Their ships had no room for the luxury of even more lifeboats on deck. The company, whose headed notepaper grandly advertised 'International Steamship Lines to the USA, Europe, Constantinople and Bombay', was outraged at the prospect of even more lifeboats:

> We find that, it would be next to an impossibility to provide the boat accommodation in accordance with the tables. Other means of buoyancy, if carried on deck, would we are afraid, seriously hamper the ship and be prejudicial to the safe working of the crew and the comfort of the passengers.

Unsurprisingly in the circumstances, ship-owner Ismay's final report in 1889 rejected the concept of lifeboats for all. Even more tragically, in the light of the future *Titanic* disaster, it failed to make any connection between the actual number of people on board any ship and the number of boats it should carry. Lifeboat provision would continue to be linked to a vessel's registered tonnage. The Ismay Committee's advice was given the force of law in that year's Merchant Shipping Life-Saving Appliances Act. It was, however, completely out of date even before the ink was dry on the paper.

Ismay's new 'lifeboat scale', only slightly modified by amendments in 1894, covered ships of up to 10,000 tons, which were now legally bound to carry sixteen standard-sized lifeboats. Any bigger ships – regardless of how much larger they actually were or how many more thousands of people they could carry – would still only need to carry sixteen boats in order to satisfy the regulations. At the time he signed the Life-Saving Appliances Committee report, Ismay knew that ships larger than 10,000 tons were already afloat; indeed, his own company owned and operated two of them ... and far bigger ships were about to be launched.[2]

In fairness to Ismay, his Life-Saving Appliances Committee probably never imagined at the time that they were shaping lifeboat policy that their regulations would still be in force two decades into the future. They must surely have believed that their rules for 10,000-ton ships would be suitably revised as larger and larger ships began sailing the seas.

They could not have been more wrong. As the first 20,000-ton ships were launched ... then 30,000 ... then 40,000 tons, the outdated regulations remained as the law of the land. If the original lifeboat scales had been a cynical mistake, then the failure to update them as year after year went by became an ongoing scandal. It was a scandal that would eventually have fearful consequence for the passengers and crew of *Titanic*. Nowhere were those consequences more dreadful than among the scores of stokers, coal heavers and engineers who stayed late at their posts, loyally continuing to do their duty in the bowels of the boiler rooms far below decks.

### Notes

1. Ismay's Admiralty suggestion was to lead to naval subsidies for many British ships for decades to come.
2. In 1889, Ismay already owned the two biggest ships afloat, the *City of New York* and the *City of Paris*; both exceeded 10,000 tons. Building on a slipway was Cunard's *Luciana* at 12,900 tons. Within a decade, Ismay would be building the *Celtic*, his first 20,000-ton ship.

# Chapter Ten

# '. . . there were eight feet of water in it'

**11.43 pm**
**Sunday 14 April 1912**
**RMS *Titanic* tank top deck**
**Dead reckoning position: 41° 46' N, 50° 41' W**
**The North Atlantic Ocean**

The noise sounded like a distant roll of thunder, a deep metallic boom that echoed around the metal walls of *Titanic's* No. 6 boiler room. The crash was loud enough to terrify leading stoker Frederick Barrett and every one of the dozen firemen and coal trimmers[1] who were working inside the hot and cramped compartment. Moments later, thousands of gallons of green, foaming seawater poured in through the starboard side of the ship. The near-freezing water gushed in 'as if from a fire-hose' through a thigh-high split that had opened up in the ship's outer hull.

Amid the splashing of running water and the shouts of panicking sailors, Barrett heard the whirr of an electric motor and the clank of moving metal. The emergency watertight door to the next compartment was slowly dropping to the floor. Along with the engineering officer, to whom he had been talking just moments before, Barrett dived through the closing hatchway and into what he hoped would be the safety of the adjacent No. 5 boiler room.

'The doors dropped instantly, automatically, from the bridge,' he later explained. 'We got through before the doors broke.'

Just thirty seconds before the water rushed in, Barrett had heard a warning bell from the bridge and had seen the boiler room's signalling system light up.

'There is like a clock rigged up in the stokehold and a red light goes up when the ship is supposed to stop – a red piece of glass and an electric light inside; a white light for full speed, and, I think it is a blue light for slow. This red light came up,' Barrett told the subsequent London Inquiry.

'I am the man in charge of the watch, and I called out, "Shut all dampers," to shut the wind off the fires. The crash came before we had them all shut. Water came pouring in 2 feet above the stokehold plate; the ship's side was torn from the third stokehold to the forward end.'

Standing on the No. 5 boiler room 'plates' – the firemen's name for the raised metal flooring[2] where they worked to feed to boiler furnaces – Barrett found his new refuge was not as safe as he had thought. The emergency door had succeeded in isolating them from the fast-flooding room No. 6, but *Titanic's* hull had been pierced even further back than that. An uncontrollable stream of water was also gushing into boiler room No. 5.[3]

Having just escaped from the adjacent room, Barrett was immediately told to go back again. A general order came from the officers on duty: 'Every man to his station. Stand by your fires.' There was no way back through the closed emergency door so, despite the ever-growing danger, Barrett and *Titanic's* Junior Assistant Second Engineer, Jonathan Shepherd, climbed up a sloping escape ladder that ran over the intervening bulkhead. They were hoping to descend a matching ladder on the other side to get back to the boilers they had abandoned in the initial panic. They needed to douse the furnace fires, but that proved to be an impossible task.

> Me and Mr Shepherd, that is the engineer who is in my section, go up the escape of No. 5 and down No. 6 escape to the boiler room, but we could not go in there because there were about 8 feet of water when we got there. Eight feet above the plates; it was not a quarter of an hour, just on ten minutes. We went back to No. 5 boiler room. Then the lights went out.

By the light of one of a dozen hurriedly gathered lanterns, Barrett checked the boiler gauges and found that the five huge boilers had all been drained of water by an emergency signal from the engine room. The near-boiling water was mixing with the ice-cold seawater still pouring through the torn seams of the hull, creating a fog so dense that it was hard to see across the room, even after the main lights first flickered and then came back to life a few moments later. Amid the growing confusion, Barrett was ordered to lift an inspection hatch that covered safety valves beneath the floor; a decision that was to have fatal consequences for one of his colleagues.

Rushing across the room, Jonathan Shepherd failed to see the open inspection hatch, fell into the hole, and fractured his leg. Ignoring the engineering officer's screams of pain, an anguished Barrett helped to lift him from the hole and carry him to the relative safety of the pump room nearby. Shepherd, badly injured in the fall and completely unable to move by himself, was never to be seen again.

Returning to his original post in boiler room No. 6, the nearest furnace room to *Titanic's* bow, Barrett realised that the floor was now sloping down slightly towards the front of the ship. Then a far more immediate danger struck:

> All at once I saw a wave of green foam come tearing through between the boilers; a rush of water came through the pass – the forward end. I did not stop to look; I jumped for the escape ladder.[4]

As Barrett and his fellow stokers finally abandoned the lowest decks of the ship, *Titanic's* fate had already been sealed. Thousands of tons of water had been pouring into each of the six most forward compartments ever since the collision. The weight was dragging the bows ever lower down in the water. Having realised, almost from the start, that *Titanic* was certain to sink, Captain Smith had long ago given the order to lower the boats. By the time Barrett and his colleagues from the lower engineering decks had climbed up to the boat decks, most of the lifeboats had gone and the few that remained were fast being loaded with women and children.

The death toll among the men who stayed at their duty stations in the engine room of *Titanic* would prove to be the highest amongst all of the crew on the ship. Under the leadership of Chief Engineer Officer Joseph Bell were twenty-four engineers, six electrical engineers, two boilermakers, and a plumber and his clerk. None of them survived. In the years following the disaster, the engineers' role in keeping power supplied to the stricken ship was largely overlooked. With no survivors from among their number to tell their tale, accounts of exactly what Bell and his team achieved amidst the engines at the rear of the ship have never been heard. But, in 1914, subscriptions from other ships' engineers around the world paid for a memorial. The impressive stone structure still stands in a municipal park in Southampton, from where many of their colleagues had set sail in *Titanic*. Its inscription is a fitting tribute to the lost heroes of the ship:

> Greater love hath no man than this. That a man lay down his life for his friends. To the memory of the engineer officers of the R.M.S *Titanic* who showed their high conception of duty and their heroism by remaining at their posts 15 April 1912. Erected by their fellow engineers and friends on 22 April 1914.

Leading stoker Frederick Barrett did, however, find a way to escape. Emergency ladders from the boiler room eventually led him to a main corridor near the top of the ship. From there he made his way towards the rear promenade deck. Once there, he was just one level below the point where the last couple of boats were being loaded. As one of those boats descended past him from the deck above, Barrett seized his chance to survive. He stepped out into the open boat, which he later said was only about 'five-sixths filled with women'. A few other men followed his lead:

> There were about three more got in after I got in, and the order was given from the boat deck, 'Let no more in that boat; the falls will break'; she was lowered away.

Even then Barrett and others in the boat were far from safe. A few feet before the lifeboat reached sea level it began filling up with water that was pouring from a pump-outlet pipe in the side of *Titanic*.

> When we found the discharge was coming out we stopped lowering and all the hose was tied up in the boat. I had a knife and I cut the hose adrift and shoved two oars over the forward end to shove the lifeboat off the ship's side. We got into the water and there was a bit of a current ... and it drifted us under No. 15 boat.

Barrett could not fight his way through the crowd of seated women to reach the central lever that would release 'the falls' – the seamen's name for the ropes that had lowered them to the sea. But with the other lifeboat now descending right on top of them, he had to act quickly. Barrett and another sailor at the front of the boat each cut through the ropes that were tethering them in place. At the last moment, their lifeboat floated clear.

At the London inquiry, Barrett admitted that he had never bothered to read the crew's boat list and had never known to which lifeboat he had been assigned. But he now found himself as the senior sailor in lifeboat No. 13.

> I did not see anybody that was going to take charge of the boat. We got the oars out; the rudder was lying in the stern at the bottom, and I shipped the rudder and took charge of the boat till after the *Titanic* sank.

Having left the heat and humidity of *Titanic*'s boiler room, Barrett could not have been more poorly dressed for the icy conditions of the open ocean, yet he stayed sat alone at the tiller for several hours. Eventually, the cold became too much to bear.

> I gave the tiller to somebody else because I was too cold; I could not feel my limbs. I had only thin gear on, coming out of the fire room. Some woman put a cloak over me, and I do not know what happened then.

Barrett was unconscious by the time his lifeboat was picked up by the first ship to arrive on the scene, the *Carpathia*. Yet he was to make a full recovery in time to tell his story to the British inquiry several weeks later.

Many of the boats, including the one in which Barrett escaped, had been lowered from *Titanic* with nowhere near their full load of women and children. Bruce Ismay's White Star shipping line had failed to give their officers any training in the correct handling of the few lifeboats that *Titanic* did possess. It was a mistake that would cost many lives that night as half-empty lifeboats were sent away from the sinking ship and desperate men were kept away from the boats by shots fired from an officer's gun.

## Notes

1. The plates were 4 to 6 feet above the Tank Top – the lowest deck of *Titanic*.
2. 'Trimmers' shifted coal from *Titanic's* many bunkers to ensure a ready supply was always available at the side of each furnace door.
3. Boiler rooms were numbered 1-6 from the rear of the ship going forwards. Each stretched across the width of the ship. Five of the rooms each held five boilers; but the foremost No. 6 room, in the narrow bows of the ship, had room for just four.
4. Barrett was asked by Lord Mersey: 'Where did the water come from?' In one of the inquiry's few lighter moments he gave the obvious reply: 'Well, out of the sea, I expect.'

# Chapter Eleven

# '. . . like wild beasts ready to spring'

11.55 am
**Lifeboat No. 14**
**Hanging alongside B deck of RMS** *Titanic*
**Dead reckoning position: 41° 46' N, 50° 41' W**
**The North Atlantic Ocean**

Scrabbling around the feet of the women and children he had loaded into *Titanic's* lifeboat No. 14, seaman Joseph Scarrott was a desperate man. He was trying to check that the 'plug' – a removable water-draining bung in the bottom of the lifeboat – was firmly in place before the boat was lowered to the ocean below. The officer who had been giving him orders had moved further down *Titanic's* deck, leaving 33-year-old Scarrott with sole responsibility for the lives of everyone in the tiny craft. Having found that the plug was properly inserted, Scarrott worked, with his fingers near-frozen, to check that the lifeboat's ropes and release gear were all operating properly. Suddenly he realised that he had a serious problem.

Until now the discipline on board *Titanic* had held firm; every passenger had respected the ancient law of the sea: 'Women and children first'. But the tilt of the ship's deck towards the bow was by then becoming more pronounced and some passengers were starting to realise that *Titanic* actually was sinking. A group of men crowded around Scarrott's boat. He later described how he tried to stop the lifeboat being overwhelmed:

> There would be twenty women got into the boat, I should say, when some men tried to rush the boats, foreigners they were, because they could not understand the order which I gave them, and I had to use a bit of persuasion. The only thing I could use was the boat's tiller.
>
> I prevented five getting in. One man jumped in twice and I had to throw him out the third time. We were practically full up.

As Scarrott won the first skirmish in his running battle to repel the 'foreigner' invaders he was joined in the boat by *Titanic's* 5th Officer, Harold Lowe. The 29-year-old junior officer had only joined the White Star Line the year before and was still thought of as something of a loner among the crew. This was Lowe's first Atlantic voyage, although he had been at sea since he was just fourteen, having run away from his home in Wales after arguing with his father.

> When Mr Lowe came I told him that I had had a bit of trouble through the rushing business, and he said, 'All right.' He pulled out his revolver and he fired two shots between the ship and the boat's side, and issued a warning to the remainder of the men that were about there. He told them that if there was any more rushing he would use it.
>
> He asked me, 'How many got into the boat?' I told him as far as I could count there were fifty-four women and four children, one of those children being a baby in arms. It was a very small baby which came under my notice more than anything, because of the way the mother was looking after it, being a very small child. I told him that was the number, and he said to me, 'Do you think the boat will stand it?' I said, 'Yes, she is hanging all right.' And he said to lower away No. 14.

Despite giving the 'lower away' order, Harold Lowe was frightened that his lifeboat was still in danger. Suspended 60 feet above the ocean, in the dark of this moonless night, *Titanic's* 5th officer was convinced that the boat was overloaded and would buckle underneath him at any moment. The officer believed that there was a lot that could go wrong. The 'falls', the heavy manila ropes attached to the davit above, could have snapped or any one of a dozen vital metal buckles and clips might have cracked apart at any moment. Worst of all, the boat, supported only at each extremity, could have snapped apart in the middle and spilled everyone on board into the freezing waters below.

Still clutching his loaded automatic pistol openly in his hand, Lowe was taking no chances. He later explained that he was certain the lifeboat could not hold more than an absolute maximum of fifty people while it was being lowered. That was why he had started to shoot.

> As we were coming down the decks, coming down past the open decks, I saw a lot of Italians, Latin people, all along the ship's rails.[1] They were all glaring, more or less like wild beasts, ready to spring. I knew, or I expected every moment, that my boat would double up under my feet. I was quite scared of it, although of course it would not do for me to mention the fact to anybody else.
>
> I had overcrowded her, but I knew that I had to take a certain amount of risk. So I thought, 'Well, I shall have to see that nobody else

gets into the boat or else it will be a case.' I thought if one additional body was to fall into that boat, that slight jerk of the additional weight might part the hooks or carry away something, no one would know what.

That is why I yelled out to 'Look out,' and let go 'Bang' right along the ship's side. I fired without intention of hurting anybody and also with the knowledge that I did not hurt anybody. I could see where I was shooting. I shot between the boat and the ship's side, so these people would hear and see the discharge.

At the American inquiry, under questioning from Chairman Senator Smith, Lowe admitted firing three shots as he descended past the open decks.

'Do you mean to tell me that these Italians were crowding around the boat deck, A deck or B deck, glaring at you?'

'They were hanging around those open decks; with the windows open, because you do not want better proof than seeing them. I shot so for them to know that I was fully armed. That is the reason.'

'And that you did not propose to have anybody else in your boat?'

'I did not. Not a single soul more. I had quite enough. The dangers are that if you overcrowd the boat the first thing that you will have will be that the boat will buckle up because she is suspended from both ends and there is no support in the middle. It was purely personal what a man considered safety.'

Each of *Titanic's* sixteen principal lifeboats had actually been built to be safely lowered with at least sixty-five fully-grown men and women. Their construction was described in a report from the builders, Harland and Wolff:

Keels of elm, stems and stern posts of oak, all clinker built of best selected well-seasoned yellow pine, double fastened with copper nails clinched over rooves; the timbers were of elm spaced about 9 inches apart, and the seats pitch-pine secured with galvanised iron double knees.

The davits and the ropes that held each boat could comfortably take the strain of lowering a fully-laden lifeboat 60 feet down the side of *Titanic* to reach the ocean surface. Edward Wilding, a former managing director of the shipbuilders Harland and Wolff, described to the inquiry how identical boats had been tested on *Titanic's* sister ship:

I had actually seen one of the lifeboats in the air, shortly before the *Olympic* left Belfast; we put into one of the lifeboats half-hundredweight weights distributed so as to represent a load equal to about sixty-five people, and then we raised and lowered the boat six times. There was nothing the matter with her; she was watertight. I do not think there was any doubt the boats were strong enough to be

lowered containing the full number of passengers. We construct them
ourselves, sufficiently strong to be lowered with that number.

Wreck Commissioner, Lord Mersey, asked whether the *Titanic's* officers had
been given the information about how many passengers the boats could safely
hold.

> Not from the builders, my Lord. As far as I know there was no special
> direct intimation given to the officers that they would carry their full
> number, but I should have thought it was a matter of general knowledge
> that they were so constructed. If I had thought there was any doubt, if
> the officers had asked about it, or had expressed any doubt about it at
> Belfast, they would have been told, and the test would have been
> mentioned to them.

Wilding was sadly mistaken in his belief that everyone knew that *Titanic's*
lifeboats could safely be lowered when packed full of people. As *Titanic* sank,
officer after officer insisted on lowering boats that, just like the boat in which
Barrett escaped, held far fewer people than they could have done. They
seemed convinced that either the boats, or the tackle, would not stand the
strain. That was the thinking behind 5th Officer Lowe's decision to fire his
pistol in lifeboat No. 14.

> The reason is that the boat is suspended from both ends, and all the
> weight is in the middle, and that being so the boat is apt to break in the
> middle and shoot the whole lot out of her.

Lowe had even less excuse than his colleagues for his ignorance about the
lifeboats built-in margins of safety. The junior officer had joined *Titanic*
before she sailed from Belfast and had then examined the lifeboats in port to
check that each was properly equipped and ready to launch.

But other officers were equally ill-informed about the boats. *Titanic*'s 3rd
officer, Herbert Pitman, had more than five years' experience working on ships
of the White Star Line all over the world. Yet even he had lowered a boat with
far fewer people than it could have held.

> I thought I had sufficient in my boat for safety in lowering. I would not
> like to fill a lifeboat with sixty people and lower it suspended at both
> ends. I think forty would be a very safe load. I do not think boats are
> ever intended to be filled from the rail.

Embarrassingly for the White Star Line, the officer's ignorance was further
highlighted at the American Senate inquiry when an ordinary seaman showed
that he knew far more about lifeboat safety than any of the men who had been
in charge of the ship. Able Seaman Frank Evans, just twenty-seven years old
but with a decade of service in the Royal Navy behind him, told the US

senators that he had seen one boat lowered from *Titanic* with a mere eight or nine people in it. He was questioned about boat capacity by the hearing's Chairman Senator Smith:

'How many will a lifeboat of that kind hold, safely?'

'It will probably hold sixty, I should say, Sir.'

'Do you wish to be understood as saying that a large lifeboat like No. 14 or No. 12 or No. 10 could be filled to its full capacity and lowered to the water with safety?'

'Yes; because we did it then, Sir.'

'That is a pretty good answer.'

Tragically, it was not the ordinary seamen such as Frank Evans who were in charge of how many people were put in each boat; that was the job of *Titanic's* 2nd officer, Charles Lightoller, the most senior officer to survive the sinking. And he revealed his complete lack of understanding about the strength of the boats when questioned at the post-sinking inquiries. He described what criteria he had used to decide on the numbers for each boat.

'It all depends on your gears, Sir; the strength of the tackle. If it were an old ship, you would barely dare to put twenty-five in. With a brand new ship, and all brand new gear, brand new boats, and everything in the pink of condition, a boat might be safely lowered – you cannot guarantee it – she might go down safely with perhaps twenty to twenty-five in her.'

'Is that due to the weak construction of the lifeboats or to the insufficiency of the falls?'

'A brand new fall, I daresay, would have lowered the boats down and carried the weight, but it would hardly be considered a seamanlike proceeding as far as the sailor side of it goes, but I certainly should not think that the lifeboats would carry it without some structural damage being done – buckling, or something like that.'

'And had you those considerations in mind in deciding how many people should go in the boat?'

'Yes.'

Lightoller admitted that he had been told that the boats could hold sixty-five people or more but that he had thought this was their 'floating capacity', not the number that could be lowered to safety. He had a ready excuse for sending the first few boats away with as few as twenty people on board:

I did not know it was urgent then. I had no idea it was urgent. I would have taken more risks. I should not have considered it wise to put more in, but I might have taken risks. I might have put a good deal more.

If the ship's most senior officers were initially kept in the dark about the seriousness of *Titanic's* plight, then the situation was far worse for the ordinary passengers. Recounting his own experiences in the lifeboats, First Class passenger Charles Stengel recalled how they had all been fooled by the officers' demeanour:

> They calmed the passengers by making them believe it was not a serious accident. In fact, most of them, after they got on board the *Carpathia*, said they expected to go back the next day and get aboard the *Titanic* again.
>
> I heard that explained afterwards by an officer of the ship, when he said, 'Suppose we had reported the damage that was done to that vessel; there would not be one of you aboard. The stokers would have come up and taken every boat, and no one would have had a chance of getting aboard one of those boats.'

Another First Class passenger also told how the crew had never revealed that *Titanic* was sinking. Mrs Lucian Smith had barely felt the collision and had no sense of the danger until her husband told her that 'as a matter of form' the ladies had to go on deck:

> That frightened me a little, but after being reassured there was no danger I took plenty of time in dressing – putting on all my heavy clothing, high shoes, and two coats, as well as a warm knit hood. I kept asking my husband if I could remain with him rather than go in a lifeboat. He promised me I could. There was no commotion, no panic, and no one seemed to be particularly frightened; I had not the least suspicion of the scarcity of lifeboats, or I never should have left my husband.
>
> He then said, 'I never expected to ask you to obey, but this is one time you must; the boat is thoroughly equipped, and everyone on her will be saved.' I asked him if that was absolutely honest, and he said, 'Yes.' I felt some better then, because I had absolute confidence in what he said. As the boat was being lowered he yelled from the deck, 'Keep your hands in your pockets; it is very cold weather.' That was the last I saw of him.

Confident that her husband's privileged position in First Class would ensure him a place in the lifeboats, Mrs Smith kept scanning other boats nearby. She fully expected to see her husband sailing to join her. She had remained convinced that they would both be saved in preference to those in the less exclusive and expensive sections of the vessel:

> We were some distance away when the *Titanic* went down. We heard the many cries for help and pitied the captain, because we knew he would have to stay with his ship. The cries we heard I thought were seamen, or possibly steerage, who had overslept, it not occurring to me for a moment that my husband and my friends were not saved.

The terrified cries of those freezing to death in the Atlantic waters were the one last horror remaining for all the lucky few who had found a place in the lifeboats. Yet, even those in boats that were half-empty refused to return to the scene; the sailors in each boat knew that well over a thousand people must have gone into the water and that their boats could be swamped were they to go near the struggling crowd.

Bruce Ismay, sitting silently in one of the last boats to escape, must have known precisely the capacity of each and every lifeboat. His father had shaped the lifeboat laws that allowed *Titanic* to sail with insufficient boats on board; he had presided over *Titanic*'s construction and decided on lifeboat numbers to be carried on board. Yet, the head of the White Star Line made no attempt whatsoever to organise the crew of his lifeboat, or that of any other, to attempt a further rescue.

In his evidence to the US inquiry, Ismay said he had seen no passengers in the water after leaving *Titanic* and had deliberately not looked back as the ship went down.

> I do not know how far we were away. I was sitting with my back to the ship. I was rowing all the time I was in the boat; we were pulling away. I did not wish to see her go down. I am glad I did not. My back was turned to her.

The British inquiry heard that only 711 people were saved in the lifeboats taken on board the rescue ship *Carpathia*.[2] The Board of Trade calculation at the time *Titanic* sailed was that her lifeboats could safely have held at least 1,167 souls. In the calm sea and benign weather conditions prevailing that night even more might have been packed into the boats in defiance of the official loading figures.

In any event, had Lightoller and the *Titanic's* other officers been better trained and had even the most basic knowledge about the lifeboats of the ship on which they served, they would have filled the boats at least to their official capacity and saved an additional 400 and more people.

The harsh truth, however, is that even had the extra 400 been saved, then more than 1,000 others would still have been left behind to die. That fact made it all the more astonishing when, in the wake of the disaster, the senior civil servant responsible for safety at sea came to a startling conclusion: he claimed that *Titanic* had too many lifeboats.

### Notes

1. The Italian Ambassador later demanded that an apology be included in the US inquiry report clearing 'Italians' of any misbehaviour on board.
2. British inquiry statistics have been used throughout, although I recognise many slightly varying figures for victims and survivors have been calculated over the years.

# Chapter Twelve

# '. . . a wanton superfluity of luxury'

3.10 pm
13 June 1912
Lord Mersey's Inquiry into the loss of *Titanic*
Scottish Hall, Buckingham Gate
London

By the twenty-third day of the British Wreck Commissioner's inquiry into the loss of the *Titanic*, the evidence from a parade of shocked survivors had become somewhat repetitive. A host of lawyers representing a dozen different interested parties had debated and argued about each and every moment of the ship's last hours. Were such a word not inappropriate to use in discussing so many needless deaths, the proceedings might have been described as boring.

Yet, on the afternoon of 13 June, the astonishing evidence of one witness made everybody in the courtroom sit up and take notice. Barely two months after 1,490 men, women and children had died because of the lack of lifeboats, former civil servant Sir Alfred Chalmers[1] expounded at length upon his own unique theory about the disaster: he believed the *Titanic* had *too many* lifeboats.

It was an astonishing statement that stopped the inquiry in its tracks; a statement made all the more astonishing in the light of the witness's most recent position of high authority. Until his retirement, just before *Titanic* was completed, Sir Alfred had been the Nautical Adviser to the Board of Trade's Marine Division. He was the official directly responsible for the undemanding lifeboat regulations in force when *Titanic* was being constructed. Lawyers representing *Titanic's* officers and crew joined Board of Trade barrister Butler Aspinall[2] in questioning Sir Alfred's controversial views:

'You think that if there had been a smaller number of boats on the deck it would have been an easier thing to have filled them, and that possibly more lives would have been saved?'

'I should say that there would have been a probability of just as many being saved. With the smaller number of boats – possibly more, because there would have been more spare room.'

'On what do you base that statement?'

'For the simple reason that, knowing they had so many boats to trust to, they probably sent the first lot away not fully loaded. I do not want to criticise the officers or the Master of the ship at all, but I assume it is probable that that may have been the case; whereas if they had had fewer boats they would have taken good care that they utilised them to the fullest extent.'

'How can you make such an assumption in view of the fact that the *Titanic* did not carry sufficient lifeboats to carry all the people on board? Even if they had been filled to their utmost capacity, there must still have been a large number of people left on board the *Titanic*?'

'Certainly, a certain percentage must be.'

'Does not that dispose of the consideration for occupying the boats to the full extent that you spoke of?'

'Yes, it does.'

'Then there is nothing in this argument of yours?'

'Oh, yes, there is. In my opinion, there is.'

'That more people would have been saved if there had been fewer boats?'

'That is my opinion. That is all I can tell you.'

Sir Alfred's evidence was so at odds with all that the court had heard in the preceding weeks that even the Wreck Commissioner himself, Lord Mersey, was moved to intervene. The court had already heard that some German liners carried far more lifeboats than their British counterparts. Lord Mersey, reluctant until then to cast doubt on any government witness, put that point to Sir Alfred:

'I am afraid – I do not want to criticise you adversely, I am sure – that your opinion flies in the face of the conduct of British ship-owners and flies in the face of the practice on German boats of a similar kind?'

'As far as the German boats are concerned, I do consider that they are encumbering their decks unduly ... and in case of a disaster I am afraid the consequences would be very bad.'

Coming just a week after one of the world's most disastrous shipwrecks and the immense loss of crew and passengers' lives on *Titanic*, it was hard to comprehend what Sir Alfred might consider to have been 'very bad' consequences. Realising how appalling an impression his witness was creating, the Board of Trade's lawyer, Mr Butler Aspinall, emphasised Sir Alfred's lengthy experience in shaping shipping regulations:

'Is this a matter that you had to consider a great deal during your term of office – the question of boats?'

'Yes, a very great deal.'

'And since this disaster happened, and you knew you were going to be called here, did you apply your mind to the experience which was to be derived from the *Titanic* disaster?'

'Yes, I did: I am still of the same opinion.'

The rules governing the number of boats on the 45,000-ton *Titanic* had last been revised eighteen years earlier when the biggest ships afloat were little more than 10,000 tons. Sir Alfred explained that there were many reasons why he had repeatedly rejected demands to update the law:

> It was the safest mode of travel in the world, and I thought it was neither right nor the duty of a State Department to impose regulations upon that mode of travel as long as the record was a clean one. Secondly, I found that, as ships grew bigger, there were such improvements made in their construction that they were stronger and better ships.

*Titanic* had carried just sixteen lifeboats under her davits. It had been more than thirty years since Sir Alfred had last served at sea, but he claimed that his experience told him that no more than sixteen boats could ever be launched by even the largest of ships. Under questioning from the seamen's union's lawyer in court, he also admitted to a concern that more boats would need more sailors to man them.

'You are providing a crew which would be carried uselessly across the ocean, that never would be required to man the boats,' said Sir Alfred.

'Would that make it unsafe for the ship – to have a number of extra hands to man the lifeboats?'

'Not unsafe, but it would take away from her commercial value.'

'Was the principal consideration that you had in adhering to the old scale, the commercial value of the ship?'

'No. The several reasons that I gave were the reasons.'

'Was it a leading consideration with you?'

'No, it was a subsidiary one.'

During his hours of evidence to the Wreck Commissioner's Inquiry, Sir Alfred maintained his absolute conviction that his antiquated lifeboat laws had needed no revisions. He was asked a specific question about *Titanic* by another union representative, the MP and barrister, Mr Clement Edwards:

'Has the *Titanic* disaster led you to believe that any single one of the Board of Trade Regulations should be modified?'

'No.'

'That is to say there are no lessons to be learned from this disaster?'

'No, because it is an extraordinary one. The Board of Trade, the Marine Department, guards against ordinary occurrences, not extraordinary.'

'It is an extraordinary Department for guarding against ordinary mishaps?'
'Perhaps so – very good.'

Sir Alfred's denial that there were any lessons to be learned from the *Titanic* disaster attracted criticism not only from British newspapers but also from others across the world. Even in New Zealand, the editor of the *Wellington Post* was moved to write a scathing editorial:

> The reasoning by which Sir Alfred Chalmers professes to arrive at sixteen as the maximum number of boats is wonderful. No larger number could, in his opinion, be handled rapidly and housed safely. When one thinks of the immense amount of space devoted on these mammoth liners to a wanton superfluity of luxury, the suggestion that room cannot be found for whatever number of boats safety may prescribe seems positively outrageous.
>
> Is so much space needed on these huge vessels for swimming baths and gymnasiums and tennis courts – golf links, we believe, are also in contemplation – that the difference between life and death is not to count? The force of official complacency could hardly further go.

It was a view that was shared by many of the survivors of the *Titanic* disaster; the men and women who had struggled to find a place in the last few lifeboats leaving the sinking ship.

### Notes

1. Chalmers' seagoing experience was limited to a number of small coastal craft.
2. Butler Aspinall was the most junior of the Board's five lawyers. He may have been selected to try and downplay the importance of Sir Alfred's controversial views.

# Chapter Thirteen

# 'The electric lights were burning right to the very last. . . '

**2.10 am**
**15 April 1912**
**The boat deck of** *Titanic*
**Dead reckoning position: 41° 46' N, 50° 41' W**
**The North Atlantic Ocean**

On the fast-sinking *Titanic*, baker Charles Joughin had finished his drink in his cabin. He once again headed for the boat deck. In the time that he had been refreshing himself below decks, *Titanic* had listed further to starboard and was now tilted several degrees down towards the bow. There were rumours among the remaining crew and the by then panicking passengers that rescue ships would arrive any moment. Joughin, however, had enough experience at sea to know that, with or without rescue ships, the near-freezing sea temperatures could kill within minutes. He knew that finding floating debris on which to lift themselves clear of the water might be the only hope for anyone left on board. Joughin hurried down to the open B deck right below. He decided to pitch anything that floated over the side of *Titanic* to try and save himself and anyone else about to end up in the water. He later explained his plan:

> I saw that all the boats had gone – all the boats were away. We all knew at least the word was passed round – that there were four or five ships rushing to us. The word was passed round, but there was nothing official. Deck-chairs were lying right along, and I started throwing deck-chairs through the large ports. It was an idea of my own. There was other people on the deck, but I did not see anybody else throwing chairs over. I was looking out for something for myself.

Moments later Joughin heard a thunderous crash of metal as an entire section of the deck appeared to buckle. Still moving the deck-chairs, he was left behind as a crowd stampeded towards the stern of the ship. In desperation

Joughin hauled himself up to the top deck again and climbed on top of the metal railings running round the starboard side of the ship. He was looking down on a scene of pure horror; hundreds, 'many hundreds I should say ...' of people were being crushed together as *Titanic* started her death-slide to the bottom of the ocean.[1]

> When I got up on top I could then see them clambering down from those decks. The electric lights were burning right to the very last. I saw the time by my watch at a quarter-past two.
>
> I kept out of the crush as much as I possibly could, and she gave a great list to port it was not going up, but the other side was going down and threw everybody in a bunch except myself. I was on the side, practically on the side then. She threw them over. I clambered on the side when she chucked them. I had tightened my belt and I had transferred some things into my stern pocket. I was just wondering what next to do when she went.
>
> I was able to straddle the starboard rail on A deck and stepped off as the ship went under. I had expected suction of some kind, but felt none. At no time was my head underwater, it may have been wetted, but no more. I just kept moving my arms and legs and kept in an upright position. No trick at all with a lift-belt on. It was just like a pond. It is only a case of keeping your head, just paddling and you keep afloat indefinitely, I should say.[2]

Almost every one of *Titanic's* passengers and crew who had been jettisoned into the open ocean were wearing life-jackets. Although primitive by today's standards, the jackets were well enough designed to keep even non-swimmers safely afloat. As a consequence, very few of *Titanic's* victims were drowning; most were being killed by the temperature of the water in which they floated.

At around eight o'clock the previous evening, the quartermaster, Robert Hitchens, had recorded the temperature of the sea around *Titanic*. Updating such weather records in the ship's logbook was a regular part of his duties. Ships routinely carried a cone-shaped waterproof, leather 'dipper' to collect water samples from the sea surface far below, but that equipment was missing on the *Titanic*. Instead, as Hitchens later reported, the crew had improvised a replacement.

> It was a small paint tin; one the quartermaster got for the occasion, because we had nothing else; it held about a quart. [It was] bent on the handle just like a bent pin; attached to a piece of line about 20 fathoms long, which we put over the lee side of the ship, and draw just sufficient water to put the instrument in to cover the mercury to make its temperature rise.

I know the thermometer was down at 31 at 8 o'clock on Sunday evening; thirty-one-and-a-half. Very intense cold; that is the only thing I do remember.

Hitchens said that he had passed on warnings to the crew that *Titanic's* drinking water supply might freeze in its tanks. According to his figures, the sea temperature was around freezing, a point at which people immersed in water will normally survive for mere minutes rather than hours. Suddenly plunging into freezing cold water provokes an instant, involuntary intake of air, a lung-filling gasp so violent that it interrupts normal breathing; the cold literally 'taking one's breath away.'

Some of *Titanic's* victims would have gasped even though their heads were underwater. They had already drowned. Others were more slowly suffocating. Their lungs unable to recover enough to suck in fresh air, they were 'dry-drowning' from lack of oxygen, even though their mouths were still above water. A few were having heart attacks as massive doses of the shock hormone, adrenalin, surged into their bloodstream, raising blood pressure and heart rate.

Almost every one of those who had survived the moment they fell in the water were still about to die. Panic quickly claimed many of them; arms and legs flailing wildly in search of support they would never find. It cost them energy reserves and heat that their bodies desperately needed to survive. Even though they wore life-jackets, some were so weighed down by their heavy, waterlogged clothes that they turned face-down in the water to drown.

Those in *Titanic's* lifeboats nearest to the point where the ship sank had to endure the horror of hearing fellow passengers and colleagues screaming for help in the inky darkness of this moonless night. For those still alive in the water, the pain of the cold was lessening but they were racked with bouts of uncontrollable shivering. Muscles constricted and then instantly released as their bodies sacrificed precious energy supplies to the desperate need for more heat. After around twenty minutes in the water, all real hope was fading. Blood was no longer flowing to their arms and legs, and muscles no longer worked in any co-ordinated way; swimmers could no longer swim and even holding onto floating debris became an impossible task.

With cold blood carrying less and less oxygen to the brain, unconsciousness and death were the inevitable result. In homage to the latest *Titanic* movie, some scientists now call this the 'DiCaprio moment' – after the scene in which actor Leonardo DiCaprio's character falls asleep, loses his grip on the wreckage and sinks into the ocean depths. In reality there was little reason for *Titanic's* life-jacketed dead victims to sink; many were doomed to stay upright, stone-cold dead, but still afloat, for days after the disaster.[3]

Amid ocean waters that were suddenly left desolate and empty in the absolute darkness that followed the sinking of the great ship, a few souls were still clinging to life. They were the passengers and crewmen who had managed to calm themselves after the gasping shock of entering the water. While their muscles still responded they had seized that brief window of opportunity to fight for survival. The most exceptional story of all was recounted by Joughin, *Titanic's* baker.

> I should say over two hours, I was just paddling and treading water. Just as it was breaking daylight I saw what I thought was some wreckage, and I started to swim towards it slowly. When I got near enough, I found it was a collapsible [lifeboat] not properly upturned but on its side, with an officer and I should say about twenty or twenty-five men standing on the side, not on the top. There was no room for any more. They were standing on it then. I tried to get on it, but I was pushed off it, and I, what you call, hung around it.
>
> I eventually got round to the opposite side, and a cook that was on the collapsible recognised me, and held out his hand and held me.

Although his legs and feet were still submerged in the freezing water, the remarkable Joughin managed to pull some of his body up onto the edge of the canvas-sided boat.

> We were hanging on to this collapsible, I should say about half an hour, and eventually a lifeboat came in sight. They got within about 50 yards and they sung out that they could only take 10. So I said 'Let go my hand', and I swam to meet it, so that I would be one of the 10.
>
> I was taken in.

Over the 100 years since Joughin 'stepped off' *Titanic's* railings and into the Atlantic, scientists have puzzled about how he survived for so very much longer than the twenty-minute 'norm' for water this cold. Obesity has helped other men in some cold water survival cases, but contemporary pictures show that, despite the culinary temptations of his job, Joughin was a slight man with a thin face – and a substantial moustache. Pulling himself partly onto the collapsible certainly saved his life – yet he had already been fully immersed for some time before reaching the boat. Even lawyers at the British inquiry were astonished that he survived to finally reach the safety of the nearest rescue ship, the *Carpathia*.[4] Joughin's ordeal in the water was summarised during his answers to final questions of the British Solicitor-General, Sir John Simon:

'You have said you thought it was about two hours before you saw this collapsible, and then you spent some time with the collapsible. How long do you suppose it was after you got to the collapsible that you were taken into the lifeboat?'

'I should say we were on the collapsible about half an hour.'

'That means that for some two and a half hours you were in the water?'

'Practically, yes.'

'I do not want to be harrowing about it, but was the water very cold?'

'I felt colder in the lifeboat – after I got in the lifeboat.'

'What condition were you in when you got to the *Carpathia*?'

'I was all right barring my feet, they were swelled.'

'Were you able to walk up the ladder?'

'No.'

'How did you get up?'

'On my knees.'

Joughin was one of little more than 700 survivors who reached the safety of the rescue ship *Carpathia*. Other ships did duly arrive, only to find no trace of *Titanic*, and only dead bodies to be 'saved'. Despite the rumours of many vessels steaming to *Titanic's* aid, her senior officers had always known that help would never arrive in time.

Perhaps the greatest scandal of the British Wreck Commissioner's inquiry was its failure to place any substantial blame for the disaster on any executives, politicians or senior civil servants whose decisions, or inaction, over decades, had contributed to the tragedy. Instead the fiercest of its criticism was reserved for the hapless captain of the *Californian*, the one ship that reportedly failed to respond to *Titanic's* pleas for help.

The truth is that *Titanic's* victims did not die because rescue ships failed to arrive as rapidly as they might have done; the great majority did not even die because some boats were sent off half-empty; they died because there were never enough lifeboats to save them. Despite 25,622 questions over thirty-six days, the British inquiry failed to discover the real reasons why *Titanic* was allowed to sail with so few lifeboats on board. To do so they would have needed to investigate not only the civil servants who failed to recommend a change in the law – but also their political masters; the men with ultimate responsibility for the death of so many people that night.

Those politicians included one young up-and-coming statesman. He was the government minister with the ultimate responsibility for safety at sea when *Titanic* was being built; a man who would go on to become Britain's most revered statesman and, arguably, the 'Greatest Briton' of all: Winston Spencer Churchill.

Churchill's illustrious political and wartime career has ensured his place in the history books. Few have ever considered his failure to act and the neglect of those in his care that characterised his role in the *Titanic* disaster. Churchill was repeatedly asked to ensure that ships like *Titanic* should have lifeboats for everybody on board. The powers he possessed as President of the Board of Trade meant that he could have changed the lifeboat rules with one stroke of his pen, rather than having to steer new legislation through the Houses of Parliament: he repeatedly refused so to do.

Many different factors were to influence Churchill's attitude towards safety at sea during the vital period when *Titanic* was being built and he was in control of the Board of Trade. One chain of events was in train even before he took office: the shipwreck of a seemingly insignificant British cargo ship in the sea off Constantinople.

### Notes

1. Joughin's account comes from a combination of his evidence to the post-sinking inquiries and letters he wrote later in life.
2. As with all of the crew, Joughin's £12 a month wages as Chief Baker were stopped by the White Star Line from the moment that *Titanic* sank.
3. Ships chartered by White Star found floating bodies for days afterwards. The law required that the dead be embalmed, but embalming fluid was in short supply. Stories have persisted that the First Class dead were embalmed, while more Third Class victims went back in the water for 'burial at sea'.
4. 'I think his getting a drink had a lot to do with saving his life,' claimed one barrister. In fact, modern research suggests that drinking should have *lessened* Joughin's chances of survival.

# Chapter Fourteen

# 'No deviation is to be permitted . . .'

**4.00 pm evening tide**
**4 December 1907**
**Danube Port of Sulina**
**Romania**

It had been a long and tiring day on board the British steamship *Grindon Hall*, laying alongside the wooden loading wharf of Europe's most easterly port. Work had started at four in the morning, with the galley boy, Thomas Govan, earning every halfpenny of his ten shillings a month pay by stoking the fires and cooking porridge for the crew – a crew still recovering from an evening's entertainment in the seafarers' bars of the Romanian town of Sulina. Unique in having no land access, the town was reachable only by ship along the wide river Danube. In those early years of the twentieth century, Sulina was the most cosmopolitan of ports. For decades it had housed international diplomats working together in the grandly named European Commission of the Danube, to ensure that no one nation controlled the vital shipping lanes of the Black Sea. That meant that the *Grindon Hall's* crew had been drinking in the Freeport bars of Sulina with sailors from a score or more of European countries and cultures.

For Captain Robert Burt the day was proving not only long, but also worrying. He had tirelessly supervised the loading of more than 200 bags of valuable maize and barley through the five different cargo hatches. Next came 44 tons of coal to feed the boilers, and water and supplies to feed the *Grindon Hall's* twenty-seven-strong crew. The captain's worry came from ensuring that the cargo could not shift and destabilise his ship on her long journey past Constantinople, through the Mediterranean and across the Bay of Biscay. He was contracted to deliver the grain safely ashore in Edinburgh. A shifting cargo had been the death of many fine ships – although the 3,000-ton *Grindon Hall* had been purpose-built in a Sunderland shipyard for just this grain-carrying task; she was more stable than many other vessels, even in rough weather.

Finally, in time to catch a tide that would see them sailing this evening and conceivably back in his Cornish home with his wife and two children by Christmas, Captain Burt finished signing the endless paperwork and walked to the nearby British Consulate. There, the master of the *Grindon Hall* registered his sworn declaration that his ship was seaworthy and correctly loaded for the voyage to come. With the good wishes of the consular clerk in his ears, the captain joined his crew, took on board the local pilot, steamed out past the mile-long artificial breakwater that formed Sulina's harbour, and headed out along the Danube. At the river's mouth, as the ship reached the open waters of the Black Sea, the pilot disembarked into his accompanying launch, and bid the captain farewell.

Neither the ship, nor its captain or crew, were ever to be seen again.

The disappearance of the *Grindon Hall* was no different from that of many other ships lost without trace in the era before ships' radios became commonplace. But this shipwreck was to have far-reaching consequences. It would soon embarrass a young Winston Churchill, newly promoted to his first Cabinet post as President of the Board of Trade. The intensely ambitious Churchill, just thirty-three years old, was then responsible for the safety at sea of all British merchant ships, and of all those who sailed in them. It was a hectic period for the new minister, and for the shipping industry over which he now had control. One spectacular shipping project would soon be underway; the simultaneous construction of the *Titanic* and her sister ship, the *Olympic* – the two biggest ships in the world.

At such a crucial time, the unhappy fate of the *Grindon Hall* would ensure that Churchill's relationship with his most senior Marine Division civil servants began in the worst possible way. That, in turn, would contribute to Churchill's failure to oversee and reform the way his antiquated government department would regulate the building of *Titanic*. The death of this one tiny British cargo steamer directly linked to the death of one of the greatest ships ever to sail the seas.

It was on New Year's Eve 1907, three months before Churchill's promotion to be President of the Board of Trade, that *The Times* newspaper carried a single paragraph of sad, maritime news. Churchill may well have read the story, but could not then have registered it as of any importance to his future career:

**FEARED LOSS OF A STEAMER**: It is feared that the Cardiff steamer, *Grindon Hall*, belonging to Messrs' Edward Nicholl and Co., of Cardiff, has been lost with all hands in the Black Sea. Nothing has been heard of her, and reports from Constantinople indicate that she never passed the Bosporus. It is, of course, just possible that she did pass the Bosporus without speaking, and, if so, there may still be hope.

Nine days later, *The Times* revealed a distressing development for the relatives of the twenty-seven crewmen on board the *Grindon Hall*:

> A damaged lifeboat of the British steamer *Grindon Hall,* believed to have sunk in the Black Sea, has been picked up in those waters. It is now practically certain that this vessel was lost about December 7.

No further trace was ever found of the *Grindon Hall*. She had become just the latest in a long list of merchant vessels that went missing at sea. In such cases there was rarely any evidence to show why, when or how they had foundered. Even so, around five months later, on 21 May 1908, magistrate Thomas William Lewis and Board of Trade adviser Captain William Barnett Bigley opened a 'preliminary inquiry' into the loss of the *Grindon Hall* at the Law Courts in her home port of Cardiff. A solicitor for the ship's owner and relatives of the missing seamen tried to attend, but were told to leave because the inquiry was 'private'.

The inquiry had little to go on: the screw-driven steamer was one of more than 200 cargo vessels built to the same design over the previous fifteen years by the respected Sunderland shipyard of William Doxford & Sons. They were known as 'turret' ships because of their distinctive design, and had a good safety record when compared with other ships of the early twentieth century.[1] The Board of Trade's assessors had copies of the missing captain's declaration, registered with authorities in Sulina. It stated that the ship was loaded in accordance with Board of Trade regulations. But, in private, they also saw written evidence from a stevedore at the Romanian port. He claimed that the ship carried tons of coal, stacked on her open deck. The hearing concluded that the captain must have been lying about the way his ship was loaded:

> The cause of the vessel not having been heard of is that she foundered in consequence of her instability as laden.

It was a damning indictment of Captain Burt; a clear suggestion that he had lied on his loading documents and led his unwitting crew to their deaths. His relatives, the ship's owners and the seamen's union were outraged. They enlisted the aid of a sympathetic peer, Lord Muskerry,[2] who demanded that public inquiries should always be held when a British ship was missing. In the House of Lords, he launched a scathing attack on Churchill and his new department, the Board of Trade, declaring:

> The tragedy of a missing ship and the unknown fate of her crew is, unfortunately, not uncommon. In justice to the widows left behind, it is

our bounden duty to cause public investigation into such disasters. But evidently missing ships receive by no means the same zealous attention at the hands of the Board of Trade.

The captain to all intents and purposes is branded as a perjurer and held responsible for the loss of his own life and the lives of his crew. It is an outrage that secret investigations may be held which drag in the mire the good names of men who have lost their lives in an honourable calling.

Board of Trade files, now in the National Archives, reveal that the criticism caused consternation among civil servants who were desperate at the time to earn their new president's approval. Churchill's office hurriedly pointed out that the cost of a public inquiry was rarely justified; the very fact that a ship was 'missing', indicated the lack of any evidence for an inquiry to consider.

The suggestion that Churchill's department was trying to save money, while British sailors' lives were being lost at sea, merely added fuel to the flames. Speaker after speaker lined up to defend the good name of British sailors and to castigate the Board of Trade. The Earl of Meath had a dire warning for the Government as a whole, and for its recently appointed cabinet minister, Winston Churchill, in particular:

To the ordinary man in the street the Board of Trade are thinking much more about the expense of investigations than of the lives of the men. If that idea once gets possession of the public, woe betide any government that permits it. Those at present in office will not sit long on the benches of power.

In the face of a house that was united against him across party lines, Churchill was humiliated into issuing a highly public apology and into promising an instant change of policy. The following morning he scrawled his own distinctive handwritten and initialled note across a Board of Trade file:

A public inquiry must be held in all cases. If the Departmental inquiry is held in private, as may sometimes be desirable to elicit full information, it must always be followed by a public judicial inquiry: WSC 7-7-08.

The file, by now marked with the word 'Immediate' in over-sized, blue crayon lettering, was sent to Sir Alfred Chalmers, the Chief Professional Adviser running the Board of Trade's Marine Division. More worryingly for Sir Alfred, it was accompanied by a new demand from Churchill that he must now be informed, personally, every week, of every British ship that might go missing, anywhere in the world. Appalled by the potential workload and expense of Churchill's new policy, one senior civil servant wrote back suggesting a compromise:

I would only suggest whether it is quite advisable that the president should so completely tie his hands as to promise that a Public inquiry should be held in every case of a missing Ship, for I think cases will surely occur in which it will be obviously useless and unnecessary to do.

The suggestion received short shrift from an embarrassed and now-angry Churchill. In a typically brief, handwritten, red-ink Churchillian memo, his instructions were clear:

No deviation is to be permitted from this rule except upon my authority WSC.

Churchill's dismay at the outcome of his first political skirmish involving the Board of Trade's Marine Division could only have been heightened by the fact that other areas of his important Cabinet post had been going so well. The boring details of regulating merchant ships were only a minor, and distinctly unglamorous, part of the job. Indeed, just weeks before, Churchill had earned the kudos of receiving a letter from the King, expressing gratitude for his new minister's help in resolving a damaging industrial dispute. Now all he was receiving was a political problem. Within days, his embarrassment was to be publicly emphasised yet again. *The Times* reported that Churchill had blamed Board of Trade investigators for the *Grindon Hall* debacle and had promised Cabinet colleagues it would not happen again. Rubbing salt into the wound, the newspaper printed a patronising open letter from an opposition peer:

I am very glad that the President of the Board of Trade has so promptly responded.

From that day onwards, the Marine Division was forced to hold 'missing ships' inquiries in public and to expend manpower on producing a detailed, weekly chart of missing ships. It was delivered to the president's desk in Whitehall each Monday morning – whether or not Churchill was in the building to view it. Clara Collett, one of the department's few female civil servants, found it amusing that Churchill was in such dominant charge of men who clearly thought themselves his intellectual superiors. She noted in her diary at the time:

I don't think the Board of Trade loves Mr Churchill, but I confess that he interests me as a human being whatever his faults may be.

Other bureaucrats in the department were not so forgiving of the 'new boy' Churchill's demanding attitude. One note in the National Archives 'missing ships' file reflects a casual disregard for outside interference:

I do not think that the Board need bother its head with any questions which Lord Muskerry or anyone else may ask. They are bound in every case to have a perfectly good answer.

Two years later, within days of Churchill leaving the department, the production of his weekly 'missing ships list' was immediately abandoned for good. The file records:

> There is nothing that binds the president to give personal attention to these cases that was a practice adopted by W. Churchill purely for his own information.

Churchill's relationship with the senior officers of the Marine Division had got off to a bad start. From then onwards, Churchill appears to have had little time or interest in that department's work. Despite having the ultimate responsibility for ensuring the safety of British ships, and British lives at sea, the new president showed little interest in reforming the rules and regulations of a department that itself had no appetite for change.

Winston Churchill was not alone in his neglect of safety policies. Successive Board of Trade presidents before him had also failed to revise the now hopelessly inadequate lifeboat rules; the rules that would shortly spell disaster for all who died on *Titanic*. But Churchill had more reason than most to have been hearing alarm bells. The shipping equivalent of an arms race was breaking out around him. On his watch at the Board of Trade, the two fastest ships in the world, Cunard's *Lusitania* and *Mauretania*, each thousands of tons bigger than any ship before, were already plying their trade across the Atlantic.

It is inconceivable that Churchill was not aware of White Star's plans to fight-back against that competition with three luxurious new ocean liners. They would be the biggest ships in the world, each in excess of 45,000 tons; and each would be governed by an old-fashioned set of rules allowing them to sail with only a fraction of the lifeboats that they needed. On top of that, Churchill was about to be given several more clear warnings that urgent action was needed to lessen the chances of a major disaster at sea. He would ignore them all.

### Notes

1. Only two of around 200 'turret ships' were reported to have been lost in the previous decade; remarkably few when compared with the poor safety record of other bulk cargo ships of the time.
2. Lord Muskerry took a lifelong interest in the plight of British seamen. He was the chief critic of the Board of Trade after *Titanic* sank.

## Chapter Fifteen

# '. . . my best love to salute you'

**8.40 am**
**12 August 1908**
**The Rose Garden**
**Blenheim Palace**
**Oxfordshire**

It was the most romantic of settings for an early morning walk with one's beloved. Early on a fine August morning the dew still glistened on the petals of the thousands of multi-coloured blooms that lined the secluded rose garden walk through the grounds of Blenheim Palace. Strolling softly, hand-in-hand, Winston Churchill and his new fiancée, Clementine, were lost in each other's company – planning how Churchill might properly announce their engagement to the friends and family with whom they had just shared breakfast.

The young politician Winston's romantic proposal of the evening before was still fresh in Clementine's memory. Although they had known each other for so little time, Winston now had an important new government job with the Board of Trade and could at last afford to take a wife. This morning had begun in even more romantic a fashion than the night before had ended. Clementine had barely awakened before a liveried footman was tapping quietly at her bedroom door. He bore a hastily scribbled note from Winston:

My dearest,
How are you? I send you my best love to salute you: & I am getting up at once in order if you like to walk to the rose garden after breakfast & pick a bunch before you start. You will have to leave here about 10:30 & I will come with you to Oxford.
Shall I not give you a letter for your Mother?
Always – W

Clementine's note by return had been equally brief:

My dearest
I am very well – Yes please give me a letter to take to Mother– I should love to go to the rose garden.

Yours always – Clementine

Such evidence suggests that Churchill had matters other than work on his mind when he first took up his position at the Board of Trade. This first Cabinet post was of vital importance to him for a number of personal and political reasons. Because ordinary MPs were unpaid, he had desperately needed a ministerial salary to help with the financial troubles that had dogged him for years. His entire political career had become dependent upon financial help from wealthy relatives and political supporters who paid all his expenses in the several different elections that Churchill had been forced to fight in the early twentieth century.[1]

His always-busy life soon threatened to overwhelm the time available for his Cabinet work. Churchill had recently lost his parliamentary constituency seat, forcing him into a by-election to get back into Parliament. He was also rebuilding his political reputation after switching political parties and was obsessively working on a biography of his late father, Randolph. Perhaps most absorbingly of all, Churchill had fallen in love.

Churchill's personal life and his chaotic political career in the years leading up to his presidency of the Board of Trade have fascinated many of his biographers. Churchill gained his first Parliamentary seat for the Tories in 1900, possibly driven by a desire to posthumously impress his cold and unloving father. In his book *Churchill – A Study in Failure 1900-1939*, historian Robert Rhodes James wrote:

… of the fact that his parents were neglectful of him and not greatly concerned in his doings there can be no doubt. His idealisation of both, and particularly of his remote, aloof father, was natural in itself, but exceptional in its intensity.

A gradual disillusionment with the Tory party had combined in Churchill's mind with the growing conviction that he was unfairly being passed over for higher office. It was to lead to a change of political allegiance. A mere four years after he was elected as a Tory he 'crossed the floor' of the House of Commons to join the Liberal Party. Many critics of Churchill's character have suggested his political conversion had more to do with his overwhelming desire for political advancement than with and deep-seated Liberal convictions. Whatever the truth of that charge, the move undoubtedly did bring immediate political rewards. Eight months later, Churchill was given a junior ministerial role in the Colonial Office and, in April 1908, he was promoted to be President of the Board of Trade. It was Churchill's first seat at the Cabinet table.

The poet Wilfred Scawen Blunt, an avid diarist of the political and social events of the era, recorded his first impressions of Churchill when he met him shortly before he joined the Liberal Government:

> He is a little, square-headed fellow of no very striking appearance, but of wit, intelligence, and originality. In mind and manner he is a strange replica of his father, with, and I should say more than his father's ability.

Churchill's early days in office were a mixture of frantic political activity and the dullest of ministerial meetings. Board of Trade records list his first decisions as being the appointment of six staff to new departmental postings and consideration of a complex Treasury Department memorandum about the office costs of the Official Receiver for Companies (Winding-Up Department). In tandem with that early banality of his ministerial 'day job', Churchill was simultaneously fighting a bitter by-election battle against a charismatic Tory opponent in a vain attempt to save his Manchester constituency seat. Having narrowly lost that battle, while still learning the ropes in his new departmental role, he then had to contest a second by-election, this time in the relatively safe Liberal seat of Dundee. Winning that election on 9 May 1908 did secure his place in Parliament and his seat at the Cabinet table but at the cost of having to undertake regular, time-consuming ten-hour train journeys to Scotland.

As if all that were not enough to deter Churchill from finding the time and inclination to tackle the many ills of the Board's troubled Marine Division, he had a more personal reason to neglect his work. He had fallen in love. In the very month that he started work at the Board of Trade Churchill began a whirlwind courtship with Miss Clementine Hozier. The couple had been briefly introduced some years earlier but it was only at this second meeting that their romance began. Four months later, Churchill asked her to marry him. Blunt, who was soon to become a close friend of both Winston and Clementine, recorded the event in August 1908:

> Blanche Hozier writes from Blenheim that her daughter Clementine is to marry Winston Churchill. She says he is gentle and tender, and affectionate to those he loves, much hated by those who have not come under his personal charm. Clementine is pretty, clever, and altogether charming, while Winston is what the world knows him, and a good fellow to boot.

Given the intensity of his new romance it is unlikely that Churchill would have taken much note of a major development in the shipping industry on the day of his betrothal. As he dallied with Clementine at Blenheim, the executives of the Darlington Forge Company in Yorkshire were celebrating a large and profitable new order: 'Three Siemens Martin steel shipframes', which together would weigh a massive 155 tons. The purchasers, Harland and Wolff, had demanded a discount of two and a half per cent and finally agreed a price of thirty shillings per hundredweight of steel. They required that the steel should be tested for quality by the Lloyd's proving house 'or its equal', and that each frame be pre-drilled with rivet holes and delivered to their shipyard in Ireland. The fittingly huge order was the first to be placed for a huge new ship: the White Star Line's *Titanic*.

Over the next two years, as *Titanic* slowly took shape on her slipway in Belfast, Winston Churchill's social, political and working life continued at the same frenetic pace. On 12 September he married Miss Clementine Hozier at St Margaret's Church, Westminster, in a ceremony attended by many of the political and social leaders of the day.[2] After the wedding Churchill was busily occupied in finding a new house for his new bride. A few months later, they moved into their new home in Ecclestone Square, Belgravia. Blunt visited them there and found the newly-weds still totally preoccupied with each other:

> I like him much. He is aux plus petits soins with his wife, taking all possible care of her. They are a very happy married pair. Clementine was afraid of wasps, and one settled on her sleeve, and Winston gallantly took the wasp by the wings and thrust it into the ashes of the fire.
>
> He had just been at the Cabinet in Downing Street, and arrived late, looking rather grave but he soon cheered up. He and Clementine are to come to Newbuildings to hear the nightingales. They are on just the same honeymoon terms as ever.

The couple's 'honeymoon' status was confirmed soon afterwards with the announcement of their 'honeymoon' baby; their first daughter, Diana, was born on 11 July 1909.[3] Most commentators agree that despite such distractions Churchill worked hard as a Cabinet minister and achieved significant successes in many areas for which he had responsibility at the Board of Trade. Revealing a genuine concern for the welfare of working men, Churchill established the first labour exchanges to help the unemployed and pushed through employment law policies to improve the lives of those who had jobs. He was directly responsible for setting the first minimum wages within some industries, and for setting limits on the working hours of Britain's miners.

He did, however, take somewhat less care of Britain's merchant seamen.

## Notes

1. A little of Churchill's first ministerial salary went on his first ever order of 1895 Pol Roget champagne. He became a customer for life
2. Churchill and Clementine remained together 'till death us do part'. In later life he summed up the relationship in one brief sentence: 'I married and lived happily ever afterwards.'
3. Churchill himself had been a 'honeymoon baby', born 'prematurely', just over seven months after his parents' sudden wedding at the British Embassy in Paris.

# *Chapter Sixteen*

# 'It was terrible cries, Sir'

**2.30 am**
**Sunday, 15 April 1912**
**Position: 49° 56' 54" W, 41° 43' 35" N**
**The now-empty waters of the North Atlantic Ocean**

In the freezing dark aftermath of *Titanic's* sinking, 2,208 men, women and children were floating amidst the ice floes and the icebergs of the North Atlantic Ocean. About 900 of them were fortunate enough to be floating in the lifeboats; the others were floating in canvas-covered, cork-filled life-jackets. All of those in the water were now rapidly drowning, or dying from the cold.

One of those lucky enough to have a seat in a lifeboat was Able Seaman Edward Burley. He was yet another crewman with many years of experience in the Royal Navy. Still only twenty-seven, he had left his home in the Hampshire village of Itchen just a week or so earlier to sign on, for £5 a month, as a deckhand with *Titanic* in the nearby Southampton Docks. Burley had been on duty since early evening, although his duties had been less demanding than usual.

> I was sitting in the mess, reading, at the time when she struck. If it was Sunday night, we never had anything to do; ordinary nights we should have been scrubbing the decks.

After the collision Burley was instructed to help other seamen prepare the ship's lifeboats. He was specifically warned not to alarm the passengers.

> The order was to tell the seamen to get together and uncover the boats and turn them out as quietly as though nothing had happened. They are on deck, and the davits are turned inboard. You have to unscrew these davits and swing the boat out over the ship's side. They turned them out in about 20 minutes.
>
> The next order was to lower them down to a line with the gunwale of the boat deck, and then fill the boats with women and children. Ours was the last boat up there, and they went around and called to see if

there were any, and they threw them in the boat at the finish, because they didn't like the idea of coming in.

I think that the majority thought that the ship would float. They thought she would go down a certain distance and stop there; several of them said they were only getting the boats out for exercise and in case of accident.

Burley escaped from *Titanic* along with a few other seamen and dozens of women and children who had been loaded into lifeboat No. 10. With too few men to row the boat properly they were no more than 250 yards away from the ship when she finally sank beneath the waves.

She went down as far as the after-funnel. First of all you could see her propellers and everything. Her rudder was clear out of the water and then there was a little roar, as though the engines had rushed forward, and she snapped in two.

We could see the outline of the ship. The lights were all out. The lights went out gradually before she disappeared. You could see she went in two, because we were quite near to her and could see her quite plainly. We could see the afterpart afloat, and there was no forepart to it. She uprighted herself for about five minutes, and then tipped over and disappeared. The people in the boat were very frightened that there would be some suction. If there had been any suction we should have been lost.

An hour later, Burley's lifeboat met up with four others that together were under the command of 5th Officer Harold Lowe. He transferred all of the passengers from his boat in order to return to the point where the ship sank and search for other survivors. Burley was one of the men rowing the rescue boat.

He went back among the wreckage to see if there were any people that had lived. There were not very many there. We got four of them. All the others were dead. Of course you could not discern them exactly on account of the wreckage; but we turned over several of them to see if they were alive. It looked as though none of them were drowned.

They looked as though they were frozen. The life belts they had on were out of the water, and their heads were laid back, with their faces on the water, several of them. Their hands were coming up; it looked as though they were frozen altogether.

After we picked up all that was alive, there was a collapsible boat we saw with a lot of people, and she was swamped, and they were up to their knees in water. We set sail and went over to them, and in a brief time picked up another boat filled with women and children, with no one to pull the oars, and we took her in tow.

In the early morning light, now securely roped together, the small flotilla of lifeboats rowed towards the steamship *Carpathia*. Even before they reached the rescue ship, some of their passengers had died.

> I think there was two died that we had saved; two men. I think it was exposure and shock. We had no stimulants in the boat to revive them, at all, and they were cold, helpless and numb. There were several in the broken boat that could not walk. Their legs and feet were all cramped. They had to stand up in the water in that boat. It was terrible cries, sir.

The same cries were heard by another sailor on board the one lifeboat that had returned to the scene of the sinking. Thirty-year-old steward George Crowe told how the crew had struggled to row the boat through the wreckage:

> We were successful in doing so and in picking one body up that was floating around in the water; when we got him into the boat – after great difficulty, he being such a heavy man – he expired shortly afterwards. Going farther in we came across one of the crew, and got him into the boat, and he was very cold and his hands were kind of stiff, but he survived; also a Japanese or Chinese young fellow that we picked up on top of some of the wreckage, it might have been a sideboard or table, that was floating around.

The story of the 'Japanese or Chinese young fellow' was later recounted by a Second Class passenger who sold her story of the sinking to an American magazine. In what was possibly a highly fanciful account, for which she was paid several hundred dollars, Charlotte Collyer claimed that the man had at first been left for dead:

> We saw a floating door that must have been torn loose. Lying upon it, face downward, was a small Japanese. He had lashed himself with a rope to his frail raft, using the broken hinges to make the knots secure. As far as we could see, he was dead. The sea washed over him every time the door bobbed up and down, and did not answer when he was hailed, and the officer hesitated about trying to save him.
>
> He had actually turned our boat around; but he changed his mind and went back. The Japanese was hauled on board, and one of the women rubbed his chest, while others chafed his hands and feet. In less time than it takes to tell, he opened his eyes and in five minutes or so had almost recovered his strength.[1]

Frank Evans, the able seaman who was later to reveal such a good knowledge of lifeboat capacity to the US inquiry, was also involved in the only rescue mission that was mounted from the lifeboats that night. He told the inquiry that all of the bodies he had seen were wearing life-jackets:

There were plenty of dead bodies about us. You couldn't hardly count them, sir. I was afraid to look over the sides because it might break my nerves down. From here upward they were clear of the water. They simply had perished. I had a thorough good look around everywhere in the wreckage. To see if I could see any live ones, any live bodies.

After finding no other people alive the lifeboat set sail again and found one of *Titanic's* collapsible lifeboats, half-submerged in the water. It was the upturned boat to which Joughin, *Titanic's* baker, was clinging. Alongside him was another, much younger crewman from the catering staff, 18-year-old Assistant Cook, John Collins. He later told his own harrowing tale of what happened in *Titanic's* last moments:

I ran to the port side on the saloon deck with another steward and a woman and two children. The steward had one of the children in his arms and the woman was crying. I took the child off of the woman and we were just turning around and making for the stern end when the wave washed us off the deck; washed us clear of it. There were hundreds on the starboard side washed off into the water.

The child was washed out of my arms; and the wreckage and the people that was around me, they kept me down for at least two or three minutes under the water. Well, it seemed that to me. I could not exactly state how long, but it seemed that to me. When I came to the surface I saw this boat that had been taken off and I swam over to it.

Having managed to climb onto the side of the barely floating lifeboat, Collins realised how fragile it was. Answering questions from the US investigators, he revealed how one brave man had sacrificed his own life for everyone on board:

'Did the men on the bottom of the collapsible boat refuse to let others get on from the water?'

'Only one, sir. If a gentleman had got on we would all have been turned over. We were all on the boat. One was running from one side to the other to keep her steady. If this man had caught hold of her he would have tumbled the whole lot of us off.'

'Who prevented him?'

'We were all telling him not to get on. He said: "That is all right, boys, keep cool, God bless you," and he bid us good-bye. He swam along for about two minutes and we seen him, but did not see him moving off; we saw his head, but we did not see him moving his hands.'

'He was not pushed off by anyone, but those on the boat asked him not to try to get on? And he acquiesced?'

'Yes, sir.'

The lack of lifeboats on *Titanic* led to many such accounts of bravery, tragedy, hope and despair emerging in the months that followed the ship's sinking. It also led to an almost instantaneous change of attitude among ship-owners all over the world. After decades of protesting that they had neither the room, nor the crewmen, to provide lifeboats for all, those problems apparently melted away overnight.[2] Ship-owners found that crews would not man the ships, nor passengers board their vessels, until the requisite number of lifeboats were provided.

Somehow those responsible for the lack of boats escaped serious censure and political shame both here and abroad. And yet, it was not as if the relevant marine regulators and the politicians supposed to be safeguarding life at sea had not been given prior warning of the problem. Some of those warning signs came not from shipwrecks in distant parts of the globe but from accidents far closer to their Westminster seats of power; from accidents in British home waters, barely outside the estuary of the river Thames.

### Notes

1. In the more imaginative parts of her story, Collyer claimed that 5th Officer Lowe had said: 'It's only a Jap,' when refusing to check if he was dead or alive.
2. Having escaped in one of the last *Titanic* boats, Bruce Ismay immediately ordered lifeboats for all on every White Star ship.

## Chapter Seventeen

# 'Who is responsible for this state of affairs?'

8.30 am
29 September 1908
The dining room of SS *Argonaut*
20 miles off Dungeness Headland
The English Channel

An excited buzz of conversation filled the busy breakfast room as the wealthy British tourists shared plans with each other for their first day at sea. Each was not quite certain of what to expect, for this was one of the first 'package holidays' ever to be organised in Britain. A fledgling travel company run by London businessman Dr Henry Lunn[1] had advertised the ease, safety and security of travelling with a group of like-minded individuals on a holiday where everything was organised in advance 'for the perfect convenience of our travellers'. So far, the trip was living up to expectations. At Tilbury Docks the evening before, around 100 enthusiastic customers had boarded their ship for this late-summer cruise along the coast of France and through the Straits of Gibraltar to the beaches of the Mediterranean. In its earlier life, and under a less-grandiose name, the holidaymakers' new 330-foot long cruise ship had been a plain tramp steamer, repetitively carrying cargo back and forth between Britain and the Caribbean. An extensive and expensive makeover had transformed her into Dr Lunn's far more luxurious and far grander sounding 'Steam Yacht *Argonaut*'.

After spending the night moored by the dockside, the ship set sail at dawn on its trip to the promised sun of the South of France. Most of the passengers had risen early to savour the novelty of the *Argonaut's* departure and were enjoying the delights of a traditional English breakfast, served by attentive stewards in the airy, top deck dining room. The 100-strong crew were all about their duties, ensuring that the ship remained on course, and on time, for her first planned continental landfall at Cherbourg. A thick sea mist had slowed the ship slightly, but nothing was to be allowed to alter the planned itinerary or spoil the holidaymakers' first morning at sea.

Barely half a mile away, the lookout on a very different breed of ship was struggling to see ahead of his vessel as it powered through the morning mist. The 2,355-ton cargo steamer *Kingswell* was only two-thirds of the size of the *Argonaut*, but carried a far heavier cargo of unprocessed iron ore. She too had slowed slightly while waiting for the weak morning sun to burn off the mist, but her captain was anxious to make port to catch a mid-morning tide in the Port of London. With visibility reduced to just a few yards, and with none of the benefits of modern navigational aids, neither captain was aware that their ships were on a collision course with each other.

The crash when it came was the rudest possible interruption to a fine morning meal; violent enough to catapult diners, their food, their chairs and many of the tables across the restaurant floor. As the *Argonaut* shuddered to a halt, those package tourists still on their feet rushed out on deck to find another huge vessel jammed across their bows. With the screech of twisted metal, the still-moving *Kingswell* drifted onwards into the fog, leaving her more luxurious victim wallowing in her wake. The *Argonaut* was holed below the waterline and was sinking rapidly. Despite the force of the impact, the only serious casualty was a junior officer with a gash to his head. As the ship settled by the bow, all of her passengers and crew assembled on deck and boarded the lifeboats. A contemporary newspaper report praised the efficiency of the captain and crew:

> Whilst everything possible was done to allay the alarm of the passengers, orders were given for the immediate launching of the lifeboats and the issue of lifebelts. So quickly did the water gain upon the steamer that after a few minutes there could be no doubt that she was doomed. In the meantime the boats had been very promptly launched. Only about 20 minutes elapsed from the time that *Argonaut* was struck until she foundered, and the haste with which she had to be abandoned by the passengers and crew was shown by the fact that all lost everything except the clothes they stood in.[2]

Adrift in the fog, many miles from the shore, it took the shocked sailors and passengers more than an hour to find the *Kingswell* still floating nearby. But having boarded the cargo ship they found that it too was on the verge of sinking. Taking to the boats once again, they were finally towed to safety by another passing steamer. The damaged *Kingswell* was deliberately beached at Dungeness to prevent it from sinking completely.

It was a fortunate end to an unfortunate accident,[3] but questions were soon being asked by the *Argonaut's* wealthy, influential and much-aggrieved clientele. On this occasion, the *Argonaut* had enough lifeboat places for all of its 130 passengers, but the yacht had been licensed to carry 338 people. Had she been fully-booked then many would have been left behind to drown as she rapidly foundered so far from the shore. For Winston Churchill, the ambitious and relatively new-in-post President of the Board of Trade, the case of the *Argonaut* was to lead to another embarrassing question in the House of Commons.

On 19 October, two weeks after the sinking, Buckinghamshire MP Herbert Arnold tabled a question asking Churchill about his department's attitude to the provision of lifeboats:

> I beg to ask the President of the Board of Trade whether there is any regulation requiring passenger vessels to be provided with lifeboat accommodation for as many passengers as they are capable of carrying; and whether he is aware that the *Argonaut*, which was capable of carrying 200 passengers, had on board only 108 passengers when she sank the other day, yet all the boats were full, so that if she had had her full complement of passengers on board a large number of people would have been unprovided for; and will he say who is responsible for this state of affairs.

As Churchill rose to speak, he would have been aware of the final preparations even then being made in Belfast for the construction of the two biggest ships in the world, *Olympic* and *Titanic*. Their slipways had been prepared, their steel had been ordered and work on their keels would start at any moment.

'There is no regulation requiring lifeboat accommodation to be provided for every person on board every passenger vessel,' said Churchill as he promised a public inquiry into the *Argonaut's* sinking. 'I am advised that it would not be practicable in the case of very large vessels to carry the number of boats that such a regulation would require.'

The *Argonaut* collision was a shipping accident on the smallest of scales: 108 passengers rescued, just one man injured, and not a single death. Yet the complacency of Churchill's reply was the clearest of signals that neither he nor anyone else within the Board of Trade was even considering the safety of passengers on board the vastly bigger ships that would soon be carrying 3,000 people and more across the Atlantic Ocean.

Churchill had been barely three months in office when the final go-ahead was given to Harland and Wolff for the construction of *Olympic* and *Titanic*. Within weeks, vast and valuable orders were flowing out from the Belfast yard to steel and iron producers all over Britain. As not only the official guardian of marine safety but also as a champion of the best of British industry, Churchill's Department of Trade was intimately involved from the start of this internationally prestigious engineering project.

From July 1908 onwards, engineers from the Marine Division were busy approving or rejecting steel and iron suppliers for the two new ships and in the testing of steel plates and bars being supplied for their construction; staff were allocated from an already stretched Surveyors' Department to liaise with the White Star Line and with Harland and Wolff. Meetings were held at Churchill's Whitehall Gardens offices to decide which of the Board's ship and engineering surveyors would inspect the continuing construction work.

As *Titanic's* construction continued throughout the following two years of Churchill's control of the Board of Trade, he was to receive – and ignore – multiple warnings about the department's long outdated regulations, the poor performance of its entire Marine Division, and of its ship surveying staff in particular. His failure to control and reform his inefficient, old-fashioned and poorly-managed ministry was to have dire consequences for British merchant shipping; it would contribute to both the safety failings and the engineering weaknesses that four years later would sink the *Titanic*. Winston Churchill presided over a vital government department that proved not fit for purpose.

Within a few weeks of the sinking of the *Argonaut*, another small cargo ship drew Churchill's attention to weaknesses in the Board of Trade's lifeboat policies. In the police courts at Swansea, the master of the steamer *Haslingden* was accused of failing to comply with lifeboat regulations. Although the outcome of the case is not recorded, the evidence of one prosecution witness fuelled a further question in the House. Joseph Havelock-Wilson, the MP and passionate champion of seamen's unions, raised the issue of the court case and went on to ask the President of the Board of Trade:

> ... whether his attention has been called to the statement of the principal officer of the Surveyor's Department of the Board of Trade for the South Wales District to the effect that there were not enough surveyors to deal with one-tenth of the vessels ... and that a vessel might go for years and never be seen by surveyors.

Havelock-Wilson pointed out that the hapless South Wales official, Captain W.B. Whall, had complained during the court case that paid surveys of new ships and boilers 'took precedence over every other duty,' including safety inspections. The MP asked Churchill:

> ... whether, in view of this state of affairs, the Board will consider the advisability of appointing additional surveyors in order that the life-saving appliances of vessels may be properly inspected.

Churchill was quick to robustly defend his Ministry's good name. He declared that criticism of the Surveyors' Department had been wrongly reported in the newspapers and added:

> Matters of safety take precedence over every other duty and if there
> were reason to think that the present staff was insufficient to secure
> proper inspection it would be increased.

The Civil Service advice on which Churchill based that answer came from his
most senior Marine Division official, Sir Walter Howell. After forty years with
the department, Sir Walter was the personification of the entire organisation;
the perfect civil servant, meticulous, careful and averse to change of any kind.
He was also well used to being 'economical with the truth' in order to protect
his position. In fact, despite the confident assessment he gave to Churchill, Sir
Walter was well aware that the Marine Surveyors' Department was grossly
under-resourced and struggling to cope with insufficient manpower, low pay
and even lower morale.

   In addition to the enforcement of lifeboat rules, the surveyors were also
responsible for surveying the hulls of all newly-built ships, including that of
*Titanic*. The Board employed both 'ship surveyors' and a more junior grade of
officer known as 'engineer surveyors', for this work. In an internal memo, Sir
Walter privately referred to earlier problems in recruiting enough competent
ship surveyors and admitted that this had affected the department's efficiency.
File No. MT/32040 in the Board of Trade's archives contains Sir Walter's
memorandum about the qualities of the two grades of survey staff:

> There are many questions connected with the survey of a steel or iron
> passenger steamer which can only properly be dealt with by a Ship
> Surveyor. But, until recent years there was difficulty in getting a supply
> of properly qualified Ship Surveyors capable of dealing with iron and
> steel ships. The survey of passenger steamers is at present mainly
> carried out by the 'Engineer Surveyors' and they have been regarded as
> being the most useful all-round men for general Board of Trade
> purposes.

It had obviously, however, been a tricky memorandum to write. The file contains
not only the final bland version admitting to a few challenges within the
department but also a more revealing, earlier draft, in which Sir Walter had been
more honest about the quality of different types of surveyors, and the rivalry
between them. He had then struck out much of what he had originally written:

> Things have from time to time come to the notice of the Board of
> Trade which have suggested that the survey of the hull of
> passenger steamers by Engineer Surveyors was not carried out as
> well as it would have been done by a competent Ship Surveyor.
> Owing to the pressure of other duties this checking work has very
> largely fallen into arrear. [sic]
>    "Secondly, the organisation of the Principal Ship Surveyors

Department should be carefully considered with a view to its complete efficiency from a business point of view. [It] has not in the past been as good as it should have been, and it is quite certain that as it stands at present, it could not stand the strain of a large volume of additional work. There has been difficulty in securing a proper delegation of duties and in preventing the head of the branch having to go into the details of each case himself.

[strike-through by hand in original]

Sir Walter went on to suggest that more skilled Ship Surveyors should be recruited as a matter of urgency. But, again, his words were then carefully revised to soften the truth of the sometimes damaging rivalry between different sets of surveyors within his organisation.

There are, however, two important other points of some importance to consider. Firstly increasing the share of 'Ship Surveyors' in the passenger survey work means to some extent decreasing that of the 'Engineer Surveyors.' a [sic] change which, if not brought about very carefully will might be much resented by the Engineer Surveyors who have had for many years the whole of this work in their own hands.

As we all know Engineers have a very strong professional feeling and there is the making of a bitter professional quarrel between the two classes. I fear some professional jealousy between the two classes, a quarrel which might not be confined to the Board's own staff but would might be taken up by the two professions and their Associations throughout the country. It is very important that in making this change the Board of Trade should, as far as possible, carry conciliate the engineers with them, or at least secure their acquiescence.

The Department of 'Trades' weaknesses at the time when *Titanic's* construction began were not a new problem. Churchill's predecessors up to and including David Lloyd-George, from whom he took over in April 1908, had similarly failed to drag the then 60-year-old organisation into the twentieth century. But none of the earlier holders of the post had ruled at a time when British shipbuilders were so in need of guidance and stricter regulation. When the Board of Trade was formed in the mid-nineteenth century, most merchant ships registered at just a few hundred tons and carried a few hundred passengers. By Churchill's day, successive waves of European emigration to the USA had fuelled a trade where ships were topping 45,000 tons and carrying 3,000 and more emigrants at a time across the Atlantic.

*Titanic's* last call after leaving Southampton and Cherbourg was to pick up America-bound passengers from the tiny port of Queenstown, now known as Cobh, on Ireland's southern coast, near Cork. Apart from the change of name, little has altered in Cobh since the days when it was a major port of exodus for hundreds of thousands of Irish men and women who migrated to the New World in the latter part of the nineteenth century. A statue on the waterfront still pays homage to the memory of local girl Annie Moore and her two young brothers, who left for America in 1891. A similar statue also stands at Ellis Island in New York, where, on 1 January the following year, Annie earned a $10 coin for being the first immigrant to pass through that New York facility.

Despite the vast increase in passenger traffic, the Board of Trade saw no reason to change their rules and regulations. They repeatedly reminded any critics that the transatlantic shipping trade had lost very few lives in recent years, and that ship-owners were voluntarily making their ships more and more unsinkable as time went by. On top of that, the Board's decision-making process was designed to move at a snail's pace.

For many years, its most senior civil servants had relied on a unique system to shield them from any criticisms that might be levelled at any of their decisions. All potentially controversial issues were referred to a committee of outside 'experts' who were asked to recommend the correct course of action. The choice of matters that were referred to the expert Merchant Shipping advisory committee, and the parameters within which that committee should operate, did, of course, remain within the department's control at all times.

For the Marine Division's top civil servants, the advisory committee system worked wonderfully well. Each committee could easily be manipulated to produce only the advice that the civil servants wanted to hear in the first place. Alternatively, in the unlikely event of a rogue committee stepping outside of its strict frame of reference and producing recommendations with which civil servants did not agree, their advice could be completely ignored if so wished. If any of the Board of Trade's decisions were ever shown to be wrong, blame could be deflected away by explaining that they had been based solely on the 'independent' advice of experts in the field.

It was a system with which Winston Churchill happily concurred when, on 26 August 1909, he approved the names of more than a dozen members of the latest Merchant Shipping advisory committee that was to proffer advice for a two-year term of office. As with every previous committee, the composition of its members was heavily weighted in favour of the shipping and shipbuilding industries. Only a minority of places were ever reserved for a few ordinary seamen and officers. Reading details of the suggested membership, Churchill would have known that this committee, like others before it, would have been unlikely candidates to suggest any radical changes to the lifeboat regulations that had been in force for so many years.

The list of potential committee members was drawn up by senior officials from the Board's Marine Division. But, unlike in some other administrative functions of the department's work, this was an area where Churchill had real personal power to approve, or reject, the membership of the committee. If he had so desired, Churchill could have chosen a group that might have been more conscious of passenger safety and less conscious of ship-owners' costs.

The advisory committee could only come into existence if Churchill signed an 'Order In Council', approving its membership. That formal document then had to be 'laid on the table' at the House of Commons for three weeks, in case any MP should object to its contents. Only then did it take effect and allow the Committee to start its deliberations.

At any time during his reign at the Board of Trade it would also have been open to Churchill to use the same 'Order In Council' procedure to make his own immediate alterations to the appallingly outdated lifeboat regulations. The 1906 Merchant Shipping Act had specifically granted that power to the president in order that rules and regulations controlling British shipping could be easily adapted to suit fast-changing times. At the time the procedure was adopted, the then head of the Board of Trade, David Lloyd-George, had explained why Orders In Council had been needed:

> It is inconvenient to require an amending Act of Parliament whenever a new regulation seems to be necessary to meet the changing circumstances of our mercantile marine. Who can foresee what may happen? What we want is to be able, by means of an Order in Council, if necessary, to introduce regulations applicable to the changing circumstances of the hour, without having to have constant resort to the House of Commons to obtain sanction for every change that may be required.

It was not, however, a power that Churchill was mindful to use. Sitting in his grand presidential office in his Whitehall headquarters, busying himself with the work of other sections of the Board of Trade, he was content to leave the Marine Division and its lifeboat rules and regulations well enough alone. As Marine Division memos languished at the bottom of his in-tray, Churchill was much engaged in plotting his own future moves in the Government. On 14 February 1910 he gained the promotion he was sure he richly deserved and became Home Secretary.

He handed over the work of regulating marine safety to his successor, Sir Sydney Buxton, a 57-year-old career politician who also saw his Board of Trade job as a stepping stone on his route to No. 10. Buxton would similarly fail to consider the safety of the thousands of passengers and crew soon to set sail across the Atlantic Ocean on the *Titanic*. It was Buxton, not Churchill, who was vilified in public when *Titanic* sank a little over two years later.

In a House of Commons debate on 7 October 1912 an attempt was made to have Buxton's conduct, and that of the Marine Division of the Board of Trade, subjected to examination by a Select Committee. Churchill's failure to act was never mentioned. The potential criticism was met with a determined assault by the powerful shipping industry lobby still working within the House. Ship-owner after ship-owner made lengthy speeches defending what to many people appeared to be the indefensible. A speech by MP Leslie Scott, a member of the Ship-owners' Parliamentary Committee, contained some typical comments made during the debate:

> It is important to remember that we must make allowance for the then prevalent belief in the unsinkability of modern ships with watertight compartments. That belief was tragically shattered by the disaster to the *Titanic*.
>
> There are some who entertain an unworthy suspicion that ship-owners make money at the risk of human life. Wrecks and loss of life are alike bad business. It is the foundation of a ship-owner's prosperity in business to win a reputation for safe ships and for not losing human lives. It is upon that that his low rates of insurance depend and that he gets his cargoes and gets his passengers. We may at once push aside that unworthy suspicion, and this House will not entertain it.

Although that 'unworthy suspicion' was precisely what some members of Parliament did entertain, few were given the opportunity to voice it. The debate was dominated by numerous lengthy speeches in support of the shipping lobby, with few other MPs getting any opportunity to contribute. At 11.00 pm the amendment criticising the Marine Division's conduct was 'talked out' of time. The debate ended without a vote. The failure of the October debate demonstrated yet again that ship-owners were a force to be reckoned with inside the British political establishment. And the power and influence of the ship-owners might also suggest a more sinister explanation for Winston Churchill's lack of action regarding the lifeboat issue while he was in charge of the Board of Trade.

In his desperation for political advancement, Churchill had left the Tory party and switched his allegiance to the Liberals. To enhance his reputation with his new colleagues he had enthusiastically embraced the Liberal Party's support of 'Home Rule' for Ireland. It would have been odd if his work on the Home Rule issue had not involved Churchill in discussions with other party supporters working towards the same end. Foremost among these was the newly ennobled Baron of Belfast, Lord William Pirrie. As the Chairman of Harland and Wolff, and the man then planning the construction of *Titanic*, Pirrie had strong commercial motivation for not increasing the number of lifeboats carried on *Titanic*.

There is no record of any discussions between Churchill and Pirrie about the lifeboat issue, or anything other than circumstantial evidence that the ship-owner unduly influenced his new Liberal colleague to leave the lifeboat regulations untouched. It is known, however, that Pirrie was concerned that new rules might be forthcoming from the Board of Trade. He was so worried that he might have to put more lifeboats on *Titanic* that he even fitted the ship with davits capable of carrying four times as many boats as he had planned to employ. In the end, the lifeboat rules were never altered, more boats were never ordered and the redundant davit capacity was never put to use.

What is also known is that the two men were close enough that they later appeared together as the main speakers at a controversial Belfast rally in favour of Home Rule. Both politicians stood united in support of a policy that was so unpopular in 'Unionist' Belfast that eggs were thrown at them and they needed police protection to arrive and depart from the meeting. It may have been that Winston Churchill failed to amend the lifeboat regulations because he was simply too busy to get around to considering the matter. Alternatively, it could be that a new minister, desperate for further political advancement, could not afford to upset some of the grandees of his own party: men just like Lord Pirrie, Chairman of Harland and Wolff, who was busy building the biggest ships in the world and who certainly did not want to 'burden them' with any more boats than were absolutely necessary.

On the day that Churchill finally moved to the Home Office, two beautiful ships were already well on their way to being completed in a bustling shipyard alongside Belfast's river Lagan. From dawn till dusk on the same day that Churchill left the shipping world behind him, more than 7,000 men were hard at work at Harland and Wolff. While Churchill shares some responsibility for the deaths on *Titanic*, there were also many other factors at work in *Titanic's* tragic story.

The builders in Belfast believed they were constructing 'almost-unsinkable' ships; ships so strong that they were to be 'their own lifeboats' and need no other means of saving the lives of passengers and crew. They were tragically mistaken. If *Titanic* had been but a little bit stronger, if she had managed to stay afloat for even a couple of hours longer than she did, then nobody need have died at all. But this massive ship, equipped with watertight compartments and bulkheads approved as fit for purpose by the British Board of Trade, failed to survive for long enough to meet the rescue ships that were steaming towards her. She sank less than three hours after hitting the iceberg.

Why did she sink so quickly? As the London inquiry into the sinking was to hear, other ocean liners in the past had hit Atlantic icebergs and survived to reach port safely. One such ship had hit the ice far harder than the *Titanic* and had suffered far more terrible damage; yet all on board had lived to tell the tale.

## Notes

1. Dr Lunn recovered from the commercial disaster of the *Argonaut* sinking. He went on to form the Lunn-Poly holiday group.

2. The Countess de Hamil de Manin lost a £6,000 fortune in jewellery in the rush for the boats. Divers regularly visit the sunken *Argonaut* but her jewels have never been found.

3. It was the unlucky *Argonaut's* second accident in less than a year; under previous owners she had run aground in Norway but was later refloated.

# Chapter Eighteen

# 'See Our Oars With Feather'd Spray'

**10.30 pm**
**7 November 1879**
**The Salon of the SS *Arizona***
**Estimated Position 47° N, 53° W**
**Northern Edge of Newfoundland Banks**
**North Atlantic Ocean**

It was not the most comfortable ship to be found on the transatlantic run. The quest for speed had given the SS *Arizona* engines that were perhaps a little too powerful for her streamlined shape. It made the ship roll more than was desirable in the heavy seas sometimes found on this trip. On this night, however, her passengers were enjoying an unusually smooth ride in unusually calm waters. It had encouraged many to stay up beyond their normal bedtime. The ladies were as usual gathered together in the ship's elegant salon among the polished wood pillars and high glass-domed roof; the gentlemen were gambling in the adjacent social hall.

The nightly auction for mileage slips predicting how far the SS *Arizona* would travel tomorrow had been a little raucous that evening, and a sizeable pile of gold and silver coins sat on the small marble table in front of the ship's self-appointed social secretary, Stephen Ingham. It was a typical evening's entertainment on board the huge ocean liner, speeding homeward-bound from New York to Liverpool with a mere 509 souls on board – far fewer than the 1,800 emigrants who had crowded into the steerage compartments on the outward leg to America.

Perhaps because of the reduced number of passengers, the crew had been a little slack of late. Stewards had been slow tonight in answering the salon's electric call bells – a modern innovation for the passengers' convenience on the newly-launched British liner. And discipline appeared to have slipped among not only the serving staff but also among the sailors on deck. Faced with freezing cold weather, the *Arizona's* lookouts had abandoned their post near the bow and were sheltering from the wind at the rear of the ship's bridge. Although they could no longer see anything dead ahead of the vessel, they could still hear the gentle sounds of the salon piano. Miss Gaslett, one of the more elderly English passengers, was entertaining the ladies with a spirited rendition of the popular song *See Our Oars With Feather'd Spray*. Even more than a century later, the lyrics have some relevance to what happened next:

> *See our Oars with Feather'd Spray, sparkle in the beam of day;*
> *In our little barque we glide, swiftly o'er the silent tide.*

It was just then that the ship ran into an iceberg.

The *New York Times* later recounted the story as told by a journalist who had been on board the badly damaged ship. Their headline would not have been out of place in a more tabloid newspaper of the day:

## BEWILDERING CONFUSION – PASSENGERS PANIC STRICKEN – COWARDICE OF THE CREW

> The hull of the steamer shook as though every rivet had burst asunder and the ladies and gentlemen were sent sprawling on the floor. A spasm of terror seized on many of the ladies, one fainted and others sobbed hysterically, but they were soon joined by husbands who hurried their fair charges to the deck.

There was a colourful account of how men in the social hall had, at first, stampeded towards the open deck:

> The prostrate were trampled on and received quite serious contusions; voices called out: 'Steady gentlemen; keep cool.' This appeal to their manhood was effective and the panic ceased almost as suddenly as it had begun. The affrighted sailors of the watch fled, and thinking only of their own safety, set to work to launch one of the boats. One of these men wept in abject terror. The sight that met the passengers' eyes was well calculated to chill the bravest heart.

What had indeed chilled the passengers' hearts as they emerged on deck was the sight of the ship jammed hard against a massive iceberg. The *Arizona*, at that time the second largest merchant ship in the world,[1] had run head-on into the ice. Contemporary descriptions suggest the iceberg may well have been even bigger than the one that, less than twenty years later, would sink the *Titanic*. From her cruising speed of around 13 knots the *Arizona* had come to a dead halt; her bow and several of her foremost compartments were crushed flat. The ship was already listing and dipping down towards the bow. The iceberg was described as 'towering overhead with large outcrops threatening to fall.'

The still terrified crew eventually lowered a boat, sailed to the front of the ship and inspected the damage. What was left of the bow structure had a gash 30 feet deep and more than 20 feet in width, although a close inspection of the watertight bulkhead, just aft of the shattered bow, found that it was still keeping out the sea. Miraculously, the now misshapen ship had a hope of staying afloat. The crew, who had earlier warned the passengers that the *Arizona's* sinking was inevitable, then inched the ship back from the ice and steamed, slow-ahead, for the nearest port. None of the passengers slept during the remainder of the night's journey but instead – in a glimpse of what the aftermath might have been like if *Titanic* had similarly stayed afloat – gathered together in the devastated salon to give thanks for their salvation with the prayer: *Praise God, from who all blessings flow*. The next day the SS *Arizona* slowly but safely limped into harbour at St John's, in Newfoundland.[2]

The survival of the SS *Arizona* was in complete contrast with the fate of the *Titanic*, although there were many similarities between the two ships. Each in its day was considered to offer the last word in luxury, each was one of the biggest ships in the world, and each struck an iceberg on a calm and clear night: and yet one reached safe harbour with no loss of life while the other sank within hours and cost the lives of 1,490 people. At the London inquiry into the sinking of *Titanic*, naval architect Edward Wilding explained the different outcomes of the two shipping disasters. He first explained his belief that the *Titanic*, unlike the *Arizona*, had struck a mere glancing blow on the ice:

> This contact seems to have been a particularly light one because we have heard the evidence that lots of people scarcely felt it; that is, that there was nothing in the nature of what is usually called impact, but that it was a comparatively light sliding blow. I mean that is the whole character of it.

Wilding modestly described himself as 'one of the people connected with the making of the design'. In fact, he had been intimately involved in *Titanic's* construction for years, working alongside Thomas Andrews, the Harland and Wolff managing director, who was credited as *Titanic's* chief designer. Andrews had died on the ship. Wilding had not been on the maiden voyage, but he knew every inch of *Titanic* better than anyone else still alive. He amazed the Wreck Inquiry by insisting that *Titanic* may well have survived and would have safely 'come in' to port if she had run headlong into the iceberg.

The inquiry had already heard that the officers on *Titanic's* bridge had ordered the ship's wheel to be put hard to starboard in a last moment attempt to avoid a head-on collision. Now both Stephen Rowlatt, one of the Board of Trade's lawyers, and the Chairman, Lord Mersey, were quick to question Wilding further:

'I am rather interested about that. Do you mean to say that if this ship had driven on to the iceberg stem on she would have been saved?'

'I am quite sure she would, my Lord. I am afraid she would have killed every fireman down in the firemen's quarters, but I feel sure the ship would have come in.'

'And the passengers would not have been lost?'

'The passengers would have come in; I am strengthened in that belief by the case which your Lordship will remember where one large North Atlantic steamer, some thirty-four years ago, did go stem on into an iceberg and did come into port, and she was going fast; the *Arizona*, my Lord.'

'You said it would have killed all the firemen: you mean the firemen in their quarters?'

'Yes, down below. We know two watches were down there. I am afraid she would have crumpled up in stopping herself. The momentum of the ship would have crushed in the bows for 80 or perhaps 100 feet. I do not think there are any Third Class passengers forward of the second bulkhead, and I believe she would have stopped before the second bulkhead was damaged. It is entirely crew there; firemen, trimmers, and greasers.'

Wilding claimed that it would have taken four or five seconds for the entire front of the ship to have crumpled up. But the destruction of the bow would have lessened the shock elsewhere in the vessel:

'Whilst it is a big pressure it is not in the nature of a sharp blow,' he explained.

'It would, I suppose, have shot everybody in the ship out of their berths?'

'I very much doubt it, my Lord. 100 feet will pull up a motor car going 22 miles an hour without shooting you out of the front.'

'What you mean is that the ship would have telescoped herself, and stopped when she telescoped enough?'

'Yes, up against the iceberg; that is what happened in the *Arizona*.'

The evidence from Wilding cast serious doubt on the wisdom of the crew's actions in trying to steer *Titanic* clear of the iceberg. Yet both he and Lord Mersey clearly felt that it would be wrong to criticise the officers who had acted quickly in what they felt was the best interests of the ship.

'An error of judgment and negligence are two different things altogether. Do you think it was an error of judgment?'

'It is very difficult to pass judgment on what would go through an officer's mind, my Lord.'

'A man may make a mistake and be very far from being negligent?'

'Yes.'

Wilding had explained how a head-on collision, rather than a glancing blow, might have left *Titanic* damaged but still safe and afloat. He did not explain why the comparatively lighter, sideswipe blow had sunk the ship so quickly. Soon after striking the iceberg *Titanic* began sending radio messages giving what Captain Smith had believed was her correct position and asking for help.

Other ships, including her sister ship *Olympic*, had picked up the distress signals and were steaming at full speed towards her. *Titanic's* final message stating 'Engine room full up to boilers' was received by the nearest ship, *Carpathia*, when that vessel was just 20 miles from the scene. Her radio operator, Thomas Cottam, later told the US Senate hearing how he had continued trying to contact the *Titanic*:

'The captain told me to go and tell the *Titanic* he was making toward the position given as quickly as possible; that he had a double watch in the engine room and she was making a good 15 and perhaps 16 knots. I repeated the message many times.'

'You repeated that message many times; but you got no answer?'

'I got no answer; no, sir.'

'And never did receive an answer to that last message?'

'No, sir.'

Both of the post-*Titanic* inquiries became obsessed with minute details of the radio messages sent to various ships that night, and whether or not those ships could have reached *Titanic* more quickly. Some of their fiercest criticism was reserved for Captain Stanley Lord, Master of the *Californian*, a ship that was alleged to have ignored *Titanic's* distress rockets and never turned to help. The case against Captain Lord was never proven, but his life was blighted forever after by the inquiry's findings.

Over the last two days of the British hearing, the Board of Trade's leading lawyer, the Attorney-General, The Right Honourable Sir Rufus Isaacs KC MP, summed up the proceedings for the benefit of the Commissioner Lord Mersey. For thirty-six days the court had heard evidence about the lack of lifeboats, the failure to fill the boats, the antiquated regulations, *Titanic's* construction, her navigation, and the moving testimony of the surviving crew and passengers. Yet Isaacs saved his most important point until the very last. The Board of Trade made a concerted effort to shift as much blame as possible from itself to the *Californian*, and the hapless Captain Lord.

'I am most anxious, and have been throughout, to find some possible excuse, for the inaction on the part of the *Californian*,' protested Isaacs. 'It is not a case of desiring to bring home to them that they did not do their duty; our anxiety would be to find some reason to explain the failure by them to take any steps when they had seen distress signals.

'I can only say that to me it is a matter of extreme regret that I have come to the conclusion that the submission I must make to you, is that there is no excuse.'

Considerably more than half of Isaacs' final day's oration was devoted to a detailed examination of the role of a sea captain whose crew may, or may not, have seen *Titanic's* distress rockets on the night of the sinking. In his anxiety to 'shoot the messenger', Isaacs and the inquiry as a whole failed to properly address the far more important question: why had *Titanic* sunk so quickly? The answer to that question had to wait for more than seventy years, until the moment when a mini-submarine searched 2½ miles down in the depths of the Atlantic Ocean – and found the *Titanic*.

### Notes

1. She was second in size only to the fabled *Great Eastern*.
2. The *Arizona* was patched up with a wooden bow and later repaired in Glasgow. She was eventually sold to the US Navy.

# Chapter Nineteen

# 'Not only the graveyard of a great ship . . .'

12.48 am
1 September 1985
The Control Room
Research Ship *Knorr*
Position: 49° 56' 54" W, 41° 43' 35" N
North Atlantic Ocean

The image on the control room television monitors had been boringly monotonous for many hours. The remotely operated camera being towed across the seafloor 2½ miles below was picking up hazy pictures of mud, mud and then more mud. Even near the start of their 'graveyard' all-night shift, it was getting more difficult for the crewmen on duty to concentrate on the screen. Their 'room' was actually the inside of two conjoined metal shipping containers strapped to the deck of the American marine research ship *Knorr*. Its primitive air-conditioning system found it hard to cope. A fug of cigarette smoke rose towards the ceiling in the heat from the mass of computer and television equipment that covered the seven different control desks that lined the container walls. Success in the mission to search the bed of the Atlantic Ocean always seemed more distant in these early hours of each morning.

Inside the container the lighting levels were being kept low to give each man and woman the best possible view of the television screens on which they were concentrating. Via a cable, stretching impossibly deep below the ship, one man was controlling how far the camera 'flew' across the seabed mud. Another was maintaining the slow progress of the ship along its predetermined search track. Others on the team were double-checking positional navigation fixes, documenting all that was seen on the screens, controlling sonar equipment or logging every scrap of data received.

The room had grown quiet since the recent changeover of shifts with the predictable chaos that came from one crew of seven handing over the search to their incoming colleagues. The routine had been the same for weeks now and a few of the team were beginning to despair of ever finding success. Suddenly an indistinct shape crossed the screen. More than seventy years since the sunken ship was last seen by human eyes, the men and women of the graveyard shift found it hard to believe what they were seeing; they had found the *Titanic*.

In his book about the discovery,[1] expedition leader Bob Ballard vividly described his feelings over the hours that followed:

> As the images on the video screen grew more and more vivid – large pieces of twisted hull plating, portholes, a piece of railing turned on its side – for the first time since I had started this quest twelve years before, the full human impact of the *Titanic's* terrifying tragedy began to sink in. Here at the bottom of the ocean lay not only the graveyard of a great ship, but the only fitting monument to the more than 1,500 people who had perished when she went down.

The discovery of the wreck of the *Titanic* was a media sensation. At a packed press conference to announce the findings of his joint American and French expedition, Ballard revealed that the wreck was sitting almost upright on the sea bed. Her stern had broken away from the bow, which had buried itself so deep in the bottom mud that it was not possible to see the part of the hull that had been damaged by the iceberg. His findings seemed to establish that the *Titanic* had broken apart as she made her final dive below the waterline but did little else to explain why she had sunk so quickly.

Ballard had conducted a brief and informal memorial service with his crew on deck on the night that *Titanic's* wreckage was discovered. He was anxious that the site should not be disturbed by a succession of treasure-hunting expeditions. For some years afterwards he had therefore refused to reveal the exact position where the ship's remains lay on the bed of the Atlantic. In time, however, it became known that the ship had sunk more than 13 miles to the south-east of where her captain and crew had thought she was at the time of the sinking. The navigators of *Titanic*, who were plotting their course that evening by dead reckoning, had got their calculations slightly wrong. They were actually a little to the south and some miles east of their charted position; the only explanation for which is that they must have been slightly over-estimating the speed at which she was travelling. It also meant that the radio distress calls that she had broadcast on the night were all based on the same navigational error; the discrepancy had, in reality, made little difference. No ships had been near enough to reach her in either her estimated, or her actual, position before she sank.

In the years since Ballard revealed exactly where *Titanic* had sunk, other expeditions have visited her frequently, some for scientific study and to take film or photographs, a rare few simply as tourists. A ticket to *Titanic* can be purchased for around £25,000. Customers buy the right to endure a four-hour descent to the wreck cramped inside one of the small Russian submersible craft now available for commercial hire.

One company was granted legal custody and control of the wreck by American courts. It has raised artefacts of all shapes and sizes from the ocean bed. Some have been relics of the beautifully-crafted fixtures and fittings that once graced the most luxurious and largest ship of her day. Others have been more personal items once held in the hands of the ill-fated passengers or crew. The removal of any items from the wreck has been fiercely opposed by those who believe that *Titanic* should be respected both as the final resting place of almost 1,500 people and as a site of unparalleled historical importance. Others argue with equal passion that the ship is even now rusting away and that all that can be lifted should be lifted. They rightly claim that all traces of human remains have long been destroyed in the deep ocean environment and, more controversially, that careful conservation on land is the only way in which any last physical traces of *Titanic* can be preserved for the wonder of future generations.

Whatever the rights or wrongs of that debate, some of the material that has been brought to the surface has given scientists the opportunity to study the metal from which the great ship was made. The steel items that have been raised include a large section of the hull, 25 feet long and 15 feet high, which was duly nicknamed the 'Big Piece'.[2] It once formed the hull around two C deck cabins high on the starboard side of *Titanic*. Tiny slivers of the Big Piece have since been shaved from one corner for the purposes of metallurgical research, and scientists have also had access to smaller steel sections of all shapes and sizes from many different locations upon and around the wreck.

Some of the earliest research into the strength of *Titanic's* steel was completed by Canadian scientists after an expedition to the wreck in 1991. Their studies appeared to show that the chemical composition of steel used in *Titanic's* hull made it unfit for use in the cold waters of the North Atlantic. In the years that followed, other researchers suggested that the original steel sample may have been unrepresentative of the hull as a whole.

Then, in 1996, American researchers from the University of Missouri-Rolla and the Bethlehem Steel Corporation carried out further tests on metal recovered in that year's expedition. Their hull pieces had been picked up from the debris field that spreads for many hundreds of yards around *Titanic* and could have come from anywhere in the central section of the ship. They investigated the relative proportions of various minerals including sulphur, phosphorous and manganese within the small metal pieces they had been given. Their results were to make headlines around the world.

All types of steel exhibit different properties at different temperatures. At normal room temperature the metal is capable of absorbing a significant impact and deforming slightly, rather than breaking into separate pieces. But as the temperature reduces, that same steel can suddenly become more brittle; more liable to fracture apart and crack under stress. The precise temperature at which this dramatic change occurs varies. It is dependent upon both the chemical composition of the steel and the way in which it has been manufactured and treated. The phenomenon has been likened to the difference between striking cold toffee with a hammer and striking it when it is warmed and softened; in one case it cracks apart, in the other it is dented.

The American metal research suggested that excess sulphur and phosphorous, along with too little manganese, would have affected the temperature at which *Titanic's* steel became more brittle. In the terminology used by metallurgists today, it would be 'dirty' steel. They believed that the near-freezing temperature of the ocean waters surrounding *Titanic's* hull on the night of the sinking would have been cold enough for the brittle–ductile transformation to occur. The plates that were bolted together to form *Titanic's* hull would therefore have become more susceptible to being fractured by the sudden shock of the iceberg strike. The toffee hammer would have been striking toffee cold enough to fracture apart. The researchers involved in the Missouri-Rolla University study had a clear conclusion:

> The lack of cleanliness of the steel had a deleterious effect on the mechanical properties ... These factors were contributing causes of the rapid sinking of the *Titanic*.

If those conclusions are correct they would help explain why the comparatively soft blow against the iceberg did so much damage. *Titanic's* hull was built up from thousands of overlapping steel plates, each riveted to the steel skeleton that gave the ship her shape and her strength.[3] The 'brittle steel' theory suggests that the plates would have fractured and cracked more easily when they struck the iceberg. The resultant damage would thus have been more widespread. It would have let in more water, more quickly, than if the plates had better resisted the impact.

Although the brittle steel theory remains controversial, one fact is certain: the steel of 1912 was less resistant to stress than the steel of today. So does that mean that *Titanic's* builders used inferior steel? Or was the metal they used the best possible quality that could have been obtained in those early years of the twentieth century? The answer to that question may help to determine how much, if any, of the blame for *Titanic's* demise can be laid at the feet of the company that constructed it – Belfast's most successful shipbuilders, Harland and Wolff.

## Notes

1. *The Discovery of the Titanic*, Robert Ballard, 1987.
2. The Big Piece, still with some of the fittings from the four portholes it contains, has been the centrepiece of various exhibitions of *Titanic* artefacts.
3. The strength of *Titanic* came from being built like a girder; her keel, the ribs and sheets of her two sides, and the steel-plated deck together formed a strong rectangular metal box.

# Chapter Twenty

# 'Having mounted a restive horse . . .'

**8.00 am**
**17 January 1855**
**The slipway**
**Robert Hickson's shipyard**
**Queen's Island**
**Belfast**

Young Edward Harland was a blunt-speaking Yorkshire lad; not a man to back away from an argument. On a frosty winter morning he was standing tall and confronting a bully-boy gang of a dozen angry workers. Behind them the bare wooden ribs of a half-built ship stuck forlornly upwards from a flimsy wooden slipway built out across the steep muddy banks of the river. Just twenty-three years old and already the manager of a financially-struggling Belfast shipyard, Harland knew full well that his entire future depended upon the completion of that vessel on time and on budget. Yet now, faced with the threat of a strike that could ruin him, he had but one message for his men: 'Strike then ... and be damned.'

The words had hardly left Harland's lips when his workers gave their instant response. The men turned as one and walked out of the yard. If the young shipbuilder felt any concern he was certainly not going to show it now. The muddy foreshore of Queen's Island was strangely silent. It seemed even more barren after the clatter and bustle of work on the ship had ceased. Little more than a decade ago the 'slob' land on which the shipyard was built had been under the brown and polluted waters of the river Lagan. Then hundreds of labourers armed with nothing more than picks, shovels and wheelbarrows had piled up thousands of tons of dark mud to form a bleak, artificial island. It stood alongside the new, straight channel that the labourers had cut to the sea; the start of the building of iron ships in Belfast.

In the attempts to ensure that the shipyard survived, it had been as good a time as any to pick a fight with its workforce. Harland knew that very little work would be completed anyway in those icy cold weeks immediately after Christmas. And he was ruthless enough to calculate that working men would find unemployment harder to bear when their families needed heat in their homes and hot food in their bellies. Left alone in the shipyard, Harland headed off across the 4-acre site to the solitary wooden shack that offered his only shelter from the morning's icy wind. The most unpopular man in Belfast needed to find new workers, or see the business die.

In an account of his life written decades later, Edward Harland, by then the owner of one of the world's largest shipyards, described the day he provoked a strike as a turning point in his illustrious shipbuilding career:

> I had been engaged to supersede a manager summarily dismissed. Although he had not given satisfaction to his employers, he was a great favourite with the men. Accordingly, my appearance as manager in his stead was not very agreeable to the employed. On inquiry I found that the rate of wages paid was above the usual value, whilst the quantity as well as quality of the work done were [sic] below the standard. I proceeded to rectify these defects, by paying the ordinary rate of wages, and then by raising the quality of the work done. I was met by the usual method – a strike.

As the bitter dispute continued, Harland tried to break the strike by importing 'blackleg' labour. He recruited workers from the shipyards of Glasgow and North East England, where he had served his own apprenticeship. But the new arrivals were soon scared away by threats of violence from the men whose jobs they were taking.[1] One friend advised Harland to 'throw up the job' as manager of Robert Hickson's yard and return to the safety of his former job in Scotland:

> My reply was, that 'having mounted a restive horse, I would ride him into the stable.' The obstacles were no doubt great; the financial difficulties were extreme; and yet there was a prospect of profit from the work in hand, provided only the men could be induced to settle steadily down to their ordinary employment.

Harland stood firm and eventually a few hungry men trickled back to work at the Queen's Island yard. Harland owned no financial stake in the business but, with the shipyard on the point of bankruptcy, he agreed to personally guarantee the wages of any man who returned to his side. More workers returned and the strike was broken. With a workforce that now accepted their new manager's orders, productivity and profitability soared.

From that time forward the works went on apace; and we finished the ships in hand to the perfect satisfaction of the owners.

It had been a baptism of fire in Ireland but Edward Harland had proven his worth as a manager. His father, William Harland, was a doctor in North Yorkshire who was related through marriage to a number of wealthy men in the booming shipping and engineering trades in the North of England. Although Dr Harland's professional qualifications were in medicine, his passion was the science of engineering. He ensured that his son grew up with design, engineering and metalwork skills that were to steer his life in only one direction. The family's friendship with George Stephenson provided Edward with an apprenticeship in the great man's new steam locomotive and railway business. Just like his father, Edward was a keen amateur inventor. One of his earliest projects was to have a strange resonance through the years for a man whose company would one day build the doomed *Titanic*. Inspired by seeing a rescue boat launched in his home town of Scarborough, Edward Harland designed a new lifeboat.

> After considerable deliberation, I matured a plan for a metal lifeboat, of a cylindrico-conical or chrysalis form, to be propelled by a screw at each end, turned by sixteen men inside, seated on water-ballast tanks; sufficient room being left at the ends inside for the accommodation of ten or twelve shipwrecked persons. The whole apparatus was almost cylindrical, and watertight, save in the self-acting ventilators which could only give access to the smallest portion of water.

Proud of his revolutionary design, that he believed could turn upside down and still continue in heavy seas with its oarsmen strapped into harnesses, the young apprentice entered a national competition to design a new boat for the 'Lifeboat Institution'. He made an intricate, one-inch-to-a-foot, working model in wood and copper, complete with miniature seats, working gears and individual metal plates cladding its hull. The model's sea trials from a rowing boat in Scarborough harbour were a resounding success; but Harland was to be sorely disappointed when he sent his design to be judged.

> I completed the prescribed drawings and specifications, and sent them, together with the model; but mine was not successful. I suspect that the extreme novelty of the arrangement deterred the adjudicators from awarding in its favour. Indeed, the scheme was so unprecedented that there was no special mention made of it in the report afterwards published.

Completing his apprenticeship and working as a journeyman in a Scottish shipyard, young Edward Harland had responded to an advertisement for a manager in a struggling shipyard in Belfast. Long before Harland's arrival in the city, there had been a record of shipbuilding there since the mid-seventeenth century. Belfast ships had traded for hundreds of years with the islands of the Caribbean. A nineteenth-century history book listed the exports they carried as: 'pork, oats, hay, butter, potatoes, lime, soot, coal, horses, and mules'. On their return journeys the ships carried only sugar.

The ships that Edward Harland went on to design in his new post with the Belfast shipyard were thankfully less revolutionary than his lifeboat. They also found more favour with his customers. The business finally began to make profits. Wealthy friends of Harland's father supported his son's new endeavour with orders for small merchant ships, and his fame grew as he designed and built several unusual metal steamships for the Bibby steamship line. The vessels had flatter bottoms than was normal and could carry greater loads. Although their safety record was no worse than other ships of the time, their distinctive box-like shape earned them the unjustified nickname of 'Bibby's Coffins'.

With the business growing rapidly Harland agreed to employ the nephew of one of his wealthy backers as his personal assistant. The young man, a German immigrant named Gustav Wolff, was not only a good worker but also had engineering training. It may have been, however, that his prime qualification for the job was the support he enjoyed from some exceedingly wealthy relatives in England.

Edward Harland was still the manager, rather than the owner, of the Belfast yard. His employer, Robert Hickson, also owned a successful iron works in the city and had diversified into shipbuilding only as a sideline, about which he had little real knowledge. Now, four years after moving to Ireland, Harland wanted to start his own business. He made inquiries about opening his own yard in Liverpool but could not find a suitable site. Instead, in September 1858, Hickson offered to sell him the Belfast yard for £5,000. He even suggested a £100 discount 'for prompt cash in the case of the purchase of the concern'.

Harland turned to Gustav Wolff and his wealthy family for help. Their agreement gave Harland funds to help buy the Queen's Island yard, but with the understanding that Gustav was to become a junior partner as soon as he gained more experience. On 1 January 1862 the two men did formally become partners with a contract allowing Harland to draw up to £700 a year in salary while Gustav could take a maximum of £500 per year as his share.[2] In return for Gustav's involvement his uncle and aunt loaned substantial working capital, and shipping companies they controlled placed orders for three new vessels. The newly-named shipbuilding firm of Harland and Wolff was successfully launched and set fair to make a fortune.

The ship designs that Edward Harland created over the next few years not only built up an enviable reputation for the new Belfast yard but also set the company on course to build bigger – and better – ships. An early twentieth century study of Irish industries described its success in glowing terms:

> It is not by mere quantity that Harland and Wolff have earned their splendid reputation. They have been pioneer builders of vessels of great size, and of a new type, which were a great advance in marine construction.[3]

Edward Harland had realised that ships made out of iron no longer had to slavishly follow the ship designs of the past. He utilised the strength of the metal to create longer ships without any increase in width. Stripped of earlier artistic flourishes such as wooden figureheads, and created to a more aerodynamic design, they could carry larger cargoes or greater numbers of passengers with a lower consumption of coal. The concept had echoes of Harland's first apprentice dreams of a lifeboat designed as a cylindrical, streamlined craft. In an 1884 article Edward Harland himself described the source of his new ideas:

> Nature seems to have furnished us with the finest design for a vessel in the form of the fish: it presents such fine lines – is so clean, so true, and so rapid in its movements. The ship, however, must float; and to hit upon the happy medium of velocity and stability seems to me the art and mystery of shipbuilding.

Harland and Wolff's 'floating fish' designs were to serve the company well for decades to come. Each ship in its time was larger and more ambitious than any that had gone before and each was one step further along the path that led inevitably to the creation of the biggest of them all: *Titanic*. But, by the time of *Titanic*, the company had changed beyond all recognition. A workforce of 100 had become a workforce of far more than 10,000; the older management generation of Edward and Gustav had given way to a newer, even more ambitious and autocratic boss. He was a man who was to drive the company forward to unprecedented success and yet also preside over its greatest disaster – the sinking of *Titanic*; a man whose greed and dishonesty would eventually bring the legacy of Edward Harland's once fine company to its knees.

None of this could possibly have been predicted when, in 1862, a fresh-faced and nervous young schoolboy walked through the company's Queen's Island gates. William Pirrie, one day to become chairman of the company, a peer of the realm, the Lord Mayor of Belfast, the wheeler-dealer behind the world's greatest shipping combine and arguably the ultimate decision maker responsible for the death of *Titanic*, was starting his very first day as a shipbuilding apprentice at Harland and Wolff.

## Notes

1. Men who failed to respond to threats were often successfully 'treated' instead. They would find themselves befriended by strangers, plied with drinks and persuaded to go home.
2. One clause allowed Gustav to draw an additional £800 lump sum 'to be married or buy a house.'
3. *The History of Belfast Shipbuilding*, by Professor C.H. Oldham, 1910.

# Chapter Twenty-One

# 'Sell out without further delay'

**6.00 am**
**Monday, 1 September 1862**
**Harland and Wolff shipyard**
**Queen's Island**
**Belfast**

It would be hard to imagine a wider social gap to bridge than the one that faced 15-year-old William James Pirrie as he started his first day at Harland and Wolff's shipyard in Belfast. He would be working among the roughest and toughest working men in Ireland. For years, young Pirrie had been cloistered amidst the academic excellence and relatively genteel surroundings of the city's Royal Belfast Academical Institute, a privileged educational existence where the wealthy sons of Ireland had been taught for generations. A little schoolboy bullying and the discipline of the institute's gentlemanly masters was poor preparation for the real world of work.

Yet Pirrie was not quite like other apprentices labouring there as 'heater boys' or 'catcher boys', high on the gantries surrounding the vast metal ships, or running errands for impatient labourers desperate for faster and more efficient work from their teams to up their piece-rate earnings. The shipyard's newest recruit was a 'gentleman apprentice'.

The many hagiographies written over the years about the teenage boy, who was destined to one day become 'Lord Pirrie', have gone out of their way to stress that Pirrie's 'gentleman apprentice' status earned him no favours in the engine room and the shipyard of Harland and Wolff; that the young lad worked his way with diligence and enthusiasm through every department in the company as every other apprentice would have done. In fact, having already paid for years of private education, the boy's wealthy Irish relatives had then paid a £100 fee to guarantee his smooth passage through the shipyard's training system and an effortless transition into a senior management post. At a time when a junior footman of Pirrie's age might expect to earn £5 to £10 a year or an agricultural labourer just £35 a year, the fee paid on Pirrie's behalf was out of the reach of all but the cream of Irish society.

Born of Irish parents in Canada, Pirrie's father, James, died when he was young, leaving his mother Eliza to return with her baby to Ireland. She was helped by her influential and wealthy relatives, including an uncle closely involved in the running of the Belfast Academy where William received his education. A favourite pastime of the institute boys was hiring boats from local fishermen for trips out on Belfast Lough, perhaps an activity that first attracted Pirrie to being involved with ships. From school he became one of a handful of premium apprentices among the 100-strong workforce. As the company expanded rapidly so did Pirrie's responsibilities. He was soon running the company's design department and in 1869, aged just twenty-two and barely out of his formal 'apprenticeship', became head draughtsman and the designer for a major new contract to build the ship *Oceanic* for the White Star Line.

In quick succession to the success of *Oceanic* came orders from White Star's owner, Thomas Ismay, for three sisters ships; all to share the same design features of part sail, part steam and with accommodation for First Class passengers to be in the greatest luxury of the day, placed amidships, where those paying the most money might enjoy the greatest comfort of ride and lack of noise from the engines.

The designs were a considerable success, marred only by the news in April 1873 that one of the sisters, *Atlantic*, had run aground on rocks off the coast of Halifax, Nova Scotia. The loss of 562 of the 933 people on board, including all but one of the women and children, would be Britain's worst civilian shipping disaster for the next forty years. It was eventually only to be surpassed when the same company's steamship, *Titanic*, sank in April 1912. In a final irony, many of the unidentifiable victims of both disasters were buried in cemeteries around the town of Halifax.

Despite the loss of *Atlantic*, which was blamed entirely on the navigational failures of her captain and crew, the Oceanic class ships were the start of a profitable working partnership between Pirrie and Thomas Ismay, the head of White Star. It was a relationship that was to see both men thrive for decades to come. By 1874, the year following the *Atlantic* disaster, both of the founders of Harland and Wolff had begun to turn their mind to other business interests and to the world of politics[1] and William Pirrie became a full partner in the company before his twenty-eighth birthday.

Under Pirrie's growing influence the shipyard flourished, despite competition from the smaller Belfast shipyard of Workman, Clarke and Co, which from 1879 onwards set up on the north side of the river Lagan, opposite

Harland's original Queen's Island site. At first employing just a few hundred men, the Workman yard would eventually grow to rival and at times even overtake the output of Harland and Wolff, possibly one of the factors that would later encourage Pirrie to take on the overwhelming challenge of building *Titanic* and her sister ships. During the decade of the 1890s, Harland and Wolff became the pre-eminent civilian shipbuilding company in the country; in nine out of ten of those years launching a greater tonnage of ships than any other yard. The decade also saw a concerted effort by William Pirrie to climb both the commercial and the social ladders of Belfast society.

Having used his family money and connections to help fight his way to his current position, Pirrie, by then married into another 'good' county family, had become the perfect social networker. His continuing relationship with Ismay ensured a steady stream of orders from the White Star Line and both men had built an impressive network of contacts within both the British and International shipping companies and inside the political establishment. Pirrie was the perfect salesman, selling both himself and his company in the search for higher profits and social advancement.

Many examples of Pirrie's complicated machinations to climb the social ladder can be seen in the files of the Public Records Office of Northern Ireland, where letters and telegrams are still on file concerning the shipbuilders' attempt to gain more respectability in a host of social and political positions. In early January 1895, for example, the death of the incumbent Deputy Lieutenant of Down left a vacancy for this largely ceremonial yet socially prestigious post. Within the week, Pirrie's brother-in-law, Alexander Carlisle, was pressed into action to drum up support for the shipbuilder's candidacy for the post.

Carlisle wrote to the influential Irish colonial politician and diplomat, the 1st Marquess of Dufferin and Ava, praising Pirrie's qualities as 'a man most suitable for such an honour'. The letter was followed by other similar sycophantic and apparently unsolicited letters from Carlisle, from Pirrie's wife Margaret and from his business contact, Joseph Ismay, in Liverpool, incidentally expressing his 'warmest wishes for his Excellency's forthcoming birthday'.

Similarly, when the even more prestigious post of Lieutenant of the County of Belfast was available a few years later, Pirrie's wife was back in action; this time writing to Lord Cadogan in similar ingratiating terms. Her letter survives as File No. T34498/9 in the Northern Ireland Records Office:

> I hope you will pardon me if I write you on a subject which you may consider outside my province but you have always in conversation spoken so nicely of my husband's good qualities – his untiring energy and his manipulation of his great works, that I venture to write you on

this subject. His appointment to the position would be a very popular one. Reasons such as that at least one eighth of the entire population of Belfast is dependent on our works etc. ... make me feel ambitious that you should if you can see your way add this additional favour to my good husband.

After a further two pages extolling her husband's multiple virtues as Mayor of Belfast, the first Freeman of the City and the creator of the longest ships ever built, Mrs Pirrie ended in self-effacing style:

I apologise for such a lengthy epistle. Perhaps you will agree with an old uncle of mine when [he] said 'what a mistake that women were ever taught to write.'

By the end of the nineteenth century the honours had cascaded in upon William Pirrie. He had become Chairman of Harland and Wolff and assumed total autocratic control with the death of Edward Harland in 1895. He was building the new generation *Oceanic*, described by a contemporary engineering magazine as 'the finest vessel ever produced.' He had been Lord Mayor of Belfast, a Privy Councillor, the High Sherriff of County Antrim, the High Sherriff of County Down and had been awarded an honorary doctorate of law from the Royal University of Ireland.

And yet, unbeknown to his high society establishment friends, Pirrie had a darker side to his character. He was not averse to massaging his accounts to make his financial position appear more secure than it really was. In years to come, following his death in 1924, it would transpire that he had been hiding his true financial position for years. Despite his outward trappings of great wealth, he would eventually leave little money for his widow and family.[2]

But for now, at the very start of the twentieth century, Pirrie was also hiding an even deeper secret. He was employing all of his well-honed networking and negotiating skills to become the catalyst for a complex international deal aimed at monopolising the North Atlantic shipping trade. The Belfast shipbuilder was at the heart of a web of clandestine negotiations in Europe and America to unite all the major international shipping lines under one American-owned banner. The discussions were being kept secret not only for sound commercial reasons but also because they had immense political ramifications.

The deals in which Pirrie was now involved would cause untold damage to both Britain's merchant marine fleet and to her vital Royal Navy interests. His actions would eventually lead him to over-stretch even the enormous resources of his cherished Harland and Wolff shipyard; and by that means would contribute directly to the death of *Titanic*. William Pirrie was about to bite off more than even he could chew.

The saga that was eventually to have such an effect on the shipbuilding work of Harland and Wolff and the future of *Titanic* began in November 1899. At the comparatively young age of sixty-two, Pirrie's long-term friend and business partner, the White Star Line owner, Thomas Ismay, died at his Liverpool home. For Pirrie this was a double blow; not only a personal loss of a good friend but also a significant business problem. From the start, the two men's individual companies had been inextricably bound together by conditions attached to the loans with which they were created. Thirty years earlier, Edward Harland had borrowed money on condition he worked with Gustav Wolff; Thomas Ismay had borrowed money from the Wolff family on the condition that his ships were built by Harland and Wolff. It had been an arranged marriage that neither company's founders had originally sought.

And yet, the marriage had worked out well. Pirrie and Thomas Ismay had grown rich together through the shipping boom years of the nineteenth century. In the decade before Thomas Ismay's death, his White Star Line had paid more than £7 million into the coffers of Harland and Wolff to purchase new ships. In return, Pirrie had put money into White Star and was a major shareholder in the company. Many of their joint deals had been sealed with little more than a handshake, and all were on a commission basis. White Star paid the basic construction costs for their new ships and then gave Harland and Wolff a percentage profit on top. Now one partner in the marriage had died.

For several years before his death, Thomas Ismay had been winding down his involvement in the business and preparing for an eventual handover to his son, Bruce. Everything had been done to prepare the boy to step into his father's shoes, but they were very big shoes to fill. Thomas Ismay had become a towering figure of success in the shipping world: respected by his peers, admired by his business contacts and called upon by governments of the day to chair prestigious shipping industry committees and conferences. By contrast, Bruce Ismay had yet to build a reputation for anything other than being his father's son. Some of the examination records from his brief attendance at Hillside House at Harrow public school in North London offer a snapshot of his academic ability:

July 1877: <u>Fourth Form Second Remove</u> – (Joseph) Bruce Ismay. 20 out of 26 in the class Classics; 12 out of 26 Modern Languages; 20 out of 26 Mathematics.
July 1877: <u>Fourth Form Head Remove</u> – (Joseph) Bruce Ismay. 32 out of 34 Classics; 19 out of 34 Modern Languages; 24 out of 34 Mathematics.

Upon leaving school the younger Ismay had completed a year's higher education in Europe, although never gaining any degree, and had worked for

The Emperor of Germany, Kasier Wilhelm II, who urged Britain to declare war on the USA because of financier J.P. Morgan's attempts to create an Atlantic shipping monopoly.

Lord Knollys. His role as Private Secretary to the Sovereign for King George V led him to be called 'the most discreet man in England'.

A young Winston Churchill.

Ticket for the Belfast 'Home Rule' political rally, which links Winston Churchill with his political ally, Lord Pirrie, of Harland & Wolff shipbuilders.

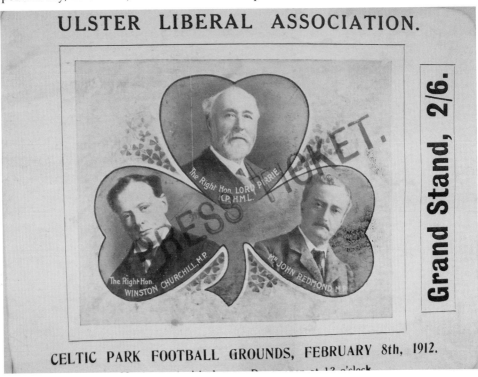

ULSTER LIBERAL ASSOCIATION.

Grand Stand, 2/6.

PRESS TICKET.

The Right Hon. LORD PIRRIE
I.P. H.M.L.

The Right Hon.
WINSTON CHURCHILL, M.P.

M^r JOHN REDMOND M.P.

CELTIC PARK FOOTBALL GROUNDS, FEBRUARY 8th, 1912.

Shipbuilder Edward
Harland, the founder
of the Harland &
Wolff yard in Belfast.

Gustav Wolff, junior partner in the firm of
Harland & Wolff.

US financier J.P. Morgan,
the banker who
effectively owned and
controlled the *Titanic*.

*Titanic* (left) and her sister ship, *Olympic*, which had been painted white for her launching ceremony. The two ships rest on their adjacent slipways under the giant Arrol crane gantry erected for their construction.

*Titanic* and *Olympic* in the background as Harland & Wolff workers knock off at the end of a working day.

Torn steel plates and rivets ripped from the hull of the *Olympic* after a collision with a naval ship at Southampton. Repairing the damage would delay the *Titanic's* construction.

*Titanic* left alone on her slipway at the Belfast shipyard.

*Titanic's* propellers while 'fitting out' in dry-dock after her launch.

*Titanic's* propeller shaft. At least one of the workers has been erased from the photographic negative by the photographer, possibly to improve the composition of his picture.

The luxurious interior of one of *Titanic's* First Class staterooms.

Sunshine pours through the elegant windows of *Titanic's* reading room.

*Titanic* takes to the water. The moment of her official launch in Belfast.

Assisted by tugs, *Titanic* leaves for sea trials in Belfast Lough.

RMS *Titanic* after sea trials in Belfast Lough.

*Titanic* prepares to depart from berth 44 of White Star dock at Southampton for her maiden voyage on 10 April 1912.

A possible suspect? An iceberg photographed from the *Carpathia* the morning after the sinking.

The richest man on board? John Jacob Astor, who drowned on the night of the sinking.

The man who escaped in the last lifeboat – head of the White Star Line, Bruce Ismay.

Thomas Andrews, the designer of the *Titanic*, who went down with the ship on her maiden voyage.

*Titanic* survivors photographed from the rescue ship, *Carpathia*.

*Titanic* passengers draw alongside the *Carpathia*. Outline by photographer on the original glass negative.

Shocked *Titanic* survivors on the deck of *Carpathia*, en-route to New York.

The *Carpathia* approaching New York harbour, with the salvaged *Titanic* lifeboats hanging from her davits.

Waiting for news of the disaster outside the White Star offices in New York City.

Thomas Henry Ismay, who drew up the lifeboat regulations two decades before *Titanic* sank.

Survivor, 'the unsinkable' Molly Brown, presents a 'loving cup' to Captain Arthur Rostron of the *Carpathia* for the ship's role in saving *Titanic's* survivors.

The crew of the *Mackay Bennett*, the ship hired by the White Star Line to salvage bodies from the Atlantic in the days after the sinking.

Viscount Mersey, the retired, elderly and near-deaf judge who chaired the British inquiry into the loss of *Titanic*.

Chair of the US Senate's *Titanic* inquiry, Senator William Alden Smith.

White Star boss, Bruce Ismay, being questioned at the US Senate inquiry in the Waldorf Astoria Hotel in New York.

Lookout Frederick Fleet shortly after giving evidence to US inquiry.

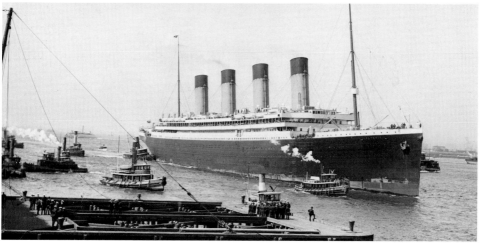

*Olympic* arriving in New York City, the destination to which *Titanic* had been heading.

A new life in America. The memorial to Irish emigration on the quayside at Cobh.

Southampton's memorial to the *Titanic's* engineers, who were all lost in the disaster. Paid for by collections from fellow engineers all over the world.

Detail of Southampton's Engineers' Memorial.

his father ever since, first with an 'apprenticeship' in England, followed by the ritual of a one-year 'grand tour' of Europe, and then several years as the White Star's 'agent' in New York, where he met and married his American wife, Julia. By the time of his father's death, Ismay had no experience outside of the family business and had been a partner in the company in England for less than ten years. He has often been described as painfully shy[3] and rumour at the time was that neither his father, nor Pirrie, were impressed or confident that the White Star Line would prosper under his command.

The upheaval Pirrie was witnessing at the White Star Line coincided with another far more seismic event in the shipping industry on the other side of the Atlantic. The American banker J.P. Morgan was secretly facilitating the merger of two major American shipping lines with one of their British-based rivals. The merger plans threatened domination of the busy transatlantic passenger shipping trade that was already suffering from an over-supply of ships and a downturn in their business.

It may be that Pirrie, with his extensive network of shipping contacts, was invited to give his confidential advice to the Americans, or it may be he heard of the negotiations and simply decided to get himself involved. Whichever was the case, Pirrie had soon insinuated himself into the heart of the plot.

As the new century dawned, Pirrie was the lynchpin around which major figures in the shipping industries of America, Britain and Germany began secretly planning to take over the transatlantic trade. In covert meetings at Pirrie's luxurious home in London he did all he could to persuade, threaten or cajole more and more shipping lines to join what was becoming known by the conspirators as 'the Morgan Combination'. The advantages that Pirrie repeatedly spelled out to potential members of the combine were substantial: J.P. Morgan was the most powerful financier in the world, a trading monopoly would control prices for all tickets between Europe and America and would rationalise the market by controlling the timetables of sailings to every destination. In addition, the combined group would be powerful enough to crush any remaining competition.

Previously confidential Foreign Office papers in the British National Archives reveal that Pirrie had become the international 'wheeler-dealer' behind J.P. Morgan's banking empire's attempt to monopolise the trade. They contain a secret report with notes from one shipping company executive who was being persuaded to sign up to the Morgan and Pirrie plans. They make it clear that Pirrie, once the new boy 'gentleman apprentice' at a Belfast shipyard, had come a long way. He was now on the international stage and setting out to impress:

> We dined again this evening at Pirrie's house, whose domestic arrangements seem to point to great riches, even measured by a London

standard. He is an earnest and I believe, clever man. Pirrie evidently had
joined a combination from which he expects, and no doubt he is right,
great advantages.

He believed, with Morgan, that an incredible waste was caused by
sailing, owing to competition, far more steamers than were actually
needed. When this matter was sensibly regulated much money would be
saved; under the circumstances it seems the best thing would be to sell
out without further delay.

William Pirrie was being well rewarded for his efforts on behalf of the
American conspirators. Once Morgan had taken over the American and
European shipping lines then Pirrie's Harland and Wolff yard would be
granted the exclusive right to build every new ship that the new combination
ordered. It was a glittering prize that would guarantee orders worth tens of
millions of pounds for the Belfast shipbuilders.

To gain that prize, Pirrie joined Morgan in playing a high-stakes poker
game in which they tried to bluff their way to a monopoly position. Pirrie lied
to prospective takeover targets by falsely claiming that the Morgan
Combination had already signed exclusive deals with all of the major
American railroad companies. It was a potent weapon of persuasion. Rival
shipping companies knew that if they were denied access to the US railway
network they would not be able to offer their passengers onward travel tickets
to all continental American destinations.

Going further, Pirrie also lied about how many of each company's
competitors had already signed up to the American deal. He warned of the
dangers of 'missing the American boat'. He stressed how impossible it would
be for any shipping company to compete if they were left out in the cold as
minor players facing a monolithic American company with unlimited financial
resources.

In fact, many of Pirrie's claims were, at first, no more than 'smoke-and-
mirrors' tricks that traded on the fearsome reputation of his backer, J.P.
Morgan. Over the past decade, the American financier had increased his
multi-million dollar fortune through a series of deals creating monopoly
'trusts' in the American railroad and steel industries. He was the most
powerful financial force in the world, consulted by governments, feared by
competitors and followed by the markets.

Morgan's reputation and Pirrie's persuasion worked well together.
Terrified of being left isolated in the battle for the North Atlantic passenger
trade, a series of European and American shipping lines now met with Pirrie
or Morgan and covertly signed up to their plot. They were all warned of the
need for secrecy. The Morgan Combination had a huge prize in their sights;
nothing less than a total monopoly of Atlantic shipping.

The plan was working out well. Despite initial resistance, it had proved easy for Pirrie to persuade the young and inexperienced Ismay to agree to sign over his British ships to the US banker's combine; now they needed to take over, by stealth or persuasion, the only remaining serious competitor, the British Cunard Line.

Unbeknown to them all, that was never going to happen. Their cover had already been blown; their secret was out.

### Notes

1. Both Edward Harland and Gustav Wolff were active in local politics and both in time withdrew some of their investment in the company and graduated to become Westminster MPs.
2. After Pirrie's death, the Board of Harland and Wolff was astonished to find he had left little money for his widow. A special pension and honorary position with the company was arranged for Lady Pirrie.
3. Ismay's reputation for shyness was reinforced by his behaviour after *Titanic* sank when he retired to a private cabin on *Carpathia* and spoke to nobody for days.

# Chapter Twenty-Two

# 'A matter certainly worth fighting for . . .'

**12 noon**
**7 August 1901**
**The German Reich-Chancellery**
**Berlin**
**Germany**

En route to what he believed was a routine diplomatic meeting in Berlin, His Majesty's Ambassador to Germany, His Excellency, Rt. Hon. Frank Lascelles was a relaxed and happy man. After years in the country, he was confident that nothing of great import would be on the agenda today. Such semi-official meetings, frequently over English tea and biscuits at the British Embassy, or, if on German soil, a small glass of schnapps, were processes that oiled the wheels of bilateral relations; informal conversations concerning, what the diplomats politely termed 'matter of mutual interest'. Even though Lascelles knew, better than most, that the British could not afford to ignore the continuing build-up of German naval power, relations had been cordial of late between the two rival, sea-faring superpowers. The tensions that would one day culminate in the mass slaughter of the First World War were still a decade and more away.

But, on the stroke of noon, as Lascelles entered the gilded offices of the Berlin Chancellery, he realised at once that this was a far from routine occasion. Waiting to greet him was not some minor German Government official but the head of the entire German nation, His Imperial Highness, Emperor Wilhelm II. This meeting was on an entirely different level to the diplomatic small talk that Lascelles had been expecting. Even so, neither of the men meeting that day had any concept of the momentous consequences that would follow as a result of their conversation.

This meeting would one day play an important role in the creation of the RMS *Titanic*, and would lead to an astonishing suggestion from the German

Emperor that Great Britain should ally itself alongside him – in a war against America.

Emperor Wilhelm was not a man to waste time on more than the briefest of diplomatic niceties. He soon forcefully spelled out the message he wanted Great Britain to understand:

> What you must realise, Lord Lascelles, is that there are real dangers to peace and stability in the world today. I am alluding to the power that comes from the enormous wealth that is now in the hands of some private individuals, chiefly Americans. The possession of such wealth constitutes a danger to the governments of some States.

As Ambassador Lascelles listened politely, but with growing astonishment, the Emperor warmed to his theme:

> I am talking, in particular, of the American banker, J.P. Morgan, who, it seems, has the aim of monopolising the navigation of the entire world. He has already brought up five of your English lines of steamers … And, according to my latest information, which may, perhaps, not have reached His Majesty's Government yet, he is now buying up the shares of the Cunard Line.

The German Emperor was a lot better informed than the British Government. Ministers in London had no clue that they were about to lose one of the country's most treasured possessions. Unbeknown to them, the American banker, J.P. Morgan, aided and abetted by the Harland and Wolff chairman, William Pirrie, was already well on his way to total control of the British Merchant Marine, the vast ocean-going trading fleet that, for centuries, had helped ensure that Britannia ruled the waves.

At the end of a thirty-minute meeting, Ambassador Lascelles headed back to the British Embassy and dictated a confidential intelligence report to his immediate superior, the newly-appointed British Foreign Secretary, Henry Charles Keith Petty-Fitzmaurice, 5th Marquess of Lansdowne. A copy of that despatch, the Ambassador's Report No. 201, still exists within the British National Archives. In it he reported all of the German Emperor's warnings to Britain: [author's italics]

> It was evident that Mr Pierpoint Morgan, as a United States citizen, would transfer the ships of these different lines to the United States' flag, and that the commercial navy of England would no longer enjoy its supremacy of numbers. H.M. considered that this was a most serious matter not only for England but for the other European powers, and he thought that it might be advisable for the German and English governments to combine to prevent it, even by force if necessary.

It was a matter that was certainly worth fighting for, and H.M. believed that, if Nelson had still been alive, the transfer of a large number of British ships to the American flag would not have been allowed.

I ventured to reply that I did not see how the shareholders in a commercial undertaking were to be prevented from selling the shares to the best advantage, and I asked whether H.M. believed that Nelson would have sunk the ships. H.M. answered that *in former times Great Britain would have gone to war*, rather than allow her commercial supremacy at sea to be taken from her.

I have etc:

[sd:] Frank C. Lascelles

The German Emperor's warnings came as a bombshell to the British Government in London. It had been publicly announced earlier in 1901 that ships of the Leyland Line, a British company, were to join an American group, but as far as was known, the tonnage involved would be relatively small. In addition, it was generally thought that the Americans had grossly overpaid for the line's few British ships. For a while J.P. Morgan had been ridiculed for his lack of business sense in paying so much for so little. Now the situation had changed dramatically; if the purchase of the Leyland ships was just the precursor for the monopoly takeover of the entire British fleet then Morgan's purchase would make far more financial sense.

The one thing that the British Government did not seriously consider at any point was the German Emperor's suggestion of using force or declaring war on America to protect our merchant fleet; but his covert warning that both the White Star Line and Cunard were potential targets for an American takeover was deeply worrying.

The British Merchant Marine was at that time the largest in the world; unequivocal proof that Britannia still did rule the waves. In a House of Commons debate the President of the Board of Trade, David Lloyd-George, had spelled out Britain's contribution to commerce around the globe:

A good deal of British ships have hardly been at home since construction. We have fifty-four per cent of the carrying trade of the world. There has not been anything like it in history. It is not merely that we carry two-thirds of our own trade, but fifty-four per cent of the trade of the whole world, and therefore, a good number of British ships trade between foreign ports and never touch home ports except once every four years for the purpose of classification at Lloyds.

The shipping industry was vital to British national interests in myriad ways. At home it provided employment not only for British sailors but also for hundreds of thousands of shipyard workers and those in the allied trades of steel production, coal mining and general engineering. At sea it was essential for maintaining links with the far-flung British Empire at a time when much of the globe was still painted red on the maps. It earned a fortune for the UK by being by far the biggest carrier of the world's trade. But most importantly of all, British merchant ships played a vital role in the defence of the realm.

For many years the British Navy had paid subsidies to British shipping lines for the production of ships that would have the dual role of being a merchant ship in times of peace and a warship in time of conflict. Some vessels, including at least fifteen ships in the White Star fleet and many others in the Cunard shipping lines, were especially strengthened in parts of their decking or hull structure to rapidly be fitted with guns in case of war. Their speed made them ideal as fast light cruisers to supplement the ships of the Royal Navy.

A secret Admiralty document submitted to the Cabinet at the time warned:

> At the present time the British Navy could not catch the fastest German merchant cruisers and that this might cause panic were it to be known to the British public.[1]

Other naval subsidies allowed for passenger or cargo ships to be available instantly when required to act as carriers of troops or equipment. Such considerations meant that the secret sale of the White Star Line and the threat that Cunard ships might also soon come under the control of an American financier was a matter of Cabinet-level importance to the British Government. With Pirrie and Morgan and Ismay still unaware that anybody knew any of the details of their monopoly plans, the British Government set out, in equal secrecy, to defeat them.

In a series of Cabinet discussions in 1901 and into 1902, ministers considered options such as a complete nationalisation of the White Star Line and Cunard fleets, or the possibility of introducing new laws making it illegal for British ships to come under the control of foreign powers. Senior Naval officials were also planning potential responses to the American threat. They considered invoking compulsory purchase clauses in their subsidy contracts with Bruce Ismay's White Star fleet; the legally binding contracts would have allowed the Admiralty to have purchased any ships they desired, with or without J.P. Morgan's approval.

After Queen Victoria's death in January 1901, her son was crowned King Edward VII. The new King was kept informed of government thinking through a series of private notes sent to him after each Cabinet meeting.

Cabinet Office file CAB 41/27/15, for example, still holds the handwritten Downing Street letter that first alerted the King:

> Lord Salisbury with his humble duty respectfully submits to Your Majesty that a Cabinet was held today at twelve o'clock.
>
> A good deal of attention was given to this great Steamship combination which has been engineered by Mr Pierpoint Morgan. Opinions were divided but the preponderant view was that it contained serious elements of danger to British commerce, and to British maritime supremacy in case of wars.
>
> Several suggestions were thrown out as to the means by which Mr Morgan might be deterred from carrying his enterprise further, or might be induced by advantageous offers to modify its character in favour of this country.

With the first hints about American plans to buy up the White Star Line by then leaking into the press, the British Government received further help from their surprising new ally, the Emperor of Germany. Another dispatch, marked 'Secret', from Ambassador Lascelles, passed on a further German message:

> Sir – In the interview which I had with the Emperor on the 3rd inst., H.M. referred at some length and with considerable vehemence to the recently formed Anglo American Shipping Syndicate which he regarded as most disastrous for England. H.M. reminded me that in August of last year he had warned me of the attempts which Mr Pierpoint Morgan was making to obtain control of the navigation of the world.
>
> H.M. could not understand how it was that England did not perceive that America was her most redoubtable rival both from a maritime and a commercial point of view. She had become a great Power both in the Pacific and Atlantic Oceans and would most certainly throw England over whenever it suited her purpose to do so. It was perhaps unfortunate that America was an English speaking country as otherwise Englishmen might be less prone to place such implicit reliance on the assurances of American friendship as to lead them to allow the control of their mercantile navy to fall into American hands.

To back up his general mischief-making comments about the relationship between Britain and her American ally, it seems that the Emperor also provided more tangible evidence to help fight off the American assault on Britain's commercial and naval interests. A short while later, the Cabinet received further secret intelligence documents, said to have come from 'a surprising new source'. In reality, that source was almost certainly the Emperor, or the German intelligence authorities acting on his behalf.

The new intelligence was in the form of a set of notes that have been preserved for posterity in the papers of Cabinet Minister Gerald Balfour. Once translated from their original German, they revealed the intimate details of discussions that had taken place during a series of meetings that had been held that year at William Pirrie's London home and at the luxurious New York apartment of banker, J.P. Morgan. Their content left no doubt that they had been written by a German shipping executive who had been trusted to know of the Morgan Combination's plans.

The papers revealed not only useful details about which companies the US financier and Pirrie, the British shipbuilder, were seeking to control but also the writer's impressions of their character and motivations:

> The visit to Morgan's house brought us his interesting acquaintance: he has an energetic face, with clever rather restless eyes dominating the rest of his features. The conference lasted about half an hour, and new lights were thrown on the story of the development of the whole affair ...
>
> ... the Morgan Combination has already taken in or absorbed all the North Atlantic Lines with the exception of Cunard, H.A.P.A.G. Lloyd, Anchor and Rotterdam-American Lines. The White Star are offering their whole affair as regard ¾ of the property, they retaining ¼ for themselves.
>
> It was further said that Europe has amused itself by picturing Morgan as a jester on a large scale, when he actually is an eminently capable man possessing an enormous shrewdness and unusually wide views. He may, for instance, be blamed for the purchase of the Leyland Line, and undoubtedly it is not a paying concern at present, but how will it be when the Combine is completed?
>
> I must confess that it has given me a very uneasy feeling, because if it is true then our own resolutions are to say the least shaky, these opponents are so strong, the ground is absolutely cut away beneath our feet, that I cannot see how we can defend ourselves.

The new intelligence was vital in helping the British Government work out ways of countering the American threat. A printed Cabinet briefing paper warned that the purchase of White Star and other British ship lines appeared to have sinister political motives:

> ... it would be unreasonable to suppose that the new policy has been dictated by commercial motives alone. For some years past it has been the policy of the United States to create a commercial navy at all costs, and to increase the War Navy *pari passu*. Indeed there can be no doubt that it is the intention of the United States Government to use the large surplus for the purpose of destroying the commerce of other nations.

The President of the Board of Trade, Gerald Balfour, told Cabinet colleagues that the Germans were taking steps to safeguard their own merchant navy. In the Cabinet's confidential briefing paper, CAB 37/61/78, he questioned the patriotism of the British ship-owners involved in J.P. Morgan's plans.

> The scrupulous care shown in the German Agreement to safeguard national interests contrasts unpleasantly with the apparent indifference of our own ship-owners to this aspect of the matter.
>
> In addition Messrs J.P. Morgan and Co. have entered into an agreement with Messrs Harland and Wolff, the terms of which are significant. While this agreement certainly appears to be a favourable one for Messrs Harland and Wolff, it is hard to see how the arrangement can be beneficial to the general interests of the ship-building industry in the United Kingdom.

The British Government requested a meeting with Bruce Ismay, head of the White Star Line, and presented him with a set of demands. In the course of a series of increasingly acrimonious meetings Ismay was told that even if his company was sold to the Americans, his ships must remain British. They were to sail under the British flag, be staffed by British officers and remain available to the Navy in case of war.

Possible alternatives such as the forcible purchase of his ships may never have been spelled out, but the Government did let Ismay, Pirrie and Morgan know that their dream of a monopoly in the Atlantic emigrant trade would never be realised. The Government had already reached a confidential agreement with Cunard that would guarantee that all of the ships of that line would stay both independent – and British.

More damagingly still for the American-backed plans, Cunard had extracted a heavy price for their loyalty to the country. The Government was lending them enough money (the equivalent of more than £100 million in today's terms) to build two new super-ships. With the help of British Government loans at low interest rates and on the easiest of repayment terms, Cunard had already begun the process of designing and ordering the new *Mauretania* and her sister ship, the *Lusitania*. They were to be built in two different British shipyards; they would be the two biggest, and fastest, ships in the world.

Faced with a new, fighting-fit rival in the form of the revitalised and 'determinedly British' Cunard Company, the Combination partners were in trouble. Morgan, Pirrie and Ismay had been comprehensively trounced. They had the White Star Line and various German companies within their fold but now they knew they were facing competition over which they had no control whatsoever.[2]

Throughout the entire affair the Cabinet had been determined to avoid any form of trade war with America. So, at this moment of apparent victory, the British Government offered J.P. Morgan 'peace terms'. In return for his agreement that the White Star Line ships should continue to sail under the British flag, he was offered a financial incentive. Britain would continue paying the valuable naval subsidies and Morgan's ships would be free to compete on equal terms with other companies for British Post Office contracts to carry mail across the Atlantic. It was a valuable concession; the money being offered could mean the difference between profit and loss for any transatlantic steamer.

It was designed to be an offer the shrewd New York financier could hardly refuse. With a jingoistic sideswipe at the Americans' ability to compete with hundreds of years of British shipping expertise, a Cabinet briefing paper neatly summed up the British Government's thinking:

> It is necessary to consider what action, if any, can be taken to avert, or diminish, the evils with which the country appears to be threatened. It is apparent that the principal, and indeed the only, object of the present proprietors of the White Star and other Lines, is to make money ... and they will have to rely on subsidies to make a future profit.
>
> It must be said that the Americans cannot build a boat – racing yachts excepted – or copy one successfully.

In a London ceremony in early 1903, representatives of the British Government and the Morgan shipping group, now officially named as the International Mercantile Marine Company (IMM), signed a legally binding deal that would last for a minimum of twenty years. It meant that, although the Americans would own the White Star Line, all of their ships, and any new ships they may build in the future, would continue to fly under the British flag and would be staffed by British officers.

In order to fulfil its promise, IMM was forced to reorganise itself into a complex business structure of interlinked British and American companies. Many years later, under questioning at the Senate hearing into the loss of *Titanic*, Phillip Franklin, one of IMM's American executives, tried to explain how it worked:

'The Oceanic Steam Navigation Co. is the managing company, the controlling company, the owning company of the White Star Line. That is the trade name under which the steamers are run as a trade name. The stock of the Oceanic Steam Navigation Co. is owned by the International Navigation Co. (Ltd.) of England, of Liverpool.'

'And the stock of the company is owned by whom?'

'It is controlled and owned by the International Mercantile Marine Co. of New Jersey through the bondholders. That is an American company.'

The practical effect was that all White Star Line's ships, including in due course *Titanic*, were nominally owned by a British company, which was owned by another British company that was controlled and owned lock, stock and barrel by the Americans.

The battle over Morgan's attempt 'to control the navigation of the world' was to have further dramatic consequences for all involved. In years to come their failure to gain monopoly powers meant that IMM would forever struggle to make a profit. It would prove to be the worst financial mistake of J.P. Morgan's life. It would one day soon lead to crushing financial pressures and an unrealistically tight timeline being brought to bear on the White Star Line and Harland and Wolff as they constructed *Titanic*. Tragically, her passengers and crew would be the ones who paid the price.

### Notes

1. Squeezing record-breaking speeds out of large ships was inordinately costly in fuel and capital cost terms. Only naval subsidies made it a commercially worthwhile proposition for any shipping line.
2. Emperor Wilhelm introduced laws ensuring that German ships remained under the majority control of German companies.

# Chapter Twenty-Three

# 'Lord Salisbury did not trust Mr Pirrie . . .'

10.30 am
17 January 1911
Harland and Wolff Boardroom
Queen's Island
Belfast

It was rapidly turning into the sort of meeting that everyone wished they had been able to avoid. Lord Pirrie, the autocratic chairman of Harland and Wolff, was being as domineering as ever, and nobody wanted to give him more bad news. Even the most senior of the companies' many managing directors were trying to avoid the great man's gaze. Eventually, Charles Payne, the executive charged with ensuring that the coming launch of *Titanic* ran smoothly[1] decided to speak out:

> There's no escaping the fact that a delay might well be necessary. An adherence to the proposed date of delivery of *Titanic* will tax the resources of my department to the utmost.

Payne, a short and somewhat overweight man with a tiny square moustache and a large forehead, from which his hair had long since receded, looked even more uncomfortable than usual in his trademark, slightly old-fashioned grey suit. Never a popular man, he looked for support from his fellow managing directors, who each ran one department of the company. He found that little help was forthcoming. All of the men present were content for Payne to be the focus of Lord Pirrie's displeasure.

'I must say this again, and say it most clearly,' Lord Pirrie responded, 'any delay will be costly and embarrassing. I've come here today with one task in mind; to impress on you all that any extra expenditure must be avoided at all costs. You must bear that in mind at all times.'

Pirrie had not been a regular attendee of the Harland and Wolff Board meetings in earlier weeks. He tended to appear only when issues of wages or costs were on the agenda, and today was no different. With 12,546 people employed in the shipyard that week, the wages bill had never been higher. Pirrie's presence at the meeting guaranteed that only he would make any decisions, although even in his absence, every matter of substance was referred to him before the Board took any action. Pirrie had already been annoyed that day by a demand from Belfast's main haulage company, John Harkness and Sons. They had sought an extra 2d per ton for deliveries to the yard.[2] Now he reluctantly agreed to change the launch date of the SS *Demosthenes*, one of the many ships simultaneously under construction. The workforce had been unable to keep up with the schedule. The delay would allow the ship to be completed without the dreaded prospect of paying overtime wages.

It was then half a century after the late Sir Edward Harland had first arrived in Belfast and the company that bore his name had changed out of all recognition. The few acres of reclaimed mud on which his first ships were built had become a sprawling, 80-acre complex of slipways, metal works, design and drawing offices spread across the Queen's Island site. The few dozen men whom Edward Harland had confronted to make the yard profitable had grown to an army of men whose living now depended upon the Belfast yard. And the orders for vessels of 1,500 tons that Edward Harland had once been so thankful to receive had grown to monstrous-sized ships of 45,000 tons and more.

The yard's humble beginnings had set Harland and Wolff on an inexorable course towards the birth – and the death – of *Titanic*.

In building *Titanic*, the company had accepted its biggest challenge yet. It was simultaneously constructing the two biggest ships in the world and planning to build a third identical sister ship immediately afterwards. Yet *Olympic*, *Titanic* and the planned *Britannic* were by no means the only jobs on the company's books. Harland and Wolff also had to fulfil contracts to build other new ships, on top of their routine repair and refurbishment work elsewhere in the vast Belfast shipyard. Between 1908, when work started on *Olympic*, and the maiden voyage of *Titanic*, in April 1912, the Queen's Island yard was to be involved in the construction or repair of no less than thirty-seven ships, ranging from the giant trio of the White Star Lines' sister ships through to eighteen others of 10,000 tons or more, and a host of smaller cargo ships and passenger vessels.

On the face of it, life had gone well for shipbuilder William Pirrie since he threw his lot in with American banker J.P. Morgan at the turn of the century. True, there had been some difficulties when the British Government had learned the full extent of Pirrie's role in helping to sell out the bulk of the British merchant fleet to its new American owners, but that had soon seemed to blow over. Lord Pirrie himself never knew that the Morgan debacle had almost cost him his cherished aristocratic title.

As far as he was concerned, his elevation in 1906 to become Baron Pirrie of Belfast had been smoothly handled by the government of the day and quickly agreed to by the King. He was unaware of letters, now stored in file D4091/A/8/5/1-15 of the Public Records Office of Northern Ireland, revealing that the King had last-minute doubts about raising Pirrie to the Peerage. King Edward VII was not satisfied that Pirrie deserved an aristocratic title. The King had been privy to some of the secret melodrama of the Morgan affair and knew that Pirrie had played a leading role.

Pirrie's supporters were, however, falsely insisting that Pirrie had only acted at the time with the full knowledge and approval of the then prime minister, the recently-deceased Lord Salisbury. Trying to establish the truth, King Edward asked his Private Secretary, Lord Knollys, to investigate as a matter of urgency.

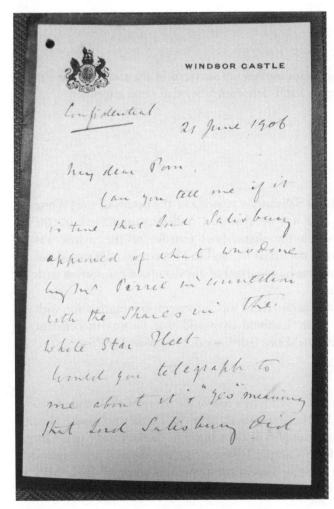

Letter written on behalf of King Edward VII seeking information about the role of Lord Pirrie in the creation of the J.P. Morgan USA shipping combine.

Lord Knollys' family had served the Kings and Queens of England for more than 300 years. He was the King's deepest confidante and was known as 'the most discreet man in England'. He sent an urgent handwritten note, on Windsor Castle notepaper, to the late Lord Salisbury's former secretary, Schomberg Kerr McDonnell:

Confidential

21 June 1906

Can you tell me if it is true that Lord Salisbury approved of what was done by Mr Pirrie in connection with the shares in the White Star fleet?
      Would you telegraph to me about it and 'yes' meaning that Lord Salisbury did know; 'no' that he did not know.

Yours ever

Francis Knollys.

The coded telegram response has not survived in the archives, but a more detailed reply was sent by hand–delivered letter that same afternoon:

Confidential

21 June 1906

My Dear Francis

It is not true that Lord Salisbury was aware of the details of the [White Star] scheme. It is not true that had Salisbury approved of the arrangement by which the shares [sic] transfer of the shares was affected. His approval not asked for: and had it been asked it would not have been given: nor was he cognisant of any details, in connection with any transfer of shares.
      I observe that it is said that I was in constant communication with Mr Pirrie at that time. I should have said that he was in constant communication with me! Lord Salisbury did not trust Mr Pirrie.

Yours ever – S. McD

It was a damning indictment of Pirrie's role in the Morgan affair and of claims that he had acted with official approval. Even so, Pirrie's political influence carried the day against the doubts of the King. The country had a new Liberal government and Sir Henry Campbell-Bannerman was the new prime minister. It was a government heavily dependent upon the votes of Irish MPs at Westminster and Pirrie was the most influential Liberal politician in Ireland.

The *London Gazette* of 20 July 1906 duly announced his new honour: henceforth William J. Pirrie would be known as 'Lord Pirrie, Baron Pirrie of the City of Belfast'.

Behind the scenes there had been other more serious developments for J.P. Morgan's shipbuilding and ship-owning co-conspirators. While Pirrie was still running Harland and Wolff, his younger and easily influenced business partner, Bruce Ismay, had seemingly gone up in the world. Whilst retaining his managing director position with the White Star Line he had also become the president of the entire International Mercantile Marine Company, the biggest ship-owning conglomerate on Earth. It was, however, something of a poisoned chalice. Since the formation of the IMM in the face of British Government opposition and their support for Cunard, the operation had proved to be a financial disaster. Ismay had reluctantly accepted the president's role after previous incumbents in the post had failed miserably to make money.

Although Ismay was nominally in charge of all of the IMM's ships and shipping lines, few doubted that the real power behind the throne was US banker, J.P. Morgan. The creation of the shipping conglomerate had cost Morgan and his worldwide banking empire a large fortune. Continuing losses year after year had eaten away at even his multi-million dollar personal wealth and had proven to be his one big business failure.

Morgan, his family and his closest banking associates had originally backed the plan with millions of dollars, knowingly paying far higher prices for the shares of shipping companies than they were really worth. The expectation had been that a monopoly position would recoup all their investment, but that had never happened. To make matters worse, a hoped-for subsidy from the American Government had failed to materialise and the worldwide shipping market had taken a downturn with the conclusion of the Boer War and the consequent slump in demand for ships to serve the British Army's needs in South Africa. Within a year the prices of IMM stock had plummeted; unable to sell their holdings, Morgan and his banker colleagues were locked into the deal. However unwillingly it had happened, J.P. Morgan was now a shipping man.[3]

After a lifetime of financial success, albeit supported throughout most of that time by his father's vast banking empire, John Pierpoint Morgan had finally made a terrible mistake. His lust for money, which had been characterised as 'impetuosity and rashness' in his banking youth, had finally got him into serious trouble. Morgan's initial decision to get involved in providing banking services to the chaotic North Atlantic shipping business was probably marginal, his subsequent decisions to invest further in trying to create the world's greatest shipping monopoly was undoubtedly a disaster.

The respected Morgan biographer, Vincent P. Carosso, described Morgan as having 'a princely income ...' but that was about to change. In the years after getting mixed up in the shipping interests of Lord Pirrie and the likes of Bruce Ismay, the hugely wealthy American's banker's income turned temporarily from that of a prince into that of a pauper.

Morgan's private financial records, now held in the New York library that he created to hold his family archives, reveal the full extent of the losses that the Morgan Combination shipping empire suffered. The accounts at the start of 1902 were hugely boosted by the vast profits accruing from the Morgan bank's involvement in the US steel industry. They showed record profits. J.P. Morgan's personal income for that year was in the region of £1.3 million, an estimated £110 million or more in today's terms. The following year, after the calamitous launch of the IMM, those profits had turned into losses.

Because they were full partners, rather than mere shareholders, Morgan and his colleagues behind the J.P. Morgan banking group not only shared in any profits, they were also liable for any losses. Morgan's personal losses that year were around £300,000. But he was not the only one suffering. The shipping disaster meant that his son Jack also lost a fortune and his other partners in New York lost millions. The financial malaise spread across the Atlantic, with their London banking partners losing money they could ill afford even less than the Morgan family could.

Morgan's other banking business continued in other years of this first decade of the twentieth century to make healthy profits, but the losses from his shipping venture must have rankled when set against Morgan's success in other fields. And J.P. Morgan was not somebody with whom most businessmen, least of all the shy and nervous Bruce Ismay, would have wanted to clash. Morgan's physical presence alone assured his domination of the room; a large man so afflicted by a deformed, reddened and bulbous nose that for most of his life he avoided being photographed. But after a lifetime of banking experience and coming from a family that had made millions from business over three generations, he was a commanding presence that few could stand up against. Morgan was used to dealing with presidents, with kings and with corporate industrial giants; the views of Bruce Ismay and his unprofitable shipping sideshow would have had little impact on his thinking.

It is inconceivable that Morgan and his colleagues, with most to lose in the continuing chaos of the IMM conglomerate, would not have demanded lower costs and higher profits throughout their involvement with the White Star Line. And a demand from J.P. Morgan was not to be ignored. Bruce Ismay and his White Star Line shareholders had come out of the original deal rather well. They had sold three-quarters of their business for considerably more than most analysts had reckoned it was worth.

Lord Pirrie, likewise, had been already well paid for his efforts in setting up the British and European deals on Morgan's behalf. He had walked away with directorships in several of Morgan's shipping companies and with the most valuable prize of all. Harland and Wolff were now the sole shipbuilders for the entire IMM fleet; all new ships of whatever shape, size and complexity would have to be built in their one riverside shipyard.

It was a welcome result for William Pirrie. For decades Harland and Wolff had been the undisputed top dog of the two British shipbuilding yards in Belfast. Looking back to 1890, there had been little comparison between the 48,633 total tonnage of ships they constructed that year and the 15,631 tons produced by the rival Workman Clarke yard alongside the city's river Lagan.

But by the turn of the century, Pirrie was watching the 'younger brother' yard grow up to rival his own empire. In 1898, Harland and Wolff's 67,905 tons was not so far ahead of Workman's 53,475; by 1902, their positions had been reversed. For the first time, Harland and Wolff became the smaller of the two Belfast shipyards, turning out just 74,497 tons against their rival's 86,712 tons. It must have been galling for Pirrie to hear Workman Clarke's managers crowing that they now worked for the 'world's finest shipyard; producing the world's finest ships'.

In the aftermath of the Morgan takeover there had been one other big winner that perhaps intensified the pain that the US bankers were feeling. Cunard had taken full advantage of the British Government's financial assistance. They were planning that the *Lusitania* and *Mauretania* should both enter service as soon as possible.

There is a popular, romantic myth about the conception and genesis of *Titanic* that has been repeated as fact in book after book over recent decades. The legend claims that the great ship was built as a result of a relaxed, postprandial discussion, in the summer of 1907, between Thomas Ismay, ostensibly the owner of the White Star Line, Lord Pirrie, the owner of Harland & Wolff shipyard, and Pirrie's nephew, the ship designer, Thomas Andrews. After dinner at Pirrie's Belgravia mansion, Downshire House, when the ladies had retired the gentlemen-trio allegedly dreamed up the idea of building, not just one magnificent ocean liner, but the three biggest ships in the world.

Over port and brandies, their imagination so ran away with them that they decided to build all three ships simultaneously, at a combined cost approaching the then incredible sum of £5 million. Common versions of the fairy story add that Pirrie then sketched out designs on the back of an envelope ... and thus, *Titanic* was born.

Nothing could be further from the truth.

The story first surfaced in a book written with the aid of Thomas Andrews' widow, Helen, many years after the event. It therefore seems likely that such a dinner party may well have taken place, but none of the three men allegedly present would then have had the authority, or the means, to take the crucial commercial decisions ascribed to them. The necessity of building *Titanic* and her sister ships was actually clear to the American financiers, the bankers who had the real power and money to make it happen, far earlier than the summer of 1907.

William Pirrie had long been working with Morgan and Ismay to decide on a strategy that could combat the threat from Cunard's magnificent new ocean liners. From the moment that the IMM combine had been formed and Cunard had begun building their super-ships, Pirrie had been working towards one end. He knew that Morgan and Ismay would need to take an enormous financial gamble. At a time when they were losing money and Cunard ships were the stars of the show, they would have to respond with new ships. From as early as 1903, Pirrie had been using his network of business contacts and his political and social standing within the Belfast establishment to good effect. The Belfast Harbour Board had agreed to build a vast new dry dock alongside the Harland and Wolff shipyard.

On the face of it, the planned 'graving dock', reputedly named after its coffin-like shape, was far bigger than it needed to be; it was longer than any ship yet planned for Belfast. Even more surprisingly, it was to be fitted with gates that could extend its length even further so that it would be longer than any ship in the world. In due course the true purpose of the dock project would become clear; its final length with its gate extension would be just a few feet longer than the eventual length of *Titanic* and her sister ships.

In addition, Harland and Wolff had been drawing up plans for a gigantic new gantry-mounted crane that could simultaneously span several of the existing slipways in the shipyard. It could be used to carry the huge hydraulic and pneumatic riveting machines and to lift the weight of steel plate that would need to be moved in the construction of enormous new ships. The complex gantry would eventually be built by Glasgow-based William Arroll and Co., which just a decade before had completed the world-famous Tower Bridge in London. William Pirrie was preparing the ground for something big.

The IMM directors had worked out a plan. The two Cunard ships could have their Blue Riband award for the speediest Atlantic crossing. IMM would instead build not just any ship; they would build the three biggest and most luxurious ships in the world, all constructed simultaneously in Lord Pirrie's yard in Belfast. Nobody had actually much considered whether or not the one single shipyard could cope with the task.

The demands on Harland and Wolff's shipyard to build *Titanic*, *Olympic* and *Britannic* were to stretch its resources to the limit. There were to be difficulties in finding sufficient high quality iron and steel from sufficient high quality foundries, problems with recruiting and retaining enough highly-skilled labourers and financial pressure from bankers to cut costs and cut corners. All reduced the possible margins of error; all were factors that caused *Titanic* to sink faster than she should have done and left the sea surface awash with the frozen bodies of *Titanic's* dead.

### Notes

1. Payne's launch arrangements did eventually go smoothly. He had the honour of starting the hydraulic rams that pushed *Titanic* into the water.

2. Harkness, whose men were known as 'the van and monkey wagon drivers', never did get the increase they wanted. The Board postponed any decision – indefinitely.

3. Despite profiting in the coming First World War, the IMM would never stop losing money. The loss of *Titanic* would contribute towards its eventual bankruptcy and demise.

## Chapter Twenty-Four

# 'I suffer from the infirmity of deafness . . .'

8.15 pm
**Sunday, 22 April 1912**
**Deck of the US cable ship** *MacKay-Bennett*
**Estimated position: 42° 58' N , 49° 21' W**
**North Atlantic Ocean**

The sodden life-jacket had been stripped from the body. The corpse was that of a young man, clearly fit and apparently uninjured in the sinking. His appearance of peaceful sleep suggested a death from exhaustion and the soul-numbing cold of the Atlantic rather than through the panic of a drowning man. None of the pockets in his cold, saturated clothing held even the slightest of clues to the identity of the dead body laid out on deck. He wore no rings, he had no tattoos and he bore no birthmark to reveal who he may have been; nothing to reveal his fate to those who may have loved him as a son, a husband or a father. Yet his calloused hands and the bulging muscles of his forearms were sure indicators that here was one of *Titanic's* missing crew.

The undertakers drying and cleaning the body knew exactly what had to be done. The corpse was hastily but tidily sewn into a clean and fresh shroud, along with pieces of scrap iron to weight its passage to the sea bed. It was prepared and prayed over before joining scores more dead bodies being consigned together forever to the ocean depths. The mass funeral service took more than an hour.

A second body in a coffin on deck had received far different treatment. As the unknown crewman's corpse splashed over the gunwales and back into the ocean, one of the undertaker's assistants was listing the possessions of a fellow *Titanic* victim. The belongings of the two men could hardly have been more different:

## NO. 124   MALE   ESTIMATED AGE 50   LIGHT HAIR & MOUSTACHE

**EFFECTS** – Gold watch; cuff links, gold with diamond; diamond ring with three stones; £225 in English notes; $2440 in notes; £5 in gold; 7s. in silver; 5 ten franc pieces; gold pencil; pocketbook.

**CLOTHING** – Blue serge suit; blue handkerchief with 'A.V.'; belt with gold buckle; brown boots with red rubber soles; brown flannel shirt; 'J.J.A.' on back of collar.

The apparent wealth suggested by the list of this body's possessions was hardly surprising; it was the body of New York hotel owner Colonel John Jacob Astor, after whom part of the famous Waldorf-Astoria hotel had been named. He was reputedly the richest man on board *Titanic* on the night she hit the iceberg. He was on his way home from an extended European honeymoon with his eighteen-year-old second wife, Madeleine. She had found a place in the lifeboats, Colonel Astor had not.

On the deck of the cable ship *Mackay-Bennett*, a professional embalmer worked to examine, undress and clean dozens of bodies being pulled from the sea. The corpses were hard to bring on board, dressed as they were in heavy, waterlogged clothing and strapped into the heavy canvas life-jackets that had kept them afloat. Despite their prolonged exposure to the water, many of the bodies had decomposed less than the undertakers had feared. Soft tissue was wrinkled, and in places disintegrating, some bodily extremities were missing but most would have been almost recognisable to those who knew them in life. It was when bodies sank to the ocean floor that the real ocean scavengers, the crabs and bottom-dwellers, could really get to work.

The embalming team recovering *Titanic*'s victims had some tough decisions to make. Several dozen of their undertaker colleagues from all over Nova Scotia were waiting in their home port of Halifax to handle the scores of bodies the ship had been expected to find. In reality this grim harvest of dead bodies from the sea had been far more productive than that. Over the course of several days of searching, hundreds of people had been sighted near the location where *Titanic* was believed to have sunk.[1] The ship was running short of supplies of ice, coffins, canvas and even embalming fluid.

Canadian law prohibited the landing of an un-embalmed dead body so those corpses that had deteriorated or been damaged to the point where there was little hope of identification were being returned to the sea. A minister on board conducted an appropriate divine service for a burial at sea. The irony of pulling bodies from the water, simply to examine and dress them and push them back in again had not been lost on those forced to take part in the ritual. But their choices were limited.

There was an unconscious class distinction also taking place in the process. Victims from First Class tended to be better dressed and have more distinctive means of identification. There were signet rings, wallets and cigarette cases for the gentlemen; purses or identifiable jewellery for the ladies. Their bodies were more likely to be embalmed and eventually landed in Halifax, for burial there or to await collection by grieving relatives or friends. Some of the wealthy families had also offered rewards for the discovery of their loved-ones' bodies.

Third Class passengers had little or no possessions that had survived the scramble to leave the sinking ship, or the prolonged immersion in Atlantic seawater. They were more likely to go back to the water. Most problematic of all were the bodies of the few stokers, the coal trimmers and engine room greasers and engineers who had escaped from the bowels of the ship. The temperatures in the boiler rooms and engine compartments meant they had worn as little as possible. There was little chance of them carrying paper identification or clothing other than overalls and a vest. They were the most likely of all to be buried at sea. Even in death, the class hierarchy of *Titanic* was being maintained.

By the end of the week more than 100 corpses had been buried at sea. The funeral ship returned to Halifax with nearly 200 bodies; three other chartered ships, between them, landed fewer than a dozen others. Teams of embalmers worked in a local indoor curling rink to prepare those landed ashore to be buried or transported by rail or sea to their final resting place. Many of the bodies were, in due course, reclaimed by their families and taken home for burial, but others were interred in the tiny cemetery in town. A handful would never be identified.[2] The ship had sighted fields of flotsam from the sinking, but more than 1,000 of the victims were never found.

It had been just one week since the *Titanic* had sunk and 1,490 people were left behind to perish as her too few lifeboats rowed or sailed away into the darkness. The shocked survivors had been safely landed in New York by the *Carpathia*. Those who could go home to their loved ones were already on their way but many of *Titanic's* officers and crew were detained in America to give evidence in the then newly-announced US Senate hearing into the loss of the ship. Travel plans initially made by the surviving White Star managing director, Bruce Ismay, had been thrown into disarray. He too was told he may not leave America until questions had been answered.

The ambitious and publicity seeking politician from Michigan, Senator William Alden Smith, was chairing the US hearing, which technically was operating as a sub-committee of the Senate Committee on Commerce. In a twist of fate, as J.J. Astor's body was being unloaded in Nova Scotia, the inquiry into the circumstances of his death, and the death of 1,399 others, was being opened at the Waldorf-Astoria Hotel in New York.

The inquiry, which was subsequently transferred to Washington, was to last almost three weeks and to hear evidence from passengers and crew, as well as from executives of the White Star Line and *Titanic's* ultimate owners, the International Mercantile Marine Company. It achieved little other than recording people's recollections of the event whilst they were still fresh in their memory. The inquiry was particularly notable for its complete failure to question anybody who could have given them expert information about the strength and the structure of the ship itself.

In London it was clear that a marine disaster on such a scale, with the loss of so many lives on a British registered ship, could not escape a far more searching and detailed investigation. The survivors, the bereaved relatives, Members of Parliament, seamen's unions and the deeply shocked British public were all demanding answers. The clamour for an inquiry held two main dangers for the Government and for the civil servants of the British Board of Trade. For more than sixty years the Board had been charged with looking after the safety of Britain's sailors and her citizens venturing out to sea. It was thus directly responsible for both the regulations governing the number of lifeboats carried on *Titanic* and for inspecting the ship's structural integrity and its strength to withstand what might befall it at sea. It was open to criticism on both counts.

Fortunately for the politicians and civil servants involved, there was a safety net. The London investigations into the death of *Titanic* were legal proceedings conducted as a 'court of summary jurisdiction'. Such a court does not require a jury. The procedure was regulated by clause five of Section 466 of the Merchant Shipping Act of 1894, which empowered the British Board of Trade to order an investigation into the loss of any ship anywhere in the world 'as long as any witness is found in the United Kingdom.' The same Act laid a duty on the body requesting the investigation to 'superintend the management of the case, and to render such assistance to the court as is in his power.'

The provisions of the then 18-year-old Act of Parliament therefore gave complete control over the investigation into the loss of *Titanic* to the one government department that was potentially most likely to be criticised by its findings. In effect, the body most likely to become a defendant in the court was also required to 'superintend the management of the case'. It was not the most promising start to an allegedly impartial study of the affair. The chances of a searching and even-handed investigation were not improved when 71-year-old retired judge, Lord Mersey, was appointed to run the proceedings.

Mersey had built his entire career as a barrister on his success in defending wealthy ship-owners and shipping companies in the courts around his home town of Liverpool. His commercial work had made him one of the wealthiest lawyers in England. His reputation was as an awkward, short-tempered and not very successful judge who had little sympathy for listening to anyone whose views differed from his own. Indeed, in his later obituary, *The Times* clearly struggled to avoid overt criticism:

> He cannot justly be placed among the greatest Judges of his time … he was far from being an eloquent or even elegant speaker; in manner he was sometimes more than brusque, though by nature he was kindly, especially to young men; to solicitors he seemed sometimes to be overbearing; and in his treatment of witnesses he was often rough.

Perhaps more importantly for the Liberal Government of the day, Mersey had also stood as a Liberal Parliamentary candidate several times before winning a seat and having a brief and totally unremarkable career as a Liberal MP. He had retired on the grounds of ill health some ten years earlier and had then been given the title 'Baron Mersey of Toxteth'.[3] It was hard to see him as the ideal choice for an impartial wreck commissioner seeking the truth about how and why *Titanic* met her doom, but the Board of Trade brushed aside criticism of his appointment and the Wreck Commissioner's Court duly began its sittings on Thursday, 2nd May 1912.

In line with their duty to manage the proceedings the Board of Trade's main lawyer, Attorney-General Sir Rufus Isaacs, expressed the Government's sympathy to the bereaved:

> My Lord, this terrible disaster in mid-ocean, both because in mere magnitude it exceeds any calamity in the history of the mercantile marine, and also because of many of its harrowing incidents, has in a profound and marked degree, touched the heart of the nation.

It was a moving opening to the proceedings but, unfortunately, very few people in the court could hear it. In the cavernous surroundings of the grand Scottish Hall at Westminster, the barristers, clerks, witnesses, reporters and the public could watch the proceedings but barely hear them. The acoustics of the hall meant that Lord Mersey himself spent a great deal of time leaning forward and straining to hear what was going on. A small, unprepossessing man, he finally admitted that he was having a problem:

> You must bear in mind that I suffer from the infirmity of deafness. You do not speak so that I can hear you. Do not whisper … Let me know what you are saying.

Despite complaints from many of the lawyers, and despite promising from the first day that the hearing would be moved to a more suitable location, Mersey then decided to press on in the same location. The acoustics were later improved by rearranging the seating but it still led to multiple cases of witnesses and lawyers being chastised by Mersey for mumbling, or of him misunderstanding or mis-hearing the evidence:

Lord Mersey: '... I am not following this.'

Sir Rufus Isaacs: 'Neither am I, my Lord; I did not even hear it. Do you mind telling us again what you said then? I could not hear you. Try to speak up?'

'Did he ever find it thick?'

'I said "thickening", my Lord.'

'I thought you said "thick"; were you in a fog when this accident happened?'

'No.'

'You must not whisper your answers. Speak up so that we can hear you.'

Throughout the thirty-six days of the Inquiry Lord Mersey reserved his harshest sarcasm and his constant interruptions for the small band of barristers whom he had reluctantly allowed into the court to represent seamen's unions and the interests of the passengers who had travelled on *Titanic's* maiden voyage. Time after time, the non-government lawyers were interrupted as they struggled to get their point across or to ask awkward questions of witnesses. Lord Mersey's final verdict on the case was to criticise the captain for travelling too fast and to offer minor criticism to the Board of Trade for their lengthy delay in updating the regulations governing lifeboat provision.

The Inquiry's biggest failure was, however, to unquestioningly accept the veracity of *Titanic's* 'Big Lie'.

All involved, from Lord Mersey downwards, apparently accepted without a qualm the supposition that *Titanic's* outer hull had no weaknesses at all. Indeed, one of the main independent voices at the London hearing, the seamen's union lawyer, Thomas Scanlan, was so convinced of *Titanic's* strength that he gave the ship a clean bill of health at the very start of his address to the court:

As to the construction of the *Titanic*, I do not think it is necessary for me to deal with this aspect of the case, because I feel I am justified to proceed on the assumption that this ship was in a perfectly seaworthy condition, and that what befell it was due not to the condition of the ship, but to the seamanship and skill, or want of seamanship and skill, and the want of proper directions as to her navigation.

The lack of any concern or investigation into the basic strength of *Titanic* was an astonishing omission in the post-sinking inquiries. Rivets were barely mentioned at the British Inquiry, and the word was never spoken at all in the

American Senate hearing. Nobody appears to have given the slightest thought to this most essential component in *Titanic's* construction.

For a century and more, few have examined the 'Big Lie' about the *Titanic*. A romantic myth has been perpetuated that the *Titanic* was the 'ship magnificent'; skilfully constructed, from the finest of materials and with no expense spared to produce the safest and most luxurious ship afloat. The legend was launched even before *Titanic* herself was launched from her Belfast slipway. Both Harland and Wolff and the White Star Line repeatedly told a respectful press and public that *Titanic* had been built by Britain's 'finest shipyard'.

It was an easy claim to make; but a claim that any critical examination would have shown has been made, since shipbuilding began, by every one of many other shipbuilders who claim to operate the 'finest shipyard' in Britain.

Equally, the claim was made that nothing as sordid as money had been allowed to interfere with Harland and Wolff's task of building the finest ship in the world. The shipyard just spent what it wanted to spend, and White Star was happy to pay all the costs – and add on a little extra payment of five per cent as a modest profit for all the shipyard's efforts.

On the grounds that if you repeat any story enough times it will be perceived as the truth, the 'Perfect *Titanic*' myth was soon being further perpetuated by the White Star Line's managing director, Bruce Ismay, at the various inquiries that followed her sinking. Even though he had, himself, barely escaped from the sinking ship, Ismay took every opportunity to drive his point home. From day one of the United States Senate hearing he conspicuously refused to apologise for the ship having sunk, and instead publicly reinforced his official message that *Titanic* had been built without regard to the cost:

> The ship was built in Belfast. She was the latest thing in the art of shipbuilding; absolutely no money was spared in her construction. She was not built by contract. She was simply built on a commission.

In later responses to the Commission Chairman, Ismay insisted once again that the shipbuilders had been encouraged to spend anything and everything they needed:

'They have carte blanche to build the ship and put everything of the very best into that ship, and after they have spent all the money they can on her they add on their commission to the gross cost of the ship, which we pay them. We would naturally try to get the best ship we possibly could. We wanted the best ship crossing the north Atlantic when we built her.'

'And you made no limitation as to cost?'

'Absolutely none.'

Ismay's apparent disregard for any form of cost-control within his company was discussed once again at the London inquiry. His account of how he gave free-rein to the shipbuilders, Harland and Wolff, was succinctly summed-up by British Attorney-General, Sir Rufus Isaacs:

'So that what it amounts to, if I follow you correctly, is, that there is no limit placed by you upon the cost of the vessel?'

'Absolutely none. All we ask them to do is to produce us the very finest ship they possibly can; the question of money has never been considered at all.'

It was an astonishing claim for any company managing director to make. Ismay was consistently claiming that he had agreed the purchase of the three biggest ships in the world – without ever considering the cost. Even more astonishing was the fact that nobody ever questioned his statement more closely. None of the official inquisitors ever asked for a shred of proof that his statements were true. Equally, none ever called, as a witness, the man who held the real power to control how, when and why *Titanic* had been built; the multi-millionaire, American banker, John Pierpoint Morgan. Indeed, the name of Morgan, the financier who pulled all of *Titanic's* strings, was mentioned just twice in the entire US Senate hearing and not at all in its British counterpart.

It was, of course, in the interests of both the American-owned company, of which Ismay was the mouthpiece, and of Harland and Wolff that nobody should ever question whether financial pressures had contributed to the loss of *Titanic*. Ismay remained adamant throughout that money was never of any importance. To quote a phrase famously uttered in a London courtroom half a century later: 'He would say that, wouldn't he?' His statements were a travesty of the truth.

*Titanic* was constructed under the constraints of enormous financial pressures from Morgan and his American banks that, to all intents and purposes, owned and controlled the ship. When *Titanic* was planned they were losing money hand-over-fist from their reluctant involvement in the Atlantic shipping trade. Moreover, the year 1907, when final plans were being made for the ship, was a particularly disastrous time for the banks. Stock market crashes around the world and an historic crisis of Wall Street confidence in 1907 were also piling up losses in other areas of their financial operations.[4]

As importantly, the ship was built in a shipyard where the workload was overstretching both men and resources, where morale was low and wage demands were getting higher by the day. The decision to build *Titanic* and her sister ships in Belfast was forced upon her owners by a confidential agreement drawn up a decade before. An agreement crafted and negotiated in secret to the lasting benefit of one man, the shrewd and calculating Chairman of Harland and Wolff, Lord William Pirrie. He was running a shipyard that was struggling to cope with demand.

## Notes

1. The incorrect radio position messages on the night of the sinking may have led the recovery ship to search the wrong area.

2. In recent years attempts have been made with varying success to identify victims by the use of DNA examination.

3. Several years after the *Titanic* court case, Baron Mersey was elevated to the rank of 1st Viscount Mersey.

4. Morgan was very well aware of the 1907 crisis. His calm demeanour in the face of huge losses was credited with restoring confidence and calming the markets.

# Chapter Twenty-Five

# 'Scaffolding not sufficient for the work . . .'

5.25 pm
13 June 1911
Scaffolding on B deck level
Ship 401
Harland and Wolff's shipyard
Queen's Island, Belfast

Nearing the end of a gruelling eleven-hour working day, the men of Harland and Wolff's Belfast shipyard were ready to go home to their families. On wooden scaffolding boards, 50 feet above No. 3 slipway of the Queen's Island yard, teams of muscular riveters lay down their heavy hammers, and retrieved the jackets and shirts they had discarded in the heat of the working day. The small charcoal braziers on which their rivets were heated were being doused and stacked-away to await the next day's shift. The scaffolding on which they had been working stood alongside the hull of '401', the shipyard number that was allocated to the vessel on the day she was ordered. Only when this ship was launched would she become the *Titanic*.

In theory, all of the men then hurriedly preparing to go home were guilty of breaking the 'Rules': the printed sheet of regulations that strictly governed the conduct of every man in the Harland and Wolff yard. Rule No. 12 was clear: 'No stopping work or preparing to stop before time.'[1] But with the great ship by then nearing completion and with the end-of-shift klaxon just a short while away, the foremen had been more relaxed of late. Discipline had slipped just a little. A tragedy was about to happen.

Others around him might have been packing up the tools from their workstations on top of the somewhat shaky, wooden platform, but rivet-counter Robert James Murphy was still hard at work – 'counting' rivets. His task was more important, and a great deal more skilful, than it sounds. Three million rivets were all that was holding *Titanic* together. The blunt-ended metal pegs fastened each steel plate of the hull to the overlapping edge of its neighbour. Heated until they expanded and softened a little, the rivets had been placed into holes already punched through the double thickness of the plates. A single head on one end of the rivet held it in place while the other end was hammered flat. The then squashed rivet pinched the two pieces of the hull together. Each rivet then cooled and contracted, shortening slightly to tighten the joint even further. In a world of engineering perfection, strong metal rivets, skilfully driven home, impart immense strength to any ship. But few jobs are ever perfect. Metal defects in the rivet, a misjudgement of the temperature to which it is heated or a misplaced blow from a riveter's hammer can all produce a faulty joint.

The rivet-counter's task was to find the faulty rivets.

In his endless search for any imperfections, Robert Murphy was armed with a small metal hammer. Walking along the scaffold boards at the side of the ship, he tapped lightly on each and every rivet head. Rather like a piano tuner on a gargantuan scale, Robert could tell a lot from the sound of a single tap on a rivet. For many years he worked as a riveter himself, hammering down the ends of millions of rivets at this Harland and Wolff yard. But the immense strength needed to swing a hammer for hour after back-breaking hour made riveting a young man's job. Then aged forty-nine and with decades of experience, Robert's ears were of more use to the shipyard than his muscles. He could instantly differentiate the telltale dull thud of a faultily-driven rivet from the ringing tone of one that had properly cooled in place and was clamping the ship's plates together with all the strength of solid iron. Some rivets that failed Robert's rivet-counting test may simply have needed additional 'caulking' – the skilled hammering of metal edges to tighten the rivet's grip; others needed to be drilled out and replaced.

Hand-riveting was among the most skilled of all shipbuilding tasks. It called for skill and judgement, not only by the man who wields the hammer, but also by the team of assistants he recruited to help him. For this was a group activity. Each riveter needed his team to run like a well-oiled machine, delivering the right size of rivet, heated to precisely the correct temperature, at just the right time, to just the right hole where it could be hammered flat in the shortest possible time. Being paid by the rivet, rather than by the hour, put pressure on everyone to work like an automaton; like the anchor chains of *Titanic*, the rivet team were only as strong as their weakest link.

The chain began with the 'heater-boy', whose job it was to tend the charcoal brazier and heat the brand new rivet. Ensuring the correct temperature of his coals was all important. Too cold and the rivet head would fail to flatten properly under the blow of the hammer; too hot and the metal of a 'burned' rivet might have weakened and distorted. With neither thermometer nor time for measurements to be taken, the heater-boy judged temperature by eye. Experience alone taught them the precise cherry-red shade that glowed from a perfectly heated rivet. For that reason, many heater-boys belied their name by being older men who knew a good hot rivet when they saw one.

From the moment that a rivet was just hot enough, time was of the essence. Snatching the rivet from the flames with his tongs, the heater-boy flung it through the air to the 'catcher-boy', who caught it in the layer of ash that lined the bottom of his leather bucket. Burns were an occupational hazard for this youngest member of the team, either from a carelessly flung and badly caught rivet, or by having the still hot metal flung back at his head by an angry riveter who believed his team were letting him down.

The penultimate man was the 'holder-up' – uniquely known in the Belfast yards as a 'houler-on' – who positioned each rivet in its hole. He used the weight of his own hammer to press the rivet in place against the thunderous quick-fire blows of the riveter himself as he flattened the end against the far side of the overlapping metal plates. On some rivet squads two hammer men were used, each of their blows perfectly synchronised, one after the other, to rhythmically shape the perfect rivet point.

For the team to earn good money in their fortnightly wage packet, they needed to repeat the same elaborate sequence to perfection, time and again, shift after shift, day after day. Harland and Wolff's riveters were paid on a piece-work basis; the faster they worked and the more perfect rivets they hammered, the greater their wages. Conversely, every defective rivet that Robert found reduced their pay. It meant that rivet counters were not always the most popular men in the yard. Robert, however, was an exception. His years of working on the rivet teams at Harland and Wolff had built up close and lasting friendships. They drank together in the pubs near Robert's family home in Hillman Street, just a short walk away from the gates of the sprawling shipyard. Many of his workmates had been guests at the wedding when Robert married his wife, Susan, fourteen years earlier, and their children had since grown up alongside the couple's own four sons and three daughters.

Riveters were known as the 'hard men' of Belfast, the undisputed kings of the shipyard jungle. Young apprentices quickly learned the old shipyard saying: 'Never ask a riveter where the last rivet goes – he just might show you.'[2] And all of them knew that old riveters never died; they came back as the seagulls, wheeling over Harland and Wolff, 'to crap on the new-fangled welders below.' Bound together by the hardships of their job, the entire riveting community had come together the previous year to help Robert and Susan cope with a devastating family tragedy. The Murphy's eldest son, Robert James 'Junior', had died in a shipyard accident. Robert's eldest son had followed in his father's, and his grandfather's, footsteps to work at Harland

and Wolff. But soon after celebrating his 'coming-of-age' twenty-first birthday, the young man had been killed while working on *Titanic's* sister ship, the *Olympic*. The boy's death was to make what happened next to Robert James 'Senior', all the harder to bear.

Accounts differed slightly in recounting the events of the late afternoon. Everyone agreed that Robert Murphy had suddenly tumbled, helplessly, straight down the side of *Titanic* to crack his skull as he landed on the concrete slipway 50 feet below. But there were differing versions as to *why* Robert fell. Reporters from the local newspaper, the *Belfast Weekly News*, got their facts from a helpful manager at the Harland and Wolff yard:[3]

### QUEEN'S ISLAND FALL

A Riveter's Terrible Fall

On the 15 inst., just before the ending of the work day at six o'clock at the Queen's Island, a riveter named Robert Murphy, Hillman Street, when employed on the *Titanic*, missed his hold and fell from one of the upper decks, a distance of 50 feet. Assistance was immediately forthcoming and the injured man was conveyed in the ambulance of the Royal Victoria Hospital. In that institution it was discovered that he was suffering from a fracture to the base of the skull. Recovery from the first was quite hopeless, and he expired sometime after admission. What makes the accident a peculiarly sad one is that a son of the deceased man, Robert Murphy, was fatally injured some time ago when working on the *Olympic*.

It was not until several days later at an inquest held on the 16 June that the true picture emerged of how Robert met his death. The Belfast City Coroner, James Graham, first heard formal evidence of identification from a member of Robert's family, and then the details of his injuries from one of the hospital doctors who had tried to save his life. The doctor informed the court that the fall had caused a compound fracture of the skull and that his patient had died of shock from the irrecoverable injuries he had received. But there was yet further evidence to come from Robert's colleagues. They revealed that the rivet counter had fallen, not because he 'missed his hold' on the high platform, but rather because part of the boarding had collapsed from underneath him and had tipped him over the side to his death.

Having considered all of the evidence, the eight men on the coroner's jury agreed that it was faulty scaffolding that had caused Robert Murphy to fall. In more recent times such a finding could have led to health and safety or criminal negligence investigations. In the less safety-conscious era of 1911, the coroner contented himself with recording that Robert's death was 'accidental' and recording a note of the jury's more detailed findings:

Mr Murphy died while working on the *Titanic*. He fell from staging which in the jury's opinion was not sufficient for the work for which it was used.

No newspapers bothered to seek any comment from Robert's employers, and there is no record of any compensation payments being made to Robert's widow and her six surviving children.[4]

Any major engineering project is, of course, a risky business, and constructing a large ship is truly 'heavy engineering'. Steel plates and castings weighing hundreds of tons swing high through the air, molten metal pours from furnaces, gigantic hydraulic presses stamp down with thousands of pounds of pressure. Men and women work with heavy machinery in hot, crowded and cramped conditions. In modern factories, despite what some would regard as a plethora of health and safety legislation, accidents do still happen. In those early years of the twentieth century, when the safety of working men was a far lesser concern for their bosses, a shipyard was an infinitely more dangerous place.

Some of those dangers were summed up by author Jean Hunter in her book *Steel Chest, Nail in the Boot and the Barking Dog*, which got its title from nicknames of riveters in the Harland and Wolff yard:

> ... accidents could easily claim a victim in the shipyard. Falls from 70-foot high gantries, electrocution, severed limbs, burns, asbestos poisoning and the blinks were just some of the dangers facing the men in the yard, as they plied their trade. The 'blinks' was an irritation of the eye caused by watching the arc light of the welding torch for too long. It has been likened to having sand thrown in your eyes. If a worker had been killed on the job, the news would pass among the men with the phrase: 'he's away to the other yard.'

Even so, the unfortunate twin deaths in the Murphy family were perhaps an indicator of a deeper malaise within the busy Belfast shipyard; one of an increasing number of signs that Harland and Wolff's management may have bitten off more than they could chew in trying to cope with the simultaneous construction of *Olympic* and *Titanic*, and the fast approaching build of their third planned sister ship, *Britannic*. Robert Senior was by no means the first man to die in the construction of *Titanic*, and he would not be the last. He was actually one of four men who died in the same month. The Murphy family's father and son had joined a steadily lengthening list of casualties by then being recorded in the Belfast yard.

The Harland and Wolff board of managing directors received regular monthly updates on every accident and fatality in both the outside yard and the engine works. As the number of employees and the workload increased, the number of accidents followed suit. In 1908 there were a total of 670 accidents;

by 1910, the figures had risen to 758, and by 1911, to 946. The tragedies occurred because of health and safety practices that seem primitive by today's standards but were normal for the early twentieth century.

The lack of any checks to see that each worker had safely left the yard at the end of their shift led to the sad case of 16-year-old George Scott in January 1911. An inquest into his death heard that he had fallen from scaffolding onto *Titanic's* lowest deck, the tank top, and fractured his skull. His body had lain undiscovered inside the ship all night until his colleagues had started work again the next morning. The coroner commented that checking each and every worker would be difficult in the yard, which at that time was employing more than 11,000 workers every day.

The accident figures reported to the board were subdivided into categories, revealing how many of the injuries were minor, how many serious, and how many had proved to be fatal. The monthly returns peaked in November 1911, when 112 men were injured in just one month. The board minutes record no expressions of regret or sympathy that may have been expressed by Harland and Wolff's directors, but they do detail the costs of each class of accident. The families of the eight men who died whilst *Titanic* was under construction received total payments of £1,133 18s 2d. The injuries of a further twenty-eight men were considered to be so severe that they would be unable to work again; they were paid a total of £2,854 13s 0d between them. Two hundred and eighteen men in the category of less serious injuries were paid compensation averaging £3 19s 2d each. To put this into perspective, the First Class parlour suites on *Titanic* cost around £660 for the one-way trip to New York, although that would cover accommodation for two and at least one servant.

At one board meeting the directors considered the 30/- a month cost of employing a 'masseur', who provided a rudimentary form of physiotherapy to badly injured workers. The Harland and Wolff official boardroom minute book contains a note of their deliberations but no indication of their final decision:

> There were suggestions that the cost was only marginally useful. One workman who severely burned both hands in an accident involving a boiling vat of pitch had agreed to give up his claim against the company and settle for the compensation on offer 'partly to avoid the pain of further treatment with the masseur.' It was pointed out to the Board that it would be useful in compensation cases reaching court to be able to say to the Judge that they had offered the masseur services.

The accident rate of any enterprise is a measure not only of how busy that business may be but also of other problems, perhaps of poor management or an inadequate workforce. Unskilled and less experienced men tend to have more accidents than their skilled and experienced counterparts, and by this stage of *Titanic's* construction, Harland and Wolff were finding skilled and experienced men harder to come by. A shortage of expertise in one particular shipbuilding trade was proving of particular concern, and would one day hasten the death of *Titanic*: they could not find enough good men for the riveting teams.

It was not a new problem for the Harland and Wolff yard or for other shipbuilders in times when new ships were being constructed as fast as the yards could turn them out. Even a decade before *Titanic* was finally launched, the *Engineer and Naval Architect* magazine was reporting that the Belfast yards were working flat out:

> Both the engine shops and parts of the boiler-shops of Messrs Harland & Wolff Limited are working double shifts, and the same remarks apply to Messrs Workman, Clark.

The same periodical also reported on a perennial problem among the 'hard men' of the shipyard; their heavy drinking, which it warned was leading to '... irregular attendance at work, especially on the part of the riveters engaged on a ship.'

> This unconscionable disregard of other people's wellbeing displayed by some of these men has become quite a scandal; for it is no uncommon thing to see groups of drillers, labourers, and rivet heaters laid idle by the wilful abstention from work of a number of the riveters engaged on a ship. It is time that this evil was seriously grappled with. If England is to hold her honourable place in the march of industry, it must be seen to that drink indulgence does not interfere with work.

As construction of *Olympic*, *Titanic* and other ships gathered pace, the board of Harland and Wolff became increasingly concerned about the problem of finding the right riveters and their teams. The 1911 Belfast Census lists more than 600 men who gave their occupation as 'riveter in the shipyard', as well as hundreds of other rivet and heater-boys.[5] Even so, there were not enough.

Against the backdrop of the White Star Line's continuing financial woes, the board, and Lord Pirrie in particular, were making every effort to cut costs and resist wages demands. In the same month that the first 3,000 tons of rivets and 13,000 tons of steel plates were delivered for *Olympic*, the directors attempted to save money by cutting wage rates throughout the yard. They were, however, worried about the prospect of their skilled riveters defecting to their rival yard on the opposite side of the river. The board minutes book records how they tried to resolve the dilemma:

> The question of reduction in wages was considered and it was moved by the Chairman that, provided Messrs. Workman Clarke intimated

their intention of taking similar action, notices of reduction in wages should be sent by today's post.

Unluckily for Harland and Wolf, their approach to their shipbuilding rivals was rebuffed the same day. Lord Pirrie was told that his rival company were 'sitting on the fence' about the issue and the plan to cut wages was then shelved indefinitely. In fact, far from reducing wages, the growing demand for skilled men forced the Harland and Wolff management to accede to a series of wage demands over the period when *Titanic* was under construction. At a late stage of the hull's construction they were forced to agree to the then sizable increase of 'one farthing an hour, or one shilling a week and five per cent extra on piece work rates' for all riveters and holder-ups.

Despite his irregular attendance at board meetings, Lord Pirrie was repeatedly involved in the search for riveters. At one stage, he told his fellow directors that he had read of another yard where work 'was a little slack' and suggested that they should be approached as a possible source of extra rivet squads. On another occasion he personally met with rival shipbuilders seeking joint agreement for a bonus scheme that would reward riveters for good attendance at work. The scheme was briefly tried but then abandoned because it had little effect on the men.

In a 1911 letter to the board, Lord Pirrie chided them for ignoring his earlier warnings that piece-work payments might be higher in other shipyard areas and this could cost them skilled men:

> As I pointed out to the Management years ago, when we could not get good riveters, it [is] essential that we should have only men of the very best class on our books, and it is obvious that they will not stay with us if they can get better pay elsewhere.

Lord Pirrie was right to have been concerned that only the very best men should be used as riveters to construct the *Titanic*. There was much that could go wrong in the process of riveting the giant steel plates of the hull to her cross-beams and spars. Each plate was secured with rows of rivets spaced just a few inches apart; sometimes two, three, four or more rows at the edge of each plate for additional strength. The riveter had to hammer the point of each rivet with just enough pressure to tighten it down, without loosening the grip of its neighbours already pounded into place.

The best riveters knew precisely when to stop 'chasing the weepers', and resist the temptation to hammer too hard. And that decision had to be correctly taken within the average three seconds that it took for the next rivet in line to be waiting for its hammer blows. Every hesitation would cost seconds and those seconds add up for a riveter driving thousands of rivets a week on a piece-rate wage.

The best riveters could 'feel' through their hammer heads if the massive steel plates had a metal burr on the faying edges being pressed together; if the hole was not perfectly aligned or mis-shapenly punched; or if the rivet temperature was not quite perfect – 'burned' by being heated too long or removed from the forge too long before the sparks started to fly.

The best riveters could pick the best teams, knowing that their heater-boys would see the correct glow, that their catcher boys would swiftly deliver, and their houler-on would correctly press the rivet head fair in its hole against the hammer blows to come. As *Practical Ship Production*, a contemporary early twentieth century handbook for riveting, explained:

> Riveting requires considerable skill and great strength and endurance. If the slightest deflection takes place some of the rivets or seams are almost sure to start leaking. If many unfair holes occur this will be a serious matter and may endanger the ship.

Over the months before *Titanic* set out on her maiden voyage there were to be more and more indications that the quality of the riveting on *Titanic* and her sister *Olympic* were perhaps not up to the task. The first clues came even before the construction of *Titanic* was finished, when *Olympic* crossed the Atlantic Ocean in one of the fiercest winter storms it would ever encounter.

### Notes

1. The 'Rules' dated from May 1888 and threatened fines or dismissal for a wide range of misdemeanours including 'Rule 9' for loss of tools, '16' for work spoiled by carelessness, '7' for neglecting a foreman's orders and '14' no smoking or preparing of food. If all else failed, the company retained a failsafe final rule of fining 'for any irregularity not mentioned in the Rules'.
2. The answer, of course, is: 'in the last hole'.
3. The newspaper (P.12, 15/06/1911) got several facts wrong. The fall occurred a little earlier in the afternoon than stated, and on the 13th of the month.
4. Harland and Wolff may eventually have paid some compensation. Susan Murphy duly inherited £84 1s.0d from her late husband's estate.
5. The Census records six woman riveters – in every case, an error on the Census form: particularly obvious because one 'riveter', named Elizabeth, was six years old.

# Chapter Twenty-Six

# 'Gigantic Waves . . . Ships in Peril'

January 14 1912
The bridge of Steamship *St Louis*
Position: 41° 37' N, 57° 48' W
600 miles from Boston
North Atlantic Ocean

It was one of the worst storms in living memory. From the bridge of the 11,000 ton transatlantic liner *St Louis*, Captain Frank Passow had ordered sand spread across the planking to help deckhands keep their feet in the heavy ice building up on the decks and rigging. In more than twenty-five years at sea, the captain had never seen such mountainous waves and freezing conditions on this regular run from Southampton to New York. In his cabin below decks the ship's surgeon, William Simpson, resorted to nailing his possessions and medical kit down onto the table, but the ship was heaving so much that it pulled the nails from the wood and flung everything he owned around the cabin. The *St Louis* was barely making its way forward in the face of the fearsome January gale.[1]

Across the Atlantic seaboard of North America hurricane force winds and record low temperatures, plunging as low as minus 40 degrees Celsius, were bringing death and destruction on land. In New York City, more than 1,000 homeless men and women sought refuge from the abnormally cold weather in emergency charity shelters. By the following morning a dozen rough-sleepers had been found frozen to death in icy doorways, on the sidewalks and in snow-covered parks across the city. Trucks supplying the ferries of the Battery in Lower Manhattan were no longer running; five of them had been blown over by the wind and lay on their sides in the street. In the Bronx, gusts of wind were so strong between the buildings that they blew two pedestrians, 18-year-old clerk Florence Seixas and 72-year-old jeweller Joseph Klipper, off their feet and into the road. Both had then been hit by cars and were now in the Lebanon Hospital. Florence went on to make a full recovery but with multiple fractures to both legs, Joseph was not expected to survive the night.

But it was at sea that the gales were threatening the greatest danger. An entire squadron of US Navy torpedo-destroyers, en route to a naval exercise off the coast of Guantanamo Bay, had been scattered by the winds. Three of the small ships were missing while five others had limped, heavily damaged, into port at Hamilton, Bermuda. Under the headline 'Gigantic Waves – Ships In Peril', the *New York Times* reported the Fleet Commander's comments: 'The worst seas I've ever known; I fear for my men.'[2] For other vessels the worst fears had already come true: off the New Jersey coast an unidentified schooner had foundered with the loss of all hands. The following day the tips of her masts and sails still showed above the waves and the wind was so fierce that it continued to push the wreck towards the shore. On the other side of the Atlantic, a further four vessels had been sunk off the coast of Scotland. In the middle of the Atlantic, heading for New York with 742 passengers on board and steaming through the heart of the storm, was the flagship of the White Star shipping line, the biggest ship afloat, the 45,000 ton Royal Mail Ship *Olympic*.

Passengers cowering below decks were terrified as the ship was repeatedly lifted high by the wave crests and then dropped into their troughs. Some waves were of such a size that they broke over her lower decks. The water surged across the ship with enough force to wrench metal fittings from their mountings and wash them overboard. Part of the deck railings were bent apart and hatch covers lifted and tore away in the wind. Even so, the *Olympic* safely came through the tempest with just a minor delay to her scheduled New York arrival time. Company executives were grateful that their ultimate boss, the American banker J.P. Morgan, who effectively owned *Olympic*, was not on board to witness and share the passengers' discomfort. Just one week earlier, the financier had travelled on *Olympic* from New York to Cherbourg, making one of his regular transatlantic trips to purchase additions to his vast collection of European works of art. The weather then had been very different; enjoying the luxury of the ship's most expensive private promenade suite, Morgan had made the trip in what he described as 'perfectly smooth sailing conditions'.

The record-breaking wind and waves of the 1912 winter are among the worst storms that the White Star Line's *Olympic* would ever have to face and yet the minor damage to the decks of the newly-launched Harland and Wolff-built ship was soon repaired. *Olympic* appeared to have survived her Atlantic ordeal with flying colours. It boded well for her sister ship, *Titanic*, then nearing completion and being readied for her own maiden voyage in three months' time. But before the *Titanic* was finished, the damage to *Olympic* would prove to be more than just skin-deep.

Even before the January 1912 storms, *Olympic* had not had the luckiest of starts to her sailing career. She had been launched amid a fanfare of publicity less than fifteen months earlier on 20 October 1910. The first of an embarrassingly large number of accidents happened on that very first day. It was, in reality, a minor bump against a buttress in the river Lagan, although the event was later spectacularly over-dramatised at the London inquiry into *Titanic's* demise. Barrister William Harbinson, representing many of the Third Class passengers, asked Harland and Wolff's naval architect, Edward Wilding, about the launch collision:

'My information is that at the launch of the *Olympic*, the sister ship of the *Titanic*, wind blew it against the side of the buttress, and the side of the ship crumpled up like tinder?'

'It did not crumple up like tinder.'

'Did you know of it crumpling up at the launch?'

'No, it did not crumple up.'

'Did it give?'

'It was slightly dented.'

'I thought so.'

The exchange drew laughter in the court and a rebuke from the Wreck Commissioner, Lord Mersey:

'If you thought it was slightly dented, why did you translate "slightly dented" into crumpling up like tinder?'

Undeterred, the lawyer persisted with his questioning of the Harland and Wolff expert:

'Would not that have suggested to you, as builders, the desirability of having a second skin in these boats up to the waterline?'

'I do not see it follows in any way. We do not build ships to bang into stone walls or come into collision.'

They may not have built them with collisions in mind, but collisions aplenty were soon occurring in quick succession. The next ones came at the end of *Olympic's* maiden voyage from Southampton to New York. Arriving at its berth on the Hudson River, *Olympic* first crushed part of a wooden pier, and shortly afterwards collided with one of the tugboats attempting to steer her safely into port. Even though the boat was officially at the time in the charge of a local pilot, the accidents were not the most auspicious of beginnings for Captain Edward Smith, the White Star Line's most senior officer – the man who would soon take command of *Titanic*. His next collision was also not the good captain's fault; but it was nevertheless spectacular.

Leaving Southampton for just her fifth voyage to the USA, *Olympic* managed to sail safely for a mere one hour and nineteen minutes before hitting another ship. On the morning of the 20 September 1911, both the White Star liner and the 8,000 ton Royal Navy cruiser HMS *Hawke* tried to pass through the same narrow passage out to open sea. The turbulence of the enormous liner passing through the narrow passage dragged the warship into its side and ripped a 20-foot wide gash in *Olympic's* side, both above and below the waterline. Under the banner headline '60 Millionaires On Board', a breathless article in the following day's *New York Times* described what happened next:

> ... suddenly unaccountably and amazingly the *Hawke* swung round and crashed into the *Olympic's* stern. The fellow in charge must have gone crazy.

Each return crossing of the Atlantic earned an estimated £150,000 profit for the White Star Line so the company's comment, 'It was the most cruel case on record,' was an understandable reaction as the entire full passenger complement, including the '60 American millionaires', disembarked in Southampton and looked for alternative travel across the Atlantic. *Olympic* was patched up in Harland and Wolff's repair facilities in Southampton docks and then sailed slowly, empty and unprofitably back to Belfast for more lasting repairs.

There was a sigh of financial relief in the company when *Olympic* was finally ready to set sail again some eight weeks after the original accident. But, a further eight weeks later, she was back in trouble once again in the unprecedented seas she encountered in the January crossing of 1912. Significantly, in view of what was later to happen to *Titanic*, the huge storm had revealed a problem with the ship's riveted seams, far below the waterline.

A memo from the Board of Trade's Belfast surveyor, Francis Carruthers, to his London office was the first indication that something was amiss. He revealed that some last minute alterations were being made to *Titanic* because of 'observations' made on the *Olympic's* crossing in heavy seas. These changes involved the fitting of a number of separate, 1-inch thick metal straps designed to strengthen *Titanic's* hull. Each strap was around 50 feet long and was to be fixed low down near the bilges, just above the keel of the giant ship. One of the straps was to be fitted to the hull near boiler room No. 6, a location that would later play a major role in the sinking of *Titanic*.

The memo has been preserved in the National Archives file MT 15/504:

Board of Trade Surveyors Office
Belfast

13 February 1912

S.S. *TITANIC*  Messrs: Harland & Wolff No 401

Sir

In connection with the scantlings of this vessel now in dry dock here, I beg to report that the builders are fitting a strip 1" thick over the landings at the upper (line) of the bilge, at both sides in the following positions:-

Forward. In way of No. 6 boiler room and extending three frame space of the W.T. bulkhead at the forward end of the boiler room, viz:- from frame 63 to 81 at the landing of J & K strakes.

Aft. In way of the turbine room & extending two frame spaces into the reciprocating room viz:- from frame 50 to 73 at the landing of K & L strakes. One extra row of holes has been drilled in the plate above the landing, making it a quadruple riveted landing.

I am informed that this strengthening is in consequence of observation made on the *Olympic* during a recent heavy [unreadable word] across the Atlantic.

I am Sir
Your obed t [sic] Servant
F. Carruthers

The fact that such changes were needed so late in the day was clearly of concern to the Board of Trade's Principal Ship Surveyor, William Archer, in London. He took the virtually unprecedented step of directly contacting Harland and Wolff's naval architect, Edward Wilding, to inquire further about what 'observations' had been made on *Olympic's* heavy sea crossing. Although no record of the conversation has survived, it is clear from the next memo to Carruthers that *Olympic's* riveted seams had been the source of the problem:

The Principal Ship Surveyor
London
15th February 1912

Sir

S.S. *Titanic*

Your report of the 13th inst. has been read with interest. I have since had a talk with Mr Wilding on the subject, and understand from him that the seams which gave trouble were double hand rivetted [sic].[3]

The position of the troublesome seams was far below the waterline so nothing could have been seen on the outside of the ship from *Olympic's* deck. It suggests that the most likely problem was water seeping into the ship through the riveted areas that Harland and Wolff later sought to strengthen. The letter asked Carruthers to find out more and he duly forwarded a sketch of the damaged areas with notes detailing how many rivets were involved at each point.

Still not satisfied, Archer in London found out that the *Olympic* was due to dock in Southampton on 29 February and wrote to the local surveyor there asking that he examine the ship:

Sirs

S.S. *Olympic*

The attached report detailing defective riveting [sic] in this vessel, and measures taken to prevent its occurrence in sister vessel *Titanic*, is forwarded for your information.

The ship or Engineer surveyor should, I think, visit the vessel and ascertain the extent of the defect whilst present passenger certificate is in force and if any other signs of stress have developed elsewhere, and report the extent in due course.

W. David Archer.

Unbeknown to the London Board of Trade officials, *Olympic* was not planning to stay in Southampton. A few days earlier the unlucky Captain Smith's ship had been involved in yet another collision at sea. She was yet again in need of emergency repairs. Nobody knows exactly what it was that the ship hit this time; the most likely candidate was some form of ship wreckage floating just underneath the surface of the sea.

The Southampton surveyor duly broke the news to his London boss:

This vessel [*Olympic*] is expected to arrive here this afternoon and will leave again tonight for Belfast, where she is to be dry-docked for the purpose of effecting repairs to [her] propeller. I therefore beg to suggest that this paper be forwarded direct to the Belfast Surveyor who last inspected the vessel and who will have an opportunity of examining the parts referred to in dry-dock. This report forwarded direct to the surveyor Belfast to save time.

Having the *Olympic* in dry dock was an unexpected yet ideal opportunity for Carruthers to look at not only the usually accessible areas of the vessel, but also the outside of the hull far below its normal waterline. His handwritten report to the Board's Principal Ship Surveyor was written on 6 March, and received in London the following day. Carruthers noted some slight signs of stress in cracking around the window frames of some of the upper deck houses and drew a diagram to illustrate the damage. Then he turned his attention to the steel plates and seams below the waterline:

MT 15/504: S.S. *Olympic* Inspection of Hull.

Sir

This vessel has been in dry dock here for the purpose of having a propeller blade fitted and the opportunity was taken for making an inspection of the hull, upon which I now beg to submit the following report.

Below the waterline. Starb d [sic] side forward in way of No. 6 Boiler room in the shell landing of J & K strakes from frame 63 to 74 about 100 rivets were slack and were drilled out and renewed. About 4 ft below this landing in the tank bar, from frame 71 to 75 about 50 slack rivets were drilled and replaced. Port side for'd [sic] in the tank bar from about frame 71 to 78, about 90 rivets were showing a little slack and were caulked.

On both sides aft in the shell landing of K & L strakes, from about frame 52 to 69, 100 rivets found slack were drilled out and replaced. I carefully inspected the vessel inside in the neighbourhood of these slack rivets but found no further signs of stress. In the stern part of the upper part of the aperture 93 rivets showing slight sign were caulked.

I am Sir
Your obed (sic) Servant
J. Carruthers
The Principal Ship Surveyor
London

Shorn of its technical jargon, the report was worryingly clear: the surveyor's inspection had revealed weaknesses in more than 400 rivets, some of them so loose that they needed to be 'drilled out' of the ship's sides and replaced with fresh rivets. It was a time-consuming and expensive business for skilled men to remove and replace the rivets and not one that Harland and Wolff would have undertaken lightly. In addition, these were all rivets that less than a year before must have passed the supposedly rigorous inspection of Harland and Wolff's team of rivet-counters and inspection from the Board of Trade's man on the spot.

The replacements involved only a minute percentage of the three million or more rivets that had been hammered into the entire ship but the position of the weakest rivets, those that needed complete replacement, may be significant. The 'starboard side forward in way of No. 6 boiler room' is one of the areas opened to the sea in *Titanic's* iceberg collision. It was the very spot where leading stoker Frederick Barrett was flooded out of No. 6 boiler room and forced to flee to No. 5 boiler room further towards the rear of the ship. In addition, the term 'J & K strakes' refers to horizontal lines of steel plate in the hull that would be far below the waterline.

One thing is certain: somebody within the Board of Trade hierarchy did believe that this particular surveyor's report on weaknesses in *Olympic's* rivets was of some importance at the time when investigations were being made into the sinking of the *Titanic*. The manila cover of the file reveals that it was booked out of the Board's archives to be read afresh in June 1912, two months after the sinking of *Titanic* and part-way through the Mersey Inquiry into the affair. Indecipherable initials in red crayon record that the file was returned to the archives on Saturday, 22 June. That was the end of the week in which the main Board of Trade witnesses had all been giving evidence.

None of that group, including the Belfast surveyor, Francis Carruthers, and the principal ship surveyor, William Archer, ever mentioned the hull rivets of *Titanic* or *Olympic*. Yet Archer's and Carruther's correspondence about *Olympic's* 'defective rivets' had been extensively annotated in the same red crayon. Each individual mention of the weakened rivets was heavily underlined but no mention had been made of the report's existence at Lord Mersey's inquiry.

Could it be that it was in nobody's interest for any questions to be raised about *Titanic's* seaworthiness and strength? She was after all a ship that had been passed as fit to sail by the British Board of Trade, with all of the disastrous consequences that followed that decision. Whether or not the 'Carruther's file' was deliberately withheld from the investigation may never be known. But the truth about the weak rivets of *Titanic* was finally to be exposed almost a century later, when twenty-first century scientists finally got the chance to examine the metal from which they were made.

### Notes

1. The *St Louis* made New York safely, two days late. Her crew used hatchets to chop 2-inch thick ice from her rigging.
2. All of the missing destroyers were later found crippled but afloat and towed to port.
3. Most rivets were inserted and compressed by hydraulic machines but manual 'hand-riveting' was still used near the bow and stern of the ship.

# Chapter Twenty-Seven

# 'There should be independent testing . . .'

Midnight
10 August 1998
The wreck of the RMS *Titanic*
12,460 feet deep
Position: 41° 43' 35" N, 49° 56' 54" W
North Atlantic Ocean

The darkness was absolute. No sunlight could penetrate to these abyssal depths. But, in the glare of the searchlights mounted on the mini-submarine approaching her bow, *Titanic* no longer looked anything like she once did on the surface. She no longer even appeared as she did when first discovered by the Ballard expedition of 1985. The photographs that the oceanographers took at the time, and which so amazed the world, were by then most definitely out of date. The deep brown 'rusticles' that hung like stalactites from every exposed metal surface of the ship had grown a little longer;[1] the entire bone structure of the ship seemed to have slumped a little more towards the muddy bottom of the sea.

Distinctive features such as the deck planking and most of the woodwork had fallen prey to the inexorable forces of decay and erosion that work deep in the ocean. Some of the largest surviving pieces of equipment had been wrenched from the deck or scavenged from the surrounding field of debris by earlier explorers in this alien undersea land. Exhibitions of *Titanic* memorabilia salvaged from the wreck and the debris field that surrounds it were drawing huge crowds and making fortunes in cities around the world. *Titanic*, herself, will not be here forever; like an old lady with her beauty long faded, she now waits to be gone. Within the next 100 years, there will be little more than a pile of rust there to mark the passing of the famous ship.

Spread across the ocean floor, around and in-between the widely separated stern and bow sections of *Titanic*, were the thousands of items that fell or were broken from the ship's structure as it plunged 2½ miles to the ocean bed. All traces of human remains had gone, leaving just the occasional pair of shoes to show that people once inhabited the ship. There had, however, been human activity down here that day. The Big Piece, a 350-square foot separated section of *Titanic's* hull had that afternoon been lifted 2½ miles to the surface of the sea; the first time it had seen sunlight since the night of the sinking a little over eighty-six years earlier. Along with a host of other metal fragments, small and large, it was providing samples for scientific study in laboratories across the world. Among those fragments were a few dozen rivets.

Defenders of Harland and Wolff's and *Titanic's* reputation argue that they always ordered the best metal that was then available without worrying about the cost. They used a well-known supplier of steel plate, the Scottish firm of David Colville & Sons, which had supplied steel for White Star ships for many years. The company was based in Motherwell, a town that had long been regarded as a centre of excellence for the British steel industry. But the sheer demand for iron and steel for all of the many ships under construction in Belfast between 1908 and 1912 forced Harland and Wolff to also look elsewhere for additional supplies.

Board of Trade files in the British National Archives show that iron and steel for *Titanic* actually came not just from their regular suppliers such as Colville & Sons but from many other sources as well. Hundreds of documents, now made public in the archives, detail the results of stress tests on samples of steel that were to be used in the ship and her sister, *Olympic*. The tests were a routine step in the process of inspection required by the Board's Engineer Surveyor-in-Chief, Alexander Boyle; without them the ships would not have been granted their licences to carry passengers. Those tests on the metal specifically ordered for *Titanic* involved no less than thirty-five different metal suppliers from numerous towns throughout Scotland and England.

Not all of the suppliers had the same reputation as Colville & Sons; some were even questioned by the Board of Trade as to their experience in supplying the type of material now being ordered by the Belfast yard. File M6414, from 1910, details an application from one Scottish steel company that had been asked, for the first time, to supply metal to Harland and Wolff for use in *Titanic*. The Waverley Iron and Steel Company was seeking approval from the Engineer Surveyor-in-Chief of the Board of Trade to join the approved list of steel manufacturers. His reply to a subordinate surveyor in Glasgow demanded a rigorous examination:

> The Surveyor should report as to the capabilities of this firm in regard to size of furnaces, size and weight of plates, angles or bars they can manufacture, and the output. He should report what experience they have had in the manufacture of steel plate, and the class of raw material they use in the manufacture of their steel.

The Board's local surveyor reported that the firm employed around 300 men in the town of Coatbridge. Iron and steel had been produced there for many years but as local supplies of a rich black ironstone ore had gradually run out the company was now using more imported foreign ore and had diversified into steel production. It ran twenty-three iron-producing 'puddling' furnaces.

The art of puddling was a skilled process that, early in the twentieth century, took a terrible toll on the health of those who carried out the work. For hours on end men used huge, long-handled metal spoons, known locally as 'rabbling bars', to stir bubbling cauldrons of molten metal. For protection against the searing heat they wore multiple layers of thick clothing and damp, rough hessian sacking wrapped tightly around each leg. Each puddler's own makeshift 'scarecrow' uniform was topped by a thick leather apron and heavy boots and gloves. Around his neck he tied one of the most important pieces of equipment – a torn rag, which he regularly dipped into a handily placed water bucket and then placed against his lips. Without the puddler's neckerchief, the tender skin of the lips would rapidly blister and burn.

The purpose of puddling was to reduce and remove impurities known as 'slag' from the molten iron mix. The more carefully and diligently the melt was stirred then the more the long strings of slag that form from chemical impurities in the ore were evenly distributed and broken up, and the less they affected the quality and strength of the final metal bar. When he judged the moment was right, the puddler rolled up a ball of molten metal at the end of his rabbling bar and pulled it from the hearth.

For higher quality iron, the molten metal could be beaten by the power of a 'shingling hammer' to crush out impurities … and then re-melted … re-puddled … re-hammered and re-rolled to refine it even further. Each new shingling created a stronger metal. 'No. 1' iron was self-evidently treated once, No. 2 twice and so on. For reasons lost in the mists of time, No. 3 iron was known as 'best' and No. 4 iron was known as 'best-best' and made very strong rivets. Harland and Wolff did not order the more expensive 'best-best' rivets for *Titanic*; they made do with just the 'best'.

Despite the Glasgow regional surveyor giving the Board of Trade a favourable report on the Waverley works at Coatbridge, the Engineer-in-Chief was clearly not impressed:

> There should be independent testing. This is especially necessary in this case where the firm has not hitherto manufactured steel material under the Board's survey. As their products are limited in variety, I suggest that the firm's name might be included in the list as makers of stay and rivet bars only – this might be agreed to, I think.

Other new companies being approached for the first time to work on *Titanic* were also having problems in passing the stringent Board of Trade tests. In December 1910, the Staffordshire-based Lilleshall Steel Company was asked to manufacture forty-one steel bars. They were to be used as 'butt straps' on the hull of *Titanic*.² The Lilleshall foundry had only recently installed a new Siemens open-hearth furnace to supplement their older Bessemer furnaces. Company records show that the new plant was markedly slower in production but 'could accept any amount of scrap in the raw material.' Board of Trade steel test No. 100-2838, from March 1910, reveals that they failed to produce steel of a good enough quality to fulfil the *Titanic* order:

> From: Engineering Surveyor-in-Chief: Ship 401 *Titanic* – The Surveyor should state why the straps were rejected. A. Boyle 13.3.11

> From: The Principal Officer, Cardiff: Ship 401 *Titanic* – Noted. The previous straps after being rolled to required shape were found to have surface defects and in order to prevent any possible delay the client decided at once to get a replacement set from another company.

There were other complications for Harland and Wolff as they widened the net in their search for new sources of the metal they needed for so many projects. The period leading up to the birth of *Titanic* was a turbulent one for industrial relations throughout British industry. The shipyard was frequently hit by wage and demarcation disputes, but the same problem regularly affected their steel suppliers all over the country. In March 1910, confidential memo CAB 37/102/4 was presented to the Cabinet with some depressing economic statistics:

> There have been 409 trade disputes affecting 299,499 workers and the engineering and shipbuilding trades remain very slack. Unemployment among trade unionists is averaging 7.7 per cent with a general decline in employment and the average number of furnaces in blast last year was 291, a reduction of 50 on two year ago.
> Of the 1,151,919 people employed around 1,129,511 sustained decreases in their wages; the principal decreases affect cotton spinners and nearly 25,000 iron and steel workers in various districts of Great Britain.

Decreasing wages and poorer working conditions were encouraging the formation of a multitude of different unions in the English and Scottish steelworks of the time. Working men were finding their voice and increasingly demanding a bigger share of the wealth being created in the nation's vast industrial plants.

At one of Harland and Wolff's steel suppliers, the Frodingham Iron and Steel Company Ltd., for example, low morale and a series of strikes were continually affecting production. The exploitation of low grade iron ore found near the Lincolnshire village in the nineteenth century had made a fortune for local landowning families. But a collapse in iron prices in 1908, just as Harland and Wolff's Queen's Island yard was building *Titanic*, led to reductions in wages and bonus payments. Strikes were called at steelworks throughout the area, including the Frodingham plant.

The lengthy dispute, organised by the National Union of Blastfurnacemen, initially involved around 400 men but soon spread further. Industrial relations were not helped when a company executive told union representatives they were 'gnat-brained extremists'. The worried owners of other steel companies attempted to help Frodingham break the strike. They supplied the strike-bound plant with metal from their own stock but were defeated when railwaymen refused to move the strikebreaking 'black' steel. In such circumstances it was hard to maintain proper quality control of the steel that was produced and passed on to customers such as Harland and Wolff.

With metal from such a wide variety of sources, it was unsurprising that quality varied. Like all shipbuilders of their day, Harland and Wolff specified that all of *Titanic's* steel should be produced to strict specifications in Siemens-Martin open-hearth furnaces. Even in these early years of the twentieth century, shipbuilders knew that the quality of the product greatly depended on the skills of the steelmaker. As early as 1901, delegates to the prestigious Steel Makers' Conference in Glasgow were receiving warnings about quality control from the distinguished chemist, Axel Wahlberg:

> It is well known to all metallurgists that, ever since the introduction of the open-hearth processes on an extensive scale, it has been impossible to obtain ingots of a perfectly homogeneous chemical composition; the exterior parts of the ingot, particularly towards the lower end, become poorer in carbon, silicon, [and] manganese. This will often prove a serious drawback in cases where material is intended for manufacturing purposes.

Wahlberg added that shipbuilders and other end-users were sometimes asking for quality that could not, in reality, be achieved:

> ... perhaps chiefly, to the fault of the manufacturers themselves, who, owing to the keen, untiring competition of the present day, are occasionally induced to accept any conditions, however absurd, for the sole purpose of securing a contract.

Yet the quality differential among the sheer number of foundries producing the metal from which *Titanic* was made, and with which it was fastened together, is not the only reason why its stress-resistance would have varied. Harland and Wolff employed thousands of men at their huge engine works attached to Queen's Island shipyard in Belfast. Some metal came ready-prepared into the yard but much of the material of *Titanic's* hull would have passed through those works. There it was heated and shaped, rolled or pressed, cut, and drilled or hole-punched into shape before being assembled on the ship slipways in the open yard. Harland and Wolff would have been well aware that the way they stored and treated *Titanic's* steel could affect its quality.

At the same Glasgow Steel Conference, another chemist, Mr C.H. Risdale, had pointed out that quality variations were not always the fault of the manufacturers:

> Steel users should take great pains to control treatment, as the makers do to control composition. The importance of composition, apart from treatment, has been over-rated. Later treatment often outweighs composition and initial treatment, and the maker can do nothing to provide against this.

Despite years of scientific research, a definitive final verdict about whether or not *Titanic's* steel was badly made, badly treated or chemically inclined to be brittle has yet to be arrived at. Scientists have even disagreed about whether the steel plates of her hull were 'brittle' or not. The difficulties and expense of recovering any material from a wreck lying 2½ miles below the surface of the sea has limited the samples from which they can work. The tiny quantities of steel so far put under the microscope are a scanty sample on which to pass judgement about so large an engineering project from so long ago. The Big Piece of hull is by far the largest object yet recovered from *Titanic*. Raising it to the surface took the efforts of two costly expeditions and hundreds of man-hours of effort.[3] And yet the 40 tons of metal in the Big Piece are but the tiniest fraction of the ship's true bulk.

The most intractable problem of all is that no scientists have ever tested, or even seen, the one section of the ship where the quality of the steel really mattered; the few hundred feet of the hull that struck the iceberg. The wreck discovered by Ballard was in two large sections, and the damaged area of the bow had buried itself deep under the mud of the ocean bottom.

In 1912, starved of any real facts, newspapers speculated that the hull had been 'gashed open', creating a huge wound from which the ship could never have recovered. But, even then, the real experts discounted such stories. However powerful the momentum of the collision was, and however hard the ice may have been, it could never have cut a gash like that through the 1-inch thick steel of *Titanic's* outer skin. At the British inquiry, Harland and Wolff's naval architect and designer, Edward Wilding, gave a clear explanation of the damage that he believed the iceberg had caused to *Titanic*.

In the weeks following the sinking, Wilding spent hours studying anew the plans of the ship. He produced intricate calculations as to how the inrushing water must have spread through *Titanic* before finally dragging her under the surface. His figures were so detailed that they even estimated how much solid fuel had been left in each bunker, and how water would have flowed between individual lumps of coal. Wilding tested the *Olympic* at sea to determine how rapidly her sister ship *Titanic* would have been able to turn. The data helped him to estimate the angle at which *Titanic* would have hit the iceberg.

Wilding finally calculated that within forty minutes of the collision, about 16,000 tons of seawater had been weighing down the bow of *Titanic*; an average of 400 tons of water per minute, or about 1,500 gallons every second, must have been gushing in through the damaged hull. He deduced that there could not have been one long uninterrupted gash in the side of *Titanic*; if there had been then the water would have flooded in far more rapidly than his calculations allowed. All Wilding's figures pointed to the iceberg having opened up a series of intermittent, unconnected slits at various points along the bow:

> I believe it must have been 'in places', that is, not a continuous rip. A hole, three-quarters of an inch wide and 200 feet long does not seem to describe to me the probable damage, but it must have averaged about that amount. My estimate of the size of the hole required   and making some allowance for the obstruction due to the presence of decks and other things – is that the total area through which water was entering the ship, was somewhere about 12 square feet.

Wilding was questioned in more detail about his findings by Stephen Rowlatt, one of the barristers working for the Board of Trade:

'I suppose it is possible that a piece of ice made a hole and then got itself broken off?'

'Yes, quite probable.'

'And then another piece of ice made another hole, and so on?'

'Yes, that is what I believe happened.'

Considering that Wilding's calculations must have involved little more than the use of a slide rule and his own intimate knowledge of the ship, they have stood the test of time remarkably well. Modern computer-aided studies have come to virtually the same conclusion as the naval architect did in the London courtroom 100 years ago. One recent research project calculated that the splits would have been spread out, as Wilding suggested, across all six forward compartments, and that their total area was 12.604644 square feet. It was a remarkable tribute to Wilding's skill in producing his century-old estimate of 'about 12 square feet'.

At the time, however, the Wreck Commissioner, Lord Mersey, and the White Star shipping line's lead barrister, Sir Robert Finlay, were not totally convinced of Wilding's findings. They debated the issue when White Star's lawyer made his final submissions to the court. Sir Robert was keen to stress that the entire disaster had only happened through an extraordinary set of circumstances:

'And the extraordinary thing is, my Lord, that they almost avoided it altogether. It was only the extraordinary circumstance of there being at the corner a projecting spike which proceeded to rip it up for six compartments, which caused this deplorable catastrophe.'

'I do not know that it was ripped up continuously. It seems to me that there were several separate holes,' responded Lord Mersey.

'That is Mr Wilding's view, my Lord. ... that it was a series of stabs.'

'It is pointed out to me that it is rather difficult to understand that. It may have been one projecting piece of the berg which ... opened it differently as it went along, that is to say the plates bulged back inwards and broke or cracked or became un-riveted in different places.'

'That is so, my Lord. Certainty is impossible, because the vessel is now 2 miles deep at the bottom of the Atlantic ... Certainty is perfectly impossible in the matter.'

Sir Robert's 1912 conviction that 2 miles of water would forever prevent further evidence being gathered on the matter was a perfectly understandable conclusion for him to draw at the time. In 1996, however, Wilding's calculations were further confirmed from an even more reliable source. An expedition to the wreck used sub-bottom profiling sonar to examine both sides of the bow buried deep in the mud. The technique employs computer analysis of reflected sound-waves to build up a picture of a buried object, in much the same way as an ultra-sound scan reveals details of a baby in the womb. The port side of the wreck was studied first for the purpose of establishing a 'base-line' picture against which the scan of the damaged starboard side could be compared. The results were clear; there was no large gash from the iceberg, just the small splits that Wilding had predicted.

The scan revealed that all of the damage occurred about 20 feet below the waterline. The seawater would have been forced inside the ship at the 'fire-hose' pressure that leading stoker Barrett had witnessed. The damage could be identified intermittently over a length of 249 feet, although the longest continuous slit seen by the sonar stretched no more than 30 feet. That most extensive slit ended just to the rear of the bulkhead dividing *Titanic's* foremost boiler rooms 6 and 5. It was the bulkhead that had featured heavily in Barrett's dramatic story of many years before.

Wilding's deduction that *Titanic* was sunk not by a gash in her side but by a series of slits had been proved to be correct once again. The horizontal slits appeared to follow the joints where steel plates overlapped each other along the hull; the seams that were fastened with rivets. It seemed that rather than the steel plates being 'gashed open', the rivets themselves had proved to be *Titanic's* weakest link.

In recent years, further tests have been conducted upon the metals recovered from the *Titanic* site. In the most authoritative study yet undertaken, American researchers Jennifer Hooper McCarty and Tim Foecke conducted their own experiments on about three dozen rivets from the ship, and gathered together data from previous academic studies into the strength of the metal used to construct *Titanic*.

In their subsequent book, *What Really Sank the Titanic*,[3] the two scientists revealed that many of the iron rivets used in the bow of the ship had such high concentrations of slag that they would have been weak points in the structure of the hull. Some of the rivets they examined were made of less than ninety per cent iron and more than ten per cent slag, often formed into long 'strings' of chemicals that significantly weakened the integrity of the whole rivet. And they believed they knew what had caused the 'feedstock metal' from which the rivets were made to be of such poor quality.

> This evidence suggests that the *Titanic* wrought iron stock was not worked for a sufficient puddling time [not enough time to mix it well] and at too low a temperature [not enough heat to squeeze out the excess slag easily] to refine the slag stringers into more consistently spherical-shaped, smaller particles. Also, the unusually large amount of total slag would suggest that the puddler was not careful about the amount of slag he left in the mix.

Their research backed up much of the other evidence that *Titanic* never had been the magnificently-constructed ship that Harland and Wolff and Ismay's White Star Line had claimed her to be. Foecke and Hooper McCarty suggested when they published their research that time pressures, rather than a desire to save money, had led the Harland and Wolff yard to source inferior materials from many sources. While it is undoubtedly true that building so many ships in the one yard at the same time did put huge pressure on the workers and management in Belfast, it is hard to deny the thought that the IMM's disastrous financial position must have played a part. Inferior wrought iron was always less expensive than buying the very best of the best.

When the starboard bow of *Titanic* hit the iceberg, steel plates were deformed rather than cut open; but that deformation put an intolerable strain on the riveted seams below the waterline of the ship. As Harland and Wolff's own expert designer, Edward Wilding, explained after the disaster:

> The 'fatal time', that is, the time when nothing that human ingenuity could do could prevent the ship sinking, is found at a much earlier time than the actual sinking of the ship.

It seemed that for want of a rivet the seams were all lost; for want of the seams, the ship was all lost. With rivets made of poorly-puddled iron and hammered together by less than perfectly skilled rivet teams, the results had a certain inevitability about them: each time one rivet snapped an even greater strain was transferred to its neighbours – the joints between some of the plates unzipped in random locations along the hull from the bow till just aft of the rear No. 6 boiler room bulkhead. With six separate compartments by then taking water, *Titanic* was doomed.

Soon after the disaster, *Titanic's* owners and builders explained why *Titanic* had never been submitted for inspection by Lloyds Register,[4] the industry's recognised experts in surveying and classifying new ships. They claimed it was because she was constructed in a way that was 'superior to their requirements'. The impression they imparted was of a ship so in advance of other vessels that outside inspection was never required. In America, Bruce Ismay made an unequivocal statement on the matter:

> So far as the White Star Line are concerned, they have never classed any of their ships, as the ships have always been built far in excess of any of those requirements. We have always been in the habit of taking out a passenger certificate on all our ships, which is a check on our own people that those ships have been kept absolutely up to the mark.

The same sentiments were repeated several times in slightly different forms during the course of the Lord Mersey Inquiry. The effect was somewhat spoiled by a letter to the editor of *The Times*, published on 8 July 1912, from Mr A. Scott, Secretary of the prestigious Lloyd's Register of British and Foreign Shipping:

> Sir,
>
> In view of the reports which have appeared in the press in connection with the inquiry into the loss of the S.S. *Titanic*, to the effect that the vessel was built considerably in excess of the requirements of Lloyd's Register, I am directed to say that these statements are inaccurate. On the contrary, in important parts of her structure the vessel as built did not come up to the requirements of Lloyd's Register for a vessel of her dimensions.

In fact, as the Lloyd's Register website now somewhat smugly points out, the only parts of *Titanic* that were surveyed by them were her anchors, '... which to this day remain intact on the seabed.'

But, if Lloyd's were never asked to survey *Titanic*, then who was checking the great ship for more than two years as 10,000 men laboured to create her and the world's largest shipping combine poured £1,500,000 into building the gigantic ship? The answer is a surprising one. It was all in the hands of one civil servant: a poorly-trained but dedicated, £7-a-week Board of Trade employee who had laboured unrecognised and without a pay rise for more than a decade.

The safety of everyone on board the *Titanic* was in the hands of the Board's most humble and obedient servant, Mr Francis Carruthers. This might yet prove a recipe for disaster.

### Notes

1. Rusticles are produced by the action of 'metal-eating' bacteria that are slowly devouring *Titanic*.
2. 'Butt straps' were laid across two metal plates 'butt jointed end to end' and then riveted to each so as to tie them together.
3. March 2008 Kensington Publishing Corp, New York.
4. Lloyd's Register is a long-established but independent body unconnected to the Lloyd's Insurance organisation.

# Chapter Twenty-Eight

# 'The Surveyor might report . . .'

**6.00 am**
**Saturday, 9 July 1910**
**The home of Francis Carruthers**
**No. 39, Ballybeen**
**Dundonald, Down**
**Belfast**

Board of Trade Engineer Surveyor, 'Second Class', Francis Carruthers, normally greeted each working day with enthusiasm, but this Saturday was different. He had a crucial meeting planned with the chief designer of the shipbuilding company Harland & Wolff, and some tricky questions to put about the construction of the two giant ships *Olympic* and *Titanic*, then taking shape under the skeleton shadows of the giant gantry crane that dominated the shipyard on nearby Queen's Island.

As the only independent inspector of the safety of the world's two biggest ships, Carruthers was aware that it was not always easy to obtain all the details of *Titanic's* construction that his superiors in Whitehall so readily demand. Awaking as usual at 6.30 am, Carruthers prepared for the meeting by dressing in his Civil Service 'uniform' of a formal black suit, black shoes, starched-collared white shirt and sober tie. He quickly ate breakfast, prepared by the family maidservant, Agnes Mwaha. The 23-year-old black domestic maid was a luxury that the Carruthers family had only recently been able to afford.

Carruthers' recent posting to Belfast had brought the first promotion; in fact, the only promotion he had enjoyed during fourteen years of loyal service with the Board. It had raised his salary to the giddy heights of almost £400 per annum. Despite their vastly different cultural backgrounds,[1] Agnes had been an invaluable help to his wife, Mary, in looking after him and 16-year-old William, the only one of their three surviving children who still lived at home with his parents. Carruthers was deeply proud of his teenage son, already showing signs of following in his father's footsteps by becoming an engineering apprentice in the town.

At the age of fifty-two, Francis Carruthers was not a forceful man, but he was loyal, dependable and had demonstrated an ability to get along with his colleagues, as well as with the ship-owners and shipbuilders with whom his working life brought him into contact. Born and bred in Cumberland, he had spent more than thirteen years at sea, starting as a lowly apprentice 3rd engineer and working his way up to become chief engineer on a cargo ship. His 'Extra First Class' Engineer's Certificate of Competency was still displayed with pride on the wall of his small office in the Customs House of Belfast Docks.

Eight years into his marriage, after the infant death of his firstborn son, Carruthers had abandoned his seafaring life and sought employment ashore. Several jobs followed, as assistant engineer in various North of England shipyards, before Carruthers' landlubber career finally washed ashore in the backwaters of the West of Scotland office of the British Board of Trade.

His was a Civil Service role that few envied. Until his recent promotion to Engineer Surveyor 'Second Class', Carruthers had earned a mere 'Third Class' salary of £5 a week – £260 a year – for a job that called upon him day or night, and heaped responsibility upon his shoulders for the safe construction of hundreds of cargo and passenger ships. Promotion came only into 'dead men's shoes' at the Board of Trade and pay scales for surveyors such as Carruthers had not been reviewed or improved for an astonishing thirty-three years. Perhaps unsurprisingly, the morale of the service was low; in fact, Carruthers' only act of gentle rebellion in his entire career had come the previous year.

Along with dozens of colleagues, Carruthers had signed his name to a document that described itself as 'A Humble Petition …' and most politely requested a salary review throughout the Marine Department. Carruthers and his colleagues were under the impression that their petition must by then already be under consideration by the President of the Board of Trade, the recently appointed Winston Churchill MP. Unfortunately, unbeknownst to them all, the department's most senior civil servant had privately ruled that Churchill was too busy to be bothered with minor matters and that the timing was 'inopportune'. He planned to delay putting it in front of the president for a further two years.

The Marine Division's confidential appraisals of Carruthers' skills had regularly shown him to be rising towards mediocrity. The staff ledgers of the service from the early 1900s are still stored in the British National Archives. Carruthers' entries are frequently the shortest on the page. 'Painstaking and reliable', and 'Performs his duties with tact', are among the recorded comments of his senior officers. Some of his colleagues over the years had left the Civil Service and sought better paid, private sector jobs with the shipping industry, but Carruthers had stayed put. By dint of his sheer perseverance he had lasted through sixteen years of service and steadily climbed the ladder of seniority. Now Carruthers had finally earned himself his one and only, much-cherished promotion to Belfast.

Having waited so long to make any sort of progress, his new job in Ireland was not a position that Carruthers wanted to jeopardise. Yet, even he was privately concerned that he may have lacked the experience necessary to carry out his important new role. He was to be the front-line judge of the quality of construction of *Olympic* and *Titanic*, the vast new ocean liners then being built half a mile away from his Belfast office.

*Olympic* was to be the biggest ship in the world when she launched a few months later, and *Titanic* would, in turn, take that title from her when she too slid down the grease-covered slipway the following year. And yet the owners and the builders of the ships had decided that they would not have the vessels inspected by Lloyd's Registry surveyors. They claimed that the ships were so large that they already outstripped the maximum size for which Lloyd's published survey regulations. The builders also claimed that they were exceeding all of Lloyd's specifications; a puzzling claim when the registration society had not yet drawn up and published any specifications for a ship of *Titanic's* size.

There was no legal requirement on White Star to have their ship inspected by Lloyds. Many ship-owners did welcome it on a voluntary basis because regular inspections by the Register's skilled surveyors were a valuable independent check on the quality of the materials and of the work that was being done. At the end of the construction process a classification from Lloyds could also greatly reduce insurance premiums. In the case of both *Titanic* and *Olympic*, the insurance issue was of lesser importance. The owners, the White Star Line, were part of the American Morgan shipping Combine and that believed it was a large enough international concern to bear part of the risk itself. Accordingly, only two-thirds of the £1,500,000 construction costs of each vessel had been insured outside of the company.

For Carruthers, the lack of a commercial survey made little difference to his work. It did mean that he did not have the comforting back-up of an independent second opinion, but he still had a legal duty to make sure that *Titanic* was structurally sound, fully equipped and seaworthy before she departed from Belfast. He would be the official who approved the two new ships' certificates, without which they could not enter service. His approval would allow *Olympic* and *Titanic* to commence carrying thousands of passengers across the Atlantic.

Carruthers, then fresh from the somewhat quieter pastures of his former posting on the west coast of Scotland, had a massive task ahead of him. With just the occasional help of a junior colleague in Belfast and a few flying visits from one of his managers in London, he somehow had to ensure the structural integrity of what were at that time the two greatest shipbuilding and engineering projects in Britain.

He had made, and would continue to make, hundreds of site visits to each of the ships in the course of their construction but the distances and the heights, the sheer quantity of metal being riveted to other metal and the complexities of the engineering issues involved were more than any one person could possibly have handled. Carruthers had seen little of his wife and family or friends in recent months; he had to rely on the assistance and guidance and continuing goodwill of Harland and Wolff's senior managers to make his job possible.

In the course of the Lord Mersey Inquiry, several of the lawyers representing passengers or the sailors from *Titanic* attempted to question Francis Carruthers about his experience and his suitability to survey the gigantic ships for which he was responsible. But on each occasion the subject was raised, either Mersey or the Attorney-General representing the Board of Trade, quickly intervened. A typical interruption came as Clement Edwards, representing the dockers' union, questioned Carruthers about how he had tested that riveted joints in the bulkheads were watertight. Just as Carruthers had admitted that his only test was looking at the rivet and feeling around the rivet head with a thin blade, Lord Mersey intervened:

> I do not know what you are doing, Mr Edwards; are you going to suggest that this gentleman did not execute his duties properly, because I do not think you ought to suggest it unless you have some charge to make against him?

A similar interruption came when a union lawyer representing *Titanic's* officers tried to suggest that Carruthers and other surveyors were never properly trained for their jobs:

> I have not a word of complaint to make against Mr Carruthers as an engineer. The complaint I am making is that the Board of Trade system is to put the wrong man to do the work, or to put a man to do work for which he is not really by his training qualified. They have six months' training, for a probationary period, he said, as shipwrights, which would seem to me to be very insufficient.

As Holmes warmed to his argument there was an immediate interruption from the Attorney-General:

> I am sorry to intervene, but I am very anxious to know what it is we have to deal with. I have found a little difficulty in following my friend's argument on the last two points and its bearing on the Enquiry before you.

Lord Mersey ruled the matter irrelevant and moved on to other things. In the end the inquiry failed to address the issue of how rigorous the Board of Trade's survey of *Titanic* had been. Statements from Harland and Wolff that the ship had not needed an independent survey of its strength appeared to have been accepted without question.

It was left to outside commentators to point out the Board of Trade's deficiencies in the months that followed. *The Times* newspaper of 8 July 1912 reminded its readers that it had previously entertained doubts about the department's ability to cope:

> It will be remembered that writing in connexion with the loss of *Titanic* our marine correspondent suggested that one of the questions which deserved consideration was whether the Board of Trade had sufficient organisation and equipment for testing the plans of vessels not built under the survey of registration societies. The question does not appear to have been fully investigated by the Court appointed to inquire into the loss of *Titanic* although the principle of an independent survey is undoubtedly one of great importance.

The newspaper's correspondent was not alone in his views. The influential *Shipping World* magazine joined in the attack on the Board's Marine Department:

> ... one would suppose that at least an attempt would be made to remedy some of the apparent defects from which this department suffers. As there is no sign of any such attempt, one can only assume that we are quite content to let matters stand as they are until some still more appalling catastrophe will awaken the public into demanding reforms.
>
> One of the greatest of these defects is the qualifications of their ship surveyors. No mention whatsoever is made of scientific experience or training. Apparently this is unnecessary.

From his outpost of the Board of Trade in Belfast Carruthers, was answerable to two bosses based in the London headquarters in Whitehall Gardens. The first was the Principal Ship Surveyor, William Archer, who expected to be kept informed of *Olympic* and *Titanic's* progress through every step of their construction. Carruthers had been filling in forms ever since the keels were laid in the adjacent slipways at Harland and Wolff. He produced a stream of tediously handwritten memoranda, each on their appropriate Board of Trade form, which were then passed back and forth between Belfast and London.

Many of the issues that Archer raised with his man on the spot in Belfast appeared only to have entered into the Board of Trade's thinking at an extraordinarily late stage of the day. By July 1910, for example, the *Olympic's* hull was completed and virtually ready for her launch, which was then barely three months away. With tens of thousands of tons of steel plates riveted irremovably onto her structure, and her internal decks completed and irreversibly sealed into her hull, it would seem an odd time for anyone to question the quality of her steel.

And yet that was precisely what the Principal Ship Surveyor proceeded to do. On 6 July the hard-pressed Carruthers received a demand for information from Archer in his London Office:

> Information required: S.S. *Olympic*
>
> Please report whether the steel plate used in the construction of the hull have been tested either at the steel works or the builders' yard. I shall be glad of any information you can obtain as to the ultimate tensile strength and elongation per cent of the material used for shell plating deck plating etc.
>
> In the case of *Lusitania* and *Mauretania* a special quality of steel was used for the upper works. Will the vessel be cleared with any of the societies?
>
> Please state what progress has been made with the construction of the hull.
>
> W. David Archer.

That memorandum was the reason why Carruthers was on his way to the shipyard on a Saturday morning. He had an appointment with *Titanic's* chief designer, Thomas Andrews, to try and answer the Board of Trade's queries. In that meeting Andrews reassured Carruthers that all was well with *Olympic* and *Titanic's* steel plates. He dismissed comparisons with the higher quality steel used on the upper decks of the two Cunard ships by pointing out that the White Star ships were far larger and more stable structures.

That same afternoon a memorandum from Carruthers was written into the file and immediately returned to London:

> Sir,
>
> In receipt of your query I saw Mr Andrews who told me that steel to Lloyd's ordinary requirements and tests was used throughout the vessel. He said that the stability of these vessels would be so much greater than that of *Lusitania* and *Mauritania* that lightness in the upper works was not a vital necessity with them as it had been in the case of these two ships.
>
> The vessels will not be cleared with any of the societies, the builders inform us. No. 400 *Olympic* is completely plated, all the bulkheads completed and steel decks completed. It is expected that she will be ready for launching about the middle of October. No. 401 *Titanic* is about three parts plated.
>
> F. Carruthers 9-7-10

Part of the sentence dealing with the 'Lloyd's ordinary requirement and tests' had been underlined (as above) in the Board's archive files, most likely when the papers were re-examined by officials after *Titanic* had sunk. It appears that Thomas Andrews's reassurance was all that the Board of Trade needed to trust that Harland and Wolff had built a strong ship. It was the last file from London to question the strength of *Titanic's* steel plate and structure.

One wonders what could conceivably have been done with two virtually completed, £1,500,000 ships if Andrews's answers had failed to satisfy their queries. With no outside inspection from the regulatory 'societies' such as Lloyds[2] and a hopelessly overstretched Board of Trade surveyor, it had in effect been left to the shipbuilders to inspect their ship themselves. Not surprisingly ... Harland and Wolff were totally happy with Harland and Wolff's creation.

However conscientiously Francis Carruthers tried to do his impossible job, it is hard to reconcile the paucity of *Titanic's* inspections with the optimistic views of Sir Walter Howell, Assistant Secretary of the Board of Trade and Head of the Marine Division. Soon after *Titanic's* sinking he gave evidence to a Royal Commission on the Civil Service:

> With regard to passenger ships and immigrant ships we do very carefully follow the design of ships and if we have the slightest suspicion that anything is going wrong in the way of construction we immediately call attention to it. Our object is the guardianship of life our sole object in interfering at all with a ship is safety of life.

Unfortunately, the Board were not doing well in Belfast with their 'guardianship of life' mission. In addition to his duties of ensuring that *Titanic* was fit to go to sea, Francis Carruthers had another heavy responsibility on his shoulders. He had to ensure that *Titanic* carried lifeboats with sufficient capacity to comply with the complex Board of Trade regulations governing boat provision on emigrant ships travelling to America. Despite the pressures of his job, Carruthers was to perform this one task with exemplary efficiency. But, seemingly like everybody else in the Board of Trade, he stuck rigidly to the letter of the law, with no thoughts as to what might actually happen were *Titanic* to sink with little more than the bare legal minimum of boats on board.

Carruthers' dual role in Belfast as an engineer *and* ship surveyor meant that he was also answerable to the Board's Engineer Surveyor-in-Chief, Alexander Boyle. The man was a frequent correspondent, rattling off frequent and terse demands for extra information. In June 1910, he also began questioning Carruthers – this time about her lifeboats.

27 June 1910
<u>From</u> A.Boyle:

> The Surveyor might report how this cases stands stating how many
> boats are to be carried on each of these vessels, and he might obtain a
> plan showing the deck arrangement. The Surveyor should report on the
> trails of the davits and gear in due course.

In responses over the next few months, Carruthers was to send several
memoranda that listed the cubic capacities of the boats to be carried. The
ancient lifeboat regulations with which the Board of Trade was concerned
bore no relation at all to how many people the ship was to carry. Instead they
were related to a ship's registered tonnage. Even that figure was not as
straightforward as it seemed; the registered tonnage was not the weight – or
the weight-of-water displacement – of the ship but was a complex calculation
of how much cargo space was enclosed by the hull of the vessel.

Under the regulations that Carruthers was seeking to enforce, any ship
with a registered tonnage of 10,000 tons or more needed to carry sixteen boats
with a total cubic capacity of 9,625 feet. A note from Carruthers in November
1910 made it clear that *Olympic*, and by implication *Titanic*, would meet the
Board's requirements:

> The Surveyor Belfast – Reply: Noted. As directed I beg to forward the
> papers dealing with the boats and davits proposed by the builders for
> this vessel. A print showing the number, dimension and arrangement of
> the boats is attached. There are fourteen boats of section A and 2 boats
> of section D. These I have measured and the dimensions and capacities
> are as follows:

> A boats; 30' x 9' x 4' = 648 cu ft
> Total for 14 boats = 9072 cu ft
> 1D boat 25.2' x 7.1 x 3.15' = 337 cu ft
> 1" 25.2 x 7.2 x 3.43 = 343

> The total capacity of the boats is therefore 9,752 cu ft. The total
> capacity required by the Regulations if 9,625 ft.

Carruthers went on to report that the davits had not yet been fitted on *Olympic*
but that they would be of the 'double-acting type', on which a total of thirty-
two boats could be hung if so desired. It was not the first time that it had been
suggested that the *Titanic* could have more than the sixteen boats required by
law. The Board of Trade had, at various times, been told that *Titanic* would
carry sixteen or thirty-two and even forty-eight lifeboats. The fact that by the
time she was launched the number had shrunk back to the legally required

sixteen (along with four collapsible bonus boats that were to be stacked on deckhouses) seemed to excite no comment at all from Carruthers or anyone at the London headquarters. It was clear that as long as the law, however outdated it may be, was complied with, then no further questions were required.

By May 1911, the Belfast surveyor was able to report that he had fully tested *Olympic's* lifeboat equipment:

> The davits and gear have been tried, all the boats being swung out and lowered, five into, and the remainder within a few of the water: obstruction at the fitting-out berth preventing the latter actually getting into the water. All the gears worked smoothly and well. The time taken to swing a boat out of the chocks and into the water a depth of about 58 feet averaging from 1 minute 40 seconds to 1 minute 55 seconds.

The response from the Engineer Surveyor-in-Chief was brief and to the point:

> Read. This appears to be in order.

In due course the same number of sixteen lifeboats and four collapsible lifeboats would be fitted and loaded and tested on the *Titanic*. Before that happened the ship would be, at long last, left standing in glorious isolation on her slipway in the Queen's Island yard. She had grown up with ship No. 400, the *Olympic*, being built on the adjacent slipway. Now *Olympic* had been launched and was floating alongside the nearby quayside for her final fitting-out.

Because *Olympic* was the first of the gigantic sister ships to be built, she had always been the 'shining star' of the Harland and Wolff yard. Like many elder sisters, *Olympic* received all of the attention. It was her hull that was painted pure white to beautify her for the launch, while *Titanic* – ship No. 401 – was left a dowdy, matt black. *Olympic* was the one whom everybody had come to see in the grand VIP launching ceremony. Those who were left working on *Titanic* feared that she would always remain the second sister, never quite as famous, never a household name. They could not have known how wrong they would be. The coming tragedy was to ensure *Titanic's* place in the record books – as the most infamous ship in history.

### Notes

1. In the Carruthers' strict Presbyterian household, their servant Agnes described her religion as 'cooneyist' in the 1911 Belfast census.
2. Lloyds Register of Shipping, the British Corporation for the Survey and Register of Shipping and Bureau Veritas of France were in competition for business in the early twentieth century.

# Chapter Twenty-Nine

# 'Happy Birthday to You . . .'

**12.13 pm**
**Wednesday, 31 May 1911**
**Slipway No. 3**
**Harland and Wolff**
**Queen's Island**
**Belfast**

The movement at first was barely perceptible; the optical illusion of an inch-by-inch progression, the way a watch hand creeps around the dial. But moments later the largest moveable object ever created by man gathered pace and steadily slid faster and faster towards the welcoming water below. The noise was truly deafening, not only from the creaks and the groans and the cracks of the grease-soaked wooden slipway but also from the thousands of people cheering and whooping and laughing for joy as the latest example of Belfast's industry and ingenuity finally took to the water. In precisely sixty-two seconds, on a warm and sunny summer afternoon, with a tidal-wave splash and a clanking of anchors and drag chains worthy of such a great vessel, *Titanic* was well and truly launched.

The pavements, roads and trams of the city of Belfast had been packed all morning with eager spectators anxious to gain a good view of the spectacle. The stands set up on each side of the ship had been full for hours and latecomers were having to make do with craning their necks for a view over the heads of the crowds in front of them. Others had spread out along every accessible part of the river bank. Some had willingly paid the penny entrance fee to stand on the next-door quayside, where all the money raised would help boost the funds of local hospitals.

In pride of place on the foremost grandstand were the men, who above all others, had made this day a possibility: Lord Pirrie, the Chairman of Harland and Wolff; Bruce Ismay, Managing Director of the White Star Line; and American financier, John Pierpoint Morgan. Few of the spectators still cheering themselves hoarse over the great British achievement of launching this great British ship had any clue that *Titanic's* real owners were Americans – the stock and bond holders of the International Mercantile Marine Company of New Jersey, USA. The formidable J.P. Morgan was the man who held the purse strings and controlled the *Titanic.*

In the nearby marquee erected to entertain the throng of newspaper journalists from all over the country, one of the Harland and Wolff managing directors was certainly not discussing the ship's American connections. Mr Saxon Payne had had the honour of pushing the button that started the huge hydraulic rams that had pushed *Titanic* into movement at the top of her slipway. Now he had drawn the short straw amongst the other directors' duties to be performed that day.

As the all-powerful Pirrie, Morgan and Ismay sat down to their exclusive luncheon with the richest and most influential guests, Payne had been deputed to look after the press. His comments about *Titanic* and her elder sister *Olympic* were decidedly patriotic:

> The two vessels are pre-eminent examples of the vitality and the progressive instincts of the Anglo–Saxon race, and by what it has done in assisting the White Star Line in its great and commendable enterprise, Belfast can lay no small share in the maintenance of the prosperity of the British Empire.

As these event go, the launch of *Titanic* could not have gone better. The ship plunged into the water with a large but manageable wave, nothing got in its way and its anchors and cables pulled it up almost immediately to be delivered into the safe hands of the waiting tugboats. The local Belfast newspaper summed it up well, although, with the benefit of hindsight, their optimism was perhaps a little misplaced:

> If the circumstances under which the launch took place can be accepted as an augury of the future, the *Titanic* should be a huge success. The weather was glorious, a multitude of people assembled to bid the vessel 'God speed', and it would be impossible to conceive of a launch for which the whole of the conditions could be more ideal.

As the crowds began to disperse, Lord and Lady Pirrie led their most privileged guests towards the Harland and Wolff boardroom for a private luncheon. The day was a special one for the couple; they were sharing their joint birthday – with each other – and with their new baby, *Titanic*.[1] They had been inundated with 'Happy Birthday to You ...' good wishes since the first guests started gathering that morning. Some Happy Birthdays had even been directed at the ship. One newspaper would later talk about the 'fortunate coincidence' of the Pirries' birthdays coinciding with the launch of *Titanic*, seemingly not realising that work on the ships had, for months now, been geared towards giving Lord Pirrie a birthday gift he could really be proud of – the biggest ship in the world.

*Titanic* was at last in the water, but still far from finished. Many months of frantic work still lay ahead to fit out the bare shell of this vessel. Work was to be completed in the nearby Thompson graving dock, or as she floated alongside the adjacent Harland and Wolff quay. Many of her luxury furnishings and interior decorations had still to be placed on board; the plumbers, the carpenters, the polishers and the men with the kitchen sinks still needed to get on board. Lifeboat davits needed to be mounted and lifeboats hoisted on deck; the sound of the riveters' hammers was to echo around *Titanic* for many months to come.

*Titanic's* finishing work went far less smoothly than had been planned in the weeks following her launch. A series of minor accidents to the *Olympic*, and one bruising collision when she and the cruiser *Hawke* crunched together at Southampton, meant that *Titanic* saw her sister ship far more often than she might have wanted. The executives of the White Star Line must have been deeply frustrated that the star of their fleet kept returning to her birth city for repairs, rather than earning her keep ferrying American millionaires back and forth to Europe. The workers trying to complete the *Titanic* were equally annoyed.

Because *Olympic* had been delivered to its owners and ought now to be earning good money, the elder sister took priority whenever she popped in for repairs. *Titanic* even suffered the indignity at one stage of being removed from dry dock in order that *Olympic* could be put there in her place. The two ships were left manoeuvring carefully around each other, and while *Titanic* came out, the *Olympic* went in, only for the entire exercise to be repeated days later after *Olympic* had been patched up and sent back to sea.

Adding insult to injury, *Olympic* even stole *Titanic's* propeller blade when in need of urgent repair after hitting a submerged obstruction mid-Atlantic. Replacement propeller parts were ordered for *Titanic* but the delays had by then begun to build up. One riveter working on *Titanic* wrote to his parents in England to complain that he was spending all day working on *Titanic* and his nights doing overtime to fix the broken *Olympic*. The planned launch date of *Titanic* had started to slip. Some have speculated over the years that just one less minor accident to *Olympic* would have altered the date of *Titanic's* departure and altered the course of maritime history.

Eventually, however, came the day when *Titanic* was finished. On Tuesday, 2 April 1912, she began her sea trials. Steaming under her own power for the first time, the ship circled and slowed and speeded up and stopped in her shortest possible distance. After a lunch at sea the manoeuvres continued until the early evening when a final test of dropping and raising her anchors was satisfactorily performed. Observing what he termed the 'steam trials' on board that day was

Board of Trade Surveyor Francis Carruthers. Shortly after 7.00 pm he signed and handed over a copy of the Board of Trade Passenger Certificate. *Titanic* was now an operational passenger ship. She departed that same evening for Southampton to be provisioned and fuelled for her first transatlantic voyage. She had one last task to perform in Belfast before her departure; she headed back towards land to drop off her non-essential crew ... and Francis Carruthers.

Although he was the man at the sharp end of the only independent oversight of the construction of *Titanic*, it would be hard to place any blame whatsoever on Carruthers for the disaster that was shortly to follow. Francis Carruthers was a symptom, rather than a cause, of a deep malaise at the heart of the Marine Division of the British Board of Trade. The department had a longstanding weakness that led to a failure of the Board's most vital function; the protection of life for passengers and crew at sea.

Even the most cursory examination of the efficiency and capabilities of the Marine Division in the early 1900s when *Titanic* and other great British ships were being planned and constructed would have revealed its deep-seated problems. In the parlance of today it was an organisation most decidedly 'Not Fit For Purpose'. One part of the tragedy of *Titanic* is that successive presidents of the Board of Trade, including Winston Churchill, came and went from the post with no more than a cursory glance at how its nautical officers were operating.

Probably its longest-standing failing was the Division's persistent and inbuilt bias towards the interests of wealthy British ship-owners, rather than the men who navigated their ships or the passengers who set sail upon them. From the mid-nineteenth century onwards, politicians and their civil servants delegated many of their decisions to be made by the advisory committees set up under the various reincarnations of the Merchant Shipping Acts. Those committees originally claimed to be representative of the industry as a whole but in the class-ridden British society of the day there was an inevitable tendency to appoint from among the great and the good; which would mean from among the ranks of wealthy men who owned vast shipping companies or built ships for a living.

Even when the advisory committees had a sprinkling of nautical men, sailors with real-life experience at sea, it was hard for their voices to be heard. The most confident, highest class of committee member would self-select as chairmen and the committee's course would be set. The system accounts for decision after decision being made for the benefit of the shipping industry rather than for those who would suffer at sea. It accounts for the way that men such as Bruce Ismay's father could recommend a lifeboat system so grossly inadequate for its task, and how committee after committee for the following two decades would fail to drag it into the modern world of *Titanic*-sized ships carrying 3,500 passengers and crew out onto the high seas.

Closely allied to the institutional class-distinction of the Board was the fear that permeated every level of the system. Reading the intricately detailed, handwritten files and reports of the Board's archive it becomes clear that underlings were scared to speak up to managers, managers were scared to speak up to their leaders, their leaders were scared to speak up to the all-powerful gods who ran the Marine Division as their personal fiefdom, hardly bothered by passing politicians. And everyone was scared of the ship-owning MPs and the power and influence that leaders of the industry could wield to make or break any career.

Some of the fear can be glimpsed in the Head of the Marine Division's evidence to a Civil Service inquiry in the year after *Titanic* had sunk. Sir Walter Howell made it clear that upsetting nobody and 'not rocking the boat' was an essential skill for surveyors such as *Titanic's* Francis Carruthers:

> A Board of Trade surveyor has the most important duties to perform; he is continually visiting the shipping on our ports and it is very necessary that he should possess tact. He has to remember that any step he takes may be a false one and he has to take any step with the greatest of care because ship-owners are very quick to resent interference with their rights, they know perfectly well what their rights are and the surveyor has a very difficult and delicate duty to perform. He may land his department in very heavy damages by one false step.

The cringing, 'take no chances' attitude leaching down from the top of the Marine Division was nowhere better illustrated than in the subservience of the staff when it came to their pay and conditions. Workloads were excessive beyond the bounds of reason for many of the regional officers struggling to investigate, regulate, assist and control a shipping industry that was growing at breakneck speed. The work of inspecting the safety of new ships being built at dozens of shipyards all over the country fell to fewer than eighty engineer-surveyors such as Carruthers at nine district offices from Scotland to the tip of Cornwall and throughout what was then a united Ireland.

As was the experience at Harland and Wolff, each yard could have ten, twenty or even more ships of different types and sizes on their slipways at any one time, each in a different stage of development and each progressing rapidly week by week. An impossible roll-call of new ships for one or two regional men to police – especially when 'tact and delicacy' to the ship-owners were the orders of the day. To add to the low morale of the surveying teams was the astonishing stagnation of wages. By the time *Titanic* was being planned, the pay scales for Carruthers and his colleagues had not been reviewed for thirty-three years. Pay in any grade could attract a £10 increment for long service but once on that top limit some officers had received no extra pay for two decades or more.[2]

In 1909, almost every engineer-surveyor in the country signed a 'humble petition' calling for a review of their wages. They pointed out that surveyors' wages in private industry had increased substantially and many revisions of the Merchant Shipping Acts had added to their duties. The response from the Board was unpromising:

> ... there is no probability of the Lords Commissioners of the Treasury entertaining any further petition from the Surveyors of this Department at present, and in the circumstances, the Board think it undesirable to accord an interview to the representatives.

For many surveyors like Carruthers there was little choice but to accept their employer's neglect. Wages were higher outside of the Civil Service but many had few practical qualifications to seek other jobs. Almost to a man, they had gone to sea at an early age and worked their way to positions as engineers and, on occasions, even master of small craft before returning to a life ashore. From that point of their careers onwards the rapid pace of technological change and new engineering techniques could have left them floundering to keep up with the demands and the challenges of modern shipbuilding. They were never well placed to argue the fine points of engineering, riveting techniques or bulkhead construction with the public school and university educated likes of Lord Pirrie, Bruce Ismay or *Titanic's* designer, Thomas Andrews. Neither did the quality of the survey team make it easy for the Board of Trade to carry out what today would be termed its 'core mission':

> The primary function of the marine Department of the Board of Trade is to safeguard human life at sea; its work therefore ... is dealing with the seaworthiness of ships and the sufficiency and efficiency of their machinery, fittings, equipment and crews.

Even after the sinking of *Titanic*, the Board of Trade escaped any meaningful examination of its working practices and institutional problems. To a large extent its civil servants even avoided criticism for outdated lifeboat laws and deficiencies in its surveying of the ship. It skilfully recruited the sympathetic Lord Mersey to steer them safely into harbour in the London inquiry and studiously ignored the existence of its American counterpart.

Even the US Senators' brief and unsatisfactory examination of the facts had found the Board of Trade at fault but, unable to subpoena any British Government officials to appear at their hearing, the Senate could do no more than issue a scathing criticism from across the ocean. Claiming that England had been struck in 'its tenderest and proudest spot', the *New York Times* reported the verdict:

> We shall leave it to the honest judgement of England its painstaking chastisement of the British Board of Trade to whose laxity of

regulation and hasty inspection the world is large indebted for this awful fatality.

If the Americans believed that England would duly take up the cudgels against its own political establishment then it was due to be disappointed. Parliamentary debates about the Marine Division fizzled out when ship-owners staged a number of co-ordinated two-hour speeches that left no time for a vote.[3] It was left to the seaman's champion, Lord Muskerry, to drive home some serious criticisms in the House of Lords in December 1912:

> Ten years ago I pointed out that the surveying and inspecting staff of the Board of Trade was hopelessly insufficient. The loss of the *Titanic* has been a terrible and costly lesson, but I trust it is not one in vain. It has opened up many matters concerning the mercantile marine which demanded ventilation and exposure, and I think it has most certainly enlisted the interest of Parliament and the public in the affairs of those who earn their living at sea. The Marine Department of the Board of Trade has shown gross neglect – I might almost say criminal neglect – of the safety of the lives of our seamen.

Lord Muskerry's claims of 'gross neglect' and 'criminal neglect' never reached the point of vote in the House of Lords debate. But, in our world 100 years later, a world of litigation, damages and more rigorous health and safety standards, he might have received a more sympathetic hearing.

If *Titanic* had sunk today, would any of the principal players in the tragedy have ended up in the dock of a courtroom? The law has certainly changed in ways that might suggest that could happen. It was a change that came about primarily as the result of one tragic event: a disastrous accident at sea.

### Notes

1. Lord Pirrie was celebrating his sixty-fifth birthday. Lady Pirrie was ten years younger.
2. When some of the Board's longest-serving surveyors did finally get a pay rise the entire department, even those with no extra reward, were required to work longer hours of duty.
3. The opposition moved to reduce the President of the Board of Trade's salary by £100 as a traditional expression of disapproval. It was 'talked-out' without a vote.

# Chapter Thirty

# '. . . infected with the disease of sloppiness'

**6.28 pm**
**6 March 1987**
*Herald of Free Enterprise* **Car Ferry**
**Zeebrugge**
**Belgium**

It happened so quickly that neither passengers nor crew could do anything to help themselves; so fast that there was not even time for an emergency radio message to call for help. As the ship first lurched violently to one side and then capsized completely, everybody on board was flung to the floor; a floor that just moments earlier had been the wall. Seawater was flooding into every cabin but the ship was no longer moving at all, not sinking lower in the water but tipped completely on its side. Many of the doors and windows were suddenly up on the ceiling. In this topsy-turvy world, where nothing was the right way up, scores of passengers were piled in a heap, crushed beneath one another, struggling to breathe and all desperately trying to comprehend what had happened. At that point the electric lights flickered … and then failed completely.

A few of the 539 people on board died within the first few minutes, trapped far below deck. As seawater soaked the engine room's electrical circuits, they had died in the dark, without even the glimmer of emergency lighting to help them escape from the cramped rooms and the labyrinth of passages below decks. Many more died over the next thirty minutes. A few of them drowned but the majority perished from cold and exposure, half-submerged in water almost as cold as the ocean was on the night that *Titanic* went down. Later that evening, in front of the television news cameras, one shocked and grieving young man described his experiences:

> It just went right over and there was nothing I could do. There was chaos and screaming and I couldn't find a way out. How can a modern ship just sink so quickly, so near to the shore?

His question was soon answered. The roll-on roll-off car ferry, *Herald of Free Enterprise*, capsized in shallow waters shortly after leaving the Belgian port of Zeebrugge because her crew had forgotten to close the bow doors. She rolled over and stuck fast on the sandy bottom, two-thirds in and one-third out of the water. Although help was quickly on the scene and divers heroically rescued scores of people over the next two hours, the eventual death toll was 193 men, women and children. It was the worst peacetime disaster on a British vessel since the loss of *Titanic*, seventy-four years earlier.

Just as in the *Titanic* case, a wreck commissioner's court investigated the circumstances of the tragedy. The commissioner, Mr Justice Sheen, concluded that the captain and several of the crew had been guilty of serious negligence but that the disaster was also partly the fault of the 'staggering complacency' of the company that owned the ship. His report commented:

> ... a full investigation into the circumstances of the disaster leads inexorably to the conclusion that underlying or cardinal faults lay higher up in the Company ... from top to bottom the body corporate was infected with the disease of sloppiness ...

With angry families demanding justice, an unsuccessful attempt was made to prosecute the company for manslaughter. It failed, primarily because of problems in identifying the process by which the company had made – or rather, had not made – decisions affecting the safety of the ship: the problem of identifying what the lawyers termed 'a single controlling mind' of the organisation.

In response to the *Herald of Free Enterprise* disaster, and other tragedies including the deaths at Aberfan, Hillsborough, King's Cross and those in the Southall train crash, the Government eventually introduced the Corporate Manslaughter and Corporate Homicide Act 2007. The law, which came into force in April the following year, allowed the prosecution of a range of corporate bodies, including private and public companies and some government departments.[1]

The new offence did not negate the entirely separate offence of 'gross negligence manslaughter'. Any individual may be guilty of that crime if he causes the death of another person by acts so negligent that they can rightly be considered as a gross breach of the duty of care he owed to the victim. How would those involved in the *Titanic* disaster have fared in the hands of our modern-day legal system?

Under various twenty-first century laws there would be a number of good candidates – both personal and corporate – for our fictitious prosecution. All were, arguably, at serious fault through their acts, or their failure to act, as *Titanic* was planned, built and allowed to sail with a hopelessly inadequate, though legally approved, complement of lifeboats. The fact that *Titanic* was a

British-registered ship would make anyone responsible for her sinking and the subsequent deaths liable to examination under a number of different British statutes.

Perhaps the first person worthy of investigation would be the government cabinet minister who was responsible for the safety of lives at sea at the time when *Titanic* was first conceived and constructed. That important responsibility fell to Winston Churchill when he became President of the Board of Trade on 12 April 1908. The contract for *Titanic's* construction was signed and handed to Harland and Wolff a little over three months later, on 31 July 1908. From then onwards, the duty of surveying *Titanic* and her sister ships' construction, and the regulation of the number of their lifeboats, came under Churchill's control.

The Marine Division of the Board of Trade, which answered directly to Churchill, would have been informed of the massive new shipbuilding project. It would also have been aware of White Star's longstanding policy of refusing to have the construction of their ships monitored by surveyors from the Lloyd's Register or any of the other ship registration societies. That put an even heavier burden of responsibility on the Board of Trade's surveyors as the only outside check on the ship's construction techniques and her safety.

Churchill was something of a 'new boy' who already had a poor relationship with his senior Marine Division officers at the time that *Titanic* was ordered. But he would have been very well acquainted with his Cabinet role and responsibilities by the time work actually started on the ship. *Titanic's* keel was laid down on 31 March 1909, almost a year after Churchill had started work at the Board of Trade. It is hard to believe that the politician in charge of the Marine Division could not have been aware of the ship's construction. The sister ships were to be the biggest vessels in the world, each supposedly a triumph of British shipbuilding expertise. And by the time that work started on *Titanic*, the construction of *Olympic* had been underway for months.

The Board of Trade's president had also by then had ample opportunities, through the necessity of answering questions in Parliament, to learn how out-of-date his department's lifeboat regulations were. He had even seen examples of how vital the boats could be for saving life at sea. In November 1909, he was told of the 'gallant conduct' of Able Seaman E. Johansen, a sailor who had saved the lives of twenty-eight shipmates by navigating a lifeboat, through heavy seas, for thirty-six hours after the sinking of the British grain ship *Matterhorn*, off the coast of Seattle.

Possibly even more damning than the lifeboat fiasco, however, was Churchill's failure to recognise and tackle the institutional problems that he inherited at the Board of Trade; the lack of properly experienced and qualified surveyors of ships and the low morale and stagnation of thought that characterised the entire Marine Division. Concentrating on his own busy personal life and on the more glamorous activities of his widespread department, Churchill failed to properly supervise his senior civil servants, or tackle his department's much-needed reform.

He even failed to act when presented with clear evidence that the Marine Division's most senior officials were engaged in some questionable arrangements with outside companies. Board of Trade file M 88, of 1909, reveals how Churchill acquiesced in a secret agreement for the Marine Division's Engineer Surveyor-in-Chief, Alexander Boyle, to also earn an outside salary for work he conducted on behalf of the independent company, the Lloyd's Register.

The agreement with the Lloyd's Register was beneficial to the Division because it supplemented the salary of a senior official at a time when Civil Service wages were so low that it was hard to attract good men. But, as a memo sent to Churchill pointed out, it also created a clear conflict of interest:

> Thus [Boyle] holds two appointments and acts in a dual capacity, being both the government inspector and the general superintendent of the machines to be inspected by that office. These are the plain facts and it must be admitted that the position is somewhat anomalous, and would not be easy to satisfactorily defend if public attention were called to the matter.

Churchill was reassured that it was 'to say the least improbable' that anyone outside of the department would learn about the arrangement, although a note from the head of the Marine Division, Sir Walter Howell, did conclude with a warning:

> Attention might however be called to the matter at any time for no specific reason by some busybody, and if a return were asked for of government servants in various Departments holding public, semi-public or private appointments, in addition to their official appointments, this dual arrangement would have to be included.

Despite the lack of transparency and the concerns about 'some busybody', Churchill had no qualms about sanctioning the affair. The bottom of the file from 16 November 1909 holds his usual scrawled handwritten note:

> The President: I approve.

*Olympic* was nearing completion and *Titanic's* hull was more than half plated by 14th February 1910 when Winston Churchill was promoted to the Home Office and thus relinquished his responsibility for the lifeboat laws. At any stage before then Churchill could have signed an 'Order In Council' to alter the lifeboat laws with a stroke of his pen. He failed to do so. Other presidents of the Board of Trade had also failed to act over many years, but none of them had witnessed the birth of the great ships that were being built while Churchill was at the helm.

The charge against the man who went on to become Britain's greatest wartime leader is clear. By his lack of vigilance, and by his readiness to accept unquestioningly the advice of his flawed Civil Service department, he neglected his duty to all who sailed on *Titanic*. With all her weak rivets, and with all her lack of lifeboats, *Titanic* was built on Winston Churchill's watch.

Hand in hand with Churchill's alleged neglect, there might, perhaps, be a more corporate prosecution of the government department he controlled: the Marine Division of the Board of Trade. Its files, still held at the British National Archives at Kew in South West London, reveal that there may be a strong case to answer. The evidence suggests that the Division was the body more responsible than any other for the tragic loss of life on board RMS *Titanic* in April 1912.

Under the 1997 Act, there are a number of elements to be considered if a charge of corporate manslaughter is to be proved. The organisation under investigation must first and foremost have owed a 'duty of care' to the victim or victims; there must have been a 'gross breach' of that duty of care; and the way in which the corporate body's activities were managed by their most senior management must have led to that breach.

In the case of the Board of Trade, each element would appear to be in place. Since the mid-nineteenth century the Board has been charged with 'the general superintendence of all matters relating to merchant ships' and has had a duty to safeguard the lives of British sailors and citizens who venture to sea. It, arguably, breached that duty of care, in a gross manner, in two areas of its activities: it failed to update lifeboats for so many years that they became no longer fit for purpose, and it failed to recruit and train sufficient surveying staff to properly fulfil their safety function of regulating the construction on ships. And lastly, both those situations arose because of the failings of the Board's most senior management officials.

The man with the greatest culpability for the archaic lifeboat regulations was Sir Alfred Chalmers. During his thirty-three-year long service with the Board of Trade, Sir Alfred was directly and personally responsible for the institutionalised lethargy about lifeboats that contributed greatly to *Titanic's* death toll. As the effective deputy-head of the department, and its most senior professional adviser for many of those years, he also bore substantial responsibility for the low morale and lack of initiative displayed by its staff.

The UK Census records trace the course of Sir Alfred's career from humble mariner to the most powerful influence in the Marine Division of the Board of Trade. After a career at sea, he had clearly changed jobs by the time of the 1881 Scottish Census. Then living with his wife, Mary, and two children in Lanarkshire, he described himself on the Census form as 'a nautical surveyor'. It seems to have paid better than his job as a sailor because the family could afford to have a 17-year-old local girl work for them as a general domestic servant. Two decades later, the English Census recorded a far grander lifestyle. Then aged fifty-five, Chalmers was listed as 'professional adviser to the Marine Department of the Board of Trade'. He and his family had swapped a small home in Scotland for the more spacious surroundings of their own London house in Russell Road, Kensington, where they employed a live-in cook and domestic, as well as a teenage housemaid.

At the Mersey Inquiry, Chalmers admitted that, although he had worked at sea for eighteen years, he had no experience whatsoever in the building of ships. His Board of Trade file in 1901 commented that he had 'no practical qualifications'. It had been Chalmers' claim that more people would have lived had *Titanic* carried fewer lifeboats that had most astonished the inquiry. He also admitted that he had never seriously contemplated updating the lifeboat rules until he learned that the *Olympic* was being built:

> I evolved it in my own mind. The 45,000-odd tons that was represented by the *Olympic* was rather a jump. I thought it might be prudent to advise the Department to refer the matter to the Advisory Committee because, although we had power to vary the Rules ourselves, it has always been the practice of the Board to refer the matter to the Advisory Committee.

The lifeboat question had then remained bogged down under consideration by committees for several more years, until the night that *Titanic* struck the iceberg and the lengthy deliberations of the Life-Saving Appliances Committee had been overtaken by harsh reality.

Despite being heavily criticised by the post-*Titanic* reports and in House of Commons debates, Sir Alfred Chalmers never expressed a moment's regret for his lifeboat decisions. He later wrote a scathing attack on the newly introduced policy of 'lifeboats for all', stating that the imposition of such costs on ship-owners was '... regulation gone mad'.

If the Board of Trade's actions – or lack of them – were driven by lethargy and institutional inertia, then almost the exact opposite forces had been driving the actions of another, more shadowy, figure in the drama of *Titanic*. The American banker J.P. Morgan had earned a formidable reputation as a man of decisive action and was the power behind the throne in all the decisions taken about the *Titanic*.

Morgan's heavy losses on his shipping investments make it certain that he would have been deeply involved in the momentous and risky decision to build *Titanic* and her sisters, all together, in Belfast. And yet there is a paucity of detailed evidence about Morgan's role. The vast archive of family and banking history that Morgan assembled in New York holds few documents that could be placed before our court of public opinion as it examines the loss of *Titanic*. Many of the US financier's letters and diaries were destroyed, or have never been made public.

In addition, Morgan was never called to give evidence at any inquiry into the sinking. Despite his own financial involvement in the most important controlling company of the International Mercantile Marine, and despite the fact that the transatlantic shipping concern had long been known as the 'Morgan Combine', Morgan's name was hardly mentioned in the quest to discover the truth about *Titanic*.

There is evidence, however, in Morgan's business history and in the dry and dusty accounts and records of his many banking companies that might explain some of what motivated him to get involved in the shipping business and in the building of *Titanic*. From his earliest adult years, struggling to emerge from the shadow of his rich and enormously successful father, he had earned a questionable reputation. Colleagues worried that the young J.P. Morgan took too many risks and made too many questionable decisions. One of the first business decisions that Morgan took independently of his father involved the purchase of a shipment of carbine rifles that were being sold off as surplus to requirements by the US Army. When it later transpired that his business partner had fraudulently sold the same consignment back to another Army department, Morgan was lucky to escape without criminal charges. There was a similar lucky escape when Morgan got involved in attempts to manipulate the price of gold. Morgan emerged from the deal with a healthy profit, not long before one of his former partners was arrested and charged with fraud.

The morality of some of Morgan's dealings worried his more staid and respectable father, Junius Morgan. The family had tried to raise their son to be a religious man.[2] Morgan's biographer, Vincent P. Carosso, recorded an occasion when the young banker received a letter from his father warning that God kept a careful eye on all of his charges:

> Act in every transaction of your life under the solemn responsibility and all will be well. Without it, and although you may acquire wealth, it is worse than useless when you consider the awful cost at which it has been accomplished.

But whatever critical opinions his banking colleagues may have voiced about J.P. Morgan's ethics and morals when he was young, they were soon forgotten when, at the age of fifty-three, he inherited a vast banking fortune from his father. Junius Morgan had never regained consciousness after a carriage accident in the South of France and had died in the spring of 1890, leaving an estimated $10 million inheritance, and a thriving international banking empire, to his son. The younger Morgan then went on to greater and greater financial triumphs by his tactics of merging companies to create the wealthy trusts that dominated the American steel and railroad industries at the turn of the twentieth century.

His involvement in the British shipping industry originally came about after he assisted in the merger of two American-owned shipping lines, but there may have been other motivations behind the scenes. Through the London branches of his banks, Morgan had been involved over several years in helping the British Government find investors to buy their war bonds. The money was needed to finance the Boer War in South Africa. But some of the deals had not gone quite as Morgan had intended. He had felt let down by the British Government, who first accepted his assistance and advice but had then failed to give him the allocation of bonds that he felt he deserved.

Could it be that his annoyance with the British Treasury had made him more receptive when he was approached with a shipping deal that would see the Morgan Combine take over control of the great bulk of Great Britain's merchant shipping fleet?

Whatever his motivations, the decision to get involved in the shipping industry cost him a small fortune. It would have made him the most deeply cost-conscious partner of the Morgan Combine as it struggled to survive in the early years of the twentieth century. Having failed in his bid to gain a total monopoly, and faced with competition from a revitalised Cunard shipping line, Morgan would have been at the heart of the decisions about building *Titanic* and her sisters.

Might the financial pressures to compete with Cunard's two fast and luxurious liners have led Morgan to encourage some rash decisions? All of the evidence is purely circumstantial and his exact role remains uncertain, but J.P. Morgan's history and his powerful and domineering character suggest that he must have exerted pressure to save money at every turn.

A stronger case may perhaps be made against Morgan's closest 'partner in crime' in the setting up of the Morgan Combine, the Chairman and autocratic boss of Harland and Wolff, William Pirrie. But what might be the charges against him? All contemporary reports suggest that it was Pirrie as chairman who ruled his Belfast shipyard with a rod of iron and that nothing of any consequence could have happened inside Harland and Wolff without Lord Pirrie's express approval.

A study of the company's records, still held for public examination by the Public Record Office of Northern Ireland, certainly backs up that impression. Boardroom decisions were constantly deferred for Pirrie's personal consideration or simply rubber-stamped by a compliant board of directors. No directors ever registered any disagreement with the Chairman's policy decisions; perhaps not surprising in an organisation where Pirrie had the sole power to decide who would serve on the board, and who would not.

In those circumstances, any shortcomings in Harland and Wolff's construction of *Titanic* must clearly be laid at the feet of Lord Pirrie. Credible scientific evidence points to the fact that *Titanic* sank more quickly than she might otherwise have done because the rivets between her hull plates were faulty. There were several possible reasons. The faults may have arisen because of the pressure of work among rivet teams struggling to earn as much money as possible under the yard's piece-work rates wages scheme. Or the rivets themselves may have been made of iron with inherent weaknesses because of a high slag content created by inefficient and insufficient puddling of their basic raw material. Or the ship may have suffered from a combination of both those factors.

Whichever possibility is correct, the fault would have been that of Harland and Wolff; compounded by the weakness of the Board of Trade's inspection regime. The yard was struggling under an intense workload, with more ships under construction than they could properly handle. That problem was not helped by the financial pressure that Pirrie exerted upon the Board at every opportunity to cut wage costs and limit overtime, even at the expense of failing to meet their planned delivery deadlines. As one of the directors of the American IMM company, Pirrie would have been very well aware of the company's parlous financial state and of Morgan's demands to save money wherever possible.

Under Pirrie's leadership, the Harland and Wolff Board showed a surprising lack of concern for the victims of *Titanic*. Some years earlier, board members had spent an entire meeting recording their individual tributes to a retiring Harland and Wolff director. The report of their glowing comments of commendation took up an entire page of the minutes' book. By contrast, in their meeting immediately after the *Titanic* disaster, the only mention of the ship was the receipt of a report detailing the money paid out in compensation for shipyard accidents during the time that she was under construction. It was not until the following month that a more formal note was recorded of the Board's 'heartfelt sympathy' for the victims.

Yet it is perhaps Pirrie's role in the formation of the International Mercantile Marine Company that offers the strongest case against him. He worked tirelessly to persuade the then inexperienced Bruce Ismay to sign over the White Star Line to the Americans; he was at the centre of negotiations with other European shipping lines. His reward was an agreement that the combine would build all of its new ships in the Harland and Wolff yard. It was a deal that was of immense benefit to Pirrie, but one that was to present the greatest risks to *Titanic's* passengers.

Other shipping lines had contracted the construction of their biggest vessels to various separate shipyards around the UK, but that was never an option for the Morgan group. The new *Titanic*, *Olympic* and *Britannic* all had to be built in Belfast, however well or badly the yard might have been able to cope with building so many great ships in such a tight timescale. The heavy workload and the overwhelming demand for metal from untested suppliers created significant dangers to the quality of the ships being produced in the shipyard. Lord Pirrie had claimed his reward – and *Titanic's* victims were to pay the cost.

The final, but by no means least likely, candidate in the legal firing line is Bruce Ismay, nominally the head of the company that owned and operated *Titanic*. Charged under his full name of Joseph Bruce Ismay, he has much to commend him as one of *Titanic's* most guilty men. He presided over the decision to order the three biggest ships in the world to be simultaneously constructed in one Belfast shipyard. Going along with Lord Pirrie's greed for the order was arguably a decision that led to the over-stretching of human and material resources that encouraged poor workmanship, the use of weaker than advisable metal, and the creation of a magnificent ship whose outer beauty concealed the ugliness of a vessel that was fundamentally flawed.

Ismay also had overall responsibility for the money spent on *Titanic*. Despite his claims that 'money was no object', might he not be guilty of penny-pinching at crucial moments? And how much of the decision to use iron rivets, rather than their stronger steel counterparts, can be laid at the door of the man controlling the cash available for *Titanic's* construction? Equally, to what extent was the number of lifeboats carried on the ship influenced by the man who would have to pay for those boats and for the wages of their crew?

'There were ...' a prosecuting counsel might claim, '... plans and designs at various times for twenty-four, thirty-six, and even forty-eight lifeboats to be carried on your ship; the davits were designed to cope with four dozen boats, and yet you ordered just sixteen to be hung from those davits. Why should that be, Mr Ismay?

'And why were the officers you chose to command the largest ship in the world so poorly trained that they failed to fill up her lifeboats completely? Not one single surviving officer knew how many of *Titanic's* passengers could have been safely lowered in her boats; they feared that lifeboats constructed and tested for total strength and security might fold in the middle if too many people were loaded. How did you allow that to happen?'

But it is in turning to Bruce Ismay's personal actions on the night *Titanic* sank that his greatest moral, if not legal, responsibility, for *Titanic* deaths is most clearly revealed. Why did he not search further afield to find more women and children to be saved in those vital last few seconds as one of *Titanic's* last boats was lowered to the sea? Does his claim that 'no one was in sight' excuse him stepping into the lifeboat? Why did he not stay the hand of the sailors lowering that boat for long enough for others to be found?

Perhaps more tellingly, why did he not suggest at any time that his lifeboat should return to the scene to save any of the hundreds of men, women and children screaming for help in the darkness as they drowned or slowly froze to the point of exhaustion in the freezing Atlantic waters? Why did he not use his position and authority to order the boats to return? It was a question never asked in the immediate aftermath of the sinking, and never remarked upon in the whitewash report of Lord Mersey.

'And yet, Mr Ismay ...' our modern-day prosecutor might comment, '... your attitude is, perhaps, best tested by examining your actions after the ship had sunk; your silence in the lifeboat, your seclusion on board *Carpathia* with no comment or concern for the shocked survivors, your lack of curiosity about who had lived ... and who had died.'

In summary of the case against Bruce Ismay, it is germane to quote from his inquisition at the 1912 London inquiry, from a line of questioning instantly brought to a halt by the sympathetic interruption of Lord Mersey as Ismay struggled to find an answer:[3]

'Has it occurred to you that, except perhaps apart from the captain, you, as the responsible managing director, deciding the number of boats, owed your life to every other person on that ship?'

'It has not.'

In response to most questions after *Titanic* sank, Bruce Ismay followed the example of Mizaru, Kikazaru and Iwazaru, Japan's three wise monkeys, who 'see no evil, hear no evil, speak no evil'.

Anyone hearing Bruce Ismay's testimony at the American and British inquiries might well have thought that this prime witness was nothing more than a casual observer, walked in off the streets, rather than the president of the most powerful shipping conglomerate ever to sail the high seas. Ismay's strategy to deflect criticism of himself and the White Star Line was clear. He had seen nothing, heard nothing, said nothing ... about any of the most controversial decisions that had led to the sinking of the *Titanic*.

He had 'not spoken' to any officers after the collision, he had 'no idea' of what radio messages were sent, of how quickly the boats could be lowered, of how many compartments *Titanic* had, of how many ships he owned or of the profits his ships might be making. He had not inspected the ship, or recognised any passengers after the collision. After a lifetime as a ship-owner he 'did not know' the Board of Trade lifeboat regulations and did not know when they were drawn up (even though his own father had been the primary architect of the law). Most importantly, he had had nothing to do with deciding the number of lifeboats: 'That was a matter for the builders, Sir.'

Had *Titanic* sunk today the outcome for Ismay, and for the others involved in her demise, could have been very different to that of 1912. The sense of public outrage, and the grief of the bereaved families, would be no less intense than it was a century ago; the demand for justice would burn as bright as ever.

Without the respect once shown by the 'lower classes' to their wealthy and aristocratic 'betters' the investigations would have been more searching, the inquiries would have been more thorough and the inquisitors less deferential in their questioning.

A hundred years after the poorly constructed and miserably ill-equipped *Titanic* sank with the loss of so many lives, it is, of course, no more than an academic exercise to judge the actions of those who owned, constructed, controlled or regulated the ship in the light of these modern-day laws. The offence of corporate manslaughter does not apply retrospectively, and the last of those who could be considered culpable have long since died.[4]

And yet, those modern laws may perhaps still shed some light on the actions of the men and the companies most to blame for failing *Titanic's* victims. There is no court of law in which now to convict, or absolve, those accused of failing *Titanic's* victims. Any legal proceedings, of course, can only remain as a fiction. You, the readers in the court of public opinion, are the only judge and jury as to the guilt or innocence of all those accused.

Each must decide the case on its merits to arrive at the final verdict: Who Sank The *Titanic*?

## Notes

1. The offence is called corporate manslaughter in England, Wales and Northern Ireland, but is known as corporate homicide in Scotland.
2. Morgan professed to be deeply religious but, although married, he had a string of mistresses throughout his life. He was reputedly staying with a favourite mistress in the South of France when he received the news of the *Titanic* disaster.
3. Lord Mersey intervened in an instant: 'I do not think that is a question to put to him; that is an observation which you may make when you come to make your speech. It is not a question for him.'
4. The last living person who had any direct connection with *Titanic* was Elizabeth Dean, known by her middle name of Millvina. She died in 2011, at the age of 97. She had been just a nine-week-old baby, the youngest person on board, when *Titanic* sank. She, her mother Georgette and her elder brother Bertram were saved; the body of her father, Bert, who had been taking the family to a new life in Kansas, was never found.

# Selected Bibliography

Many hundreds of books and many millions of words have been written about RMS *Titanic* in the 100 years since the night of the tragedy. Any author writing about the ship is of necessity following in the footsteps of many who have gone before. I am grateful to the following books, periodicals, technical journals and internet websites that have proved of particular help along the way.

## BOOKS
Anderson, Roy, *White Star*, T. Stephenson & Sons, Prescot, 1964.

Baker, E., *An Introduction to Steel Shipbuilding*, McGraw Hill, London, 1943.

Ballard, Dr Robert D., *The Discovery of the Titanic*, Hodder & Stoughton, London, 1987.

Beesley, Lawrence, *The Loss of the Titanic: Its Story and its Lesson*, Heinemann, London, 1912.

Beveridege, Bruce and Hall, Steve, *Olympic and Titanic: The Truth Behind the Conspiracy*, Six Star Publishing, London, 2004.

Booth, John, and Coughlan, Sean, *Titanic: Signals of Disaster*, White Star, Westbury, 1993.

Brown, Richard, *Voyage of the Iceberg: The Story of the Iceberg that Sank the Titanic*, Bodley Head, London, 1985.

Bullock, Shan F., *A Titanic Hero: Thomas Andrews Shipbuilder, 1865-1935*, Maunsell, Dublin and London, 1912.

Burk, Kathleen, *Morgan Grenfell 1838-1988, The Biography of a Merchant Bank*. Oxford University Press, Oxford, 1989.

Cahill, Richard A., *Disasters at Sea: Titanic to Exxon Valdez*, Century, London, 1990.

Cannadine, David, *The Aristocratic Adventurer*, Penguin Books, London, 1994.

Carosso, Vincent P., *The Morgans: Private International Bankers 1854-1913*, Harvard University Press, Cambridge, Massachusetts, 1987.

Chernow, Ron, *The House of Morgan: An American Banking Dynasty and the Rise of Modern Finance*, Grove Press, New York, 2001.

Chirnside, Mark, *RMS Olympic: Titanic's Sister*, Tempus Publishing, London, 2004.

Chirnside, Mark, *The 'Olympic' Class Ships: Olympic, Titanic & Britannic*, Tempus Publishing, London, 2004.

Cooper, Gary, *The Man Who Sank the Titanic: The Life and Times of Captain Edward J. Smith*, Witan Books, London, 1992.

Costello, Philip, *Titanic: The Tragedy that Became a Legend,* Titanic Products, Portsmouth, 1986.

Davie, Michael, *Titanic: The Full Story of a Tragedy,* Bodley Head, London, 1986.

Eaton, John P., and Haas, Charles A., *Titanic: Destination Disaster, The Legends and the Reality,* Patrick Stephens, Wellingborough, 1987.

Eaton, John P., and Haas, Charles A., *Falling Star: Misadventures of White Star Line Ships,* Patrick Stephens, Wellingborough, 1989.

Eaton, John P., and Haas, Charles A., *Titanic: Triumph and Tragedy,* Patrick Stephens, Wellingborough, 1994.

Gardiner, Robin, and Van der Vat, Dan, *The Riddle of the Titanic,* Weidenfeld and Nicolson, London, 1995.

Garrett, Richard, *Atlantic Disaster: The Titanic and Other Victims of the North Atlantic,* Buchan & Enright, London, 1986.

Goldsmith, Frank J. W., *Echoes in the Night: Memories of a Titanic Survivor,* Titanic Historical Society, Massachusetts, 1991.

Gracie, Archibald, *The Truth About the Titanic,* Mitchell, Kennerley, New York, 1913.

Green, Rod, *Building the Titanic: An Epic Tale of Human Endeavour and Modern Engineering,* Carlton Books, London, 2005.

Harrison, Leslie, *Titanic Myth: The Californian Incident,* William Kimber, London, 1986.

Hart, Eva M., and Denney, Ronald, *Shadow of the Titanic: A Survivor's Story,* Greenwich University, Dartford, 1994.

Haws, Duncan, *Merchant Fleets Vol.19: White Star Line, Oceanic Steam Navigation Company,* TCL Publications, Hereford, 1990.

Hobson, Dominic, *The Pride of Lucifer: Unauthorised Biography of a Merchant Bank,* Hamish Hamilton, London, 1990.

Hooper McCarty, Jennifer, and Foecke, Tim, *What Really Sank the Titanic,* Citadel Press, New York, 2008.

Hoffman, William, and Grimm, Jack, *Beyond Reach: The Search for the Titanic,* Paul Harris, Edinburgh 1984.

Hutchinson, Gillian, *The Wreck of the Titanic,* National Maritime Museum, London, 1994.

Hyman Alan, *The Rise & Fall of Horatio Bottomley: The Biography of a Swindler,* Cassell, London, 1972.

Hyslop, Donald, *Titanic Voices,* Southampton City Council, Southampton, 1994.

Jackson, Stanley, *The Rise and Fall of a Banker,* William Heinemann, London, 1984.

Jefferson, Herbert, *Viscount Pirrie of Belfast,* Mullan, Belfast, 1948.

Lord, Walter, *A Night to Remember*, Penguin, London 1976.

Lynch, Don, *Titanic: An Illustrated History*, Hodder and Stoughton, London, 1992.

MacInnis, Joseph, *Titanic in a New Light*, Thomasson-Grant, Virginia, 1992.

Marcus, Geoffrey, *The Maiden Voyage*, Allen and Unwin, London, 1969.

Moss, Michael, and Hume, John R., *Shipbuilders to the World: 125 Years of Harland and Wolff, Belfast, 1861–1986*, Blackstaff, Belfast, 1986.

Oldham, Wilton J., *The Ismay Line: The White Star Line and the Ismay Family Story*, Journal of Commerce, Liverpool, 1961.

Padfield, Peter, *The Titanic and the Californian*, Hodder, London, 1965.

Pellegrino, Charles, *Her Name, Titanic: The Untold Story of the Sinking and Finding of the Unsinkable Ship*, Robert Hale, London, 1990.

Pollard, Sydney, and Robertson, Paul, *The British Shipbuilding Industry 1870–1914*, Harvard University Press, Cambridge, Massachusetts, 1979.

Ticehurst, Brian, *The Titanic: Southampton's Memorials*, Waterfront, Poole, 1987.

Thearle, S., *Modern Practice of Shipbuilding in Iron and Steel*, Collins, London, 1891.

Vale, Vivian, *The American Peril: The Challenge to Britain on the North Atlantic, 1901–04*, Manchester University Press, Manchester, 1984.

Wade, Wyn Craig, *The Titanic: End of a Dream*, Weidenfeld & Nicolson, London, 1980.

Walton, T., *Steel Ships, Construction and Maintenance*, Griffin, London, 1904.

Watson, Arnold and Betty, *Roster of Valor: The Titanic Halifax Legacy*, 7-C's Press, Connecticut, 1984.

Wilkins, Mira, *The Emergence of Multinational Enterprise: American Business Abroad from the Colonial Era to 1914*, Harvard University Press, Cambridge, Massachusetts, 1986.

Young, Filson, *Titanic*, Grant Richards, London, 1912.

**PERIODICALS**

*Business History Review*, 28 December 1954: Navin, Thomas R. and Sears, Marian V., *A study in Merger Formation of the International Mercantile Marine Company*.

*Engineering*: October 1910, *The White Star Liner Olympic*; May 1911, *The White Star Liner Titanic;* April 1912, *The Lessons of the Titanic Disaster*; June 1912, *The Titanic Investigation Report.*

*The Engineer*: June 1910, *The White Star Line*; June 1911, *The Launch of the Titanic*; March 1911, *White Star Liners Olympic and Titanic.*

*International Marine Engineering Journal*: July 1911, *Launch of Titanic.*

*Marine Review*: May 1912, *Loss of the Steamship Titanic*; September 1912, *Final Reports of Titanic Inquiries in America and England*.
*Marine Technology*: October 1996, *The Titanic and Lusitania: A Final Forensic Analysis*.
*National Geographic*: December 1985, Ballard, Robert D., *How We Found Titanic;* December 1986, Ballard, Robert D., *A Long Last Look at Titanic*.
*Scientific American*, supplement No. 1,850, June 1911, *The Olympic and Titanic – Two Giant Ocean Steamships*.
*The Journal of Commerce*, 1961: Oldham Wilton J., *The Ismay Line*.
*The Shipbuilder 6*, Special Number, 1911, *Olympic and Titanic*.


## GOVERNMENT REPORTS
British Wreck Commissioner's Court (London: HMSO, 1912): *Formal investigation into the loss of the SS Titanic. Evidence, appendices and index.*

British Wreck Commissioner's Court (London: HMSO, 1912): *Report of a formal investigation into the circumstances attending the foundering on 15th April, 1912, of the British steamship Titanic of Liverpool, after striking ice in or near latitude 41° 46' N, longitude 50° 14' W, North Atlantic, whereby loss of life ensued.*

Committee on Commerce, United States Senate (Washington: Government Printing Office 1912): *Titanic Disaster: hearings of a subcommittee of the pursuant to S. Res. 283, directing the Committee on Commerce to investigate the causes leading to the wreck of the White Star liner Titanic.*


## INTERNET WEBSITES
Among the vast numbers of websites dedicated to *Titanic* are many seekers after the truth of the event. The following, in particular, have proved of great help:
www.encyclopedia-titanica.org
www.titanic-titanic.com
www.titanic.com
www.markchirnside.co.uk
www.titanichistoricalsociety.org
www.titanic-model.com
www.titaniccities.org.uk

# Index